Graham Scho

1991

ESSENTIAL LAW FOR LANDOWNERS AND FARMERS

Essential Law for Landowners and Farmers

Second Edition

Michael Gregory and Margaret Parrish

Collins
Professional
Books

Collins Professional Books
William Collins Sons & Co. Ltd
8 Grafton Street, London W1X 3LA

First published in Great Britain by
Granada Publishing – Technical Books Division 1980
Second edition published by
Collins Professional Books 1987

Distributed in the United States of America
by Sheridan House, Inc.

British Library Cataloguing in Publication Data
Gregory, Michael, 1925 –
Essential law for landowners and farmers.
— 2nd ed.
1. Agricultural laws and legislation —
England   2. Land use, Rural — Law and
Legislation — England
I. Title   II. Parrish, Margaret R.K.
344.2064'676   KD2241

ISBN 0–00–383269–4

Printed and bound in Great Britain by
Mackays of Chatham, Kent

Contents

Foreword

Historically the ownership and occupancy of land has led to dispute and misunderstanding, to argument and bloodshed. Today the issues and emotions surrounding these proprietory interests are no less heated but we can resolve the conflicts that arise by litigation or arbitration. Increasingly landowners are realising that compromise and negotiation can often pre-empt conflict and create mutually beneficial agreements. Such enlightenment is not possible where ignorance of the law exists. It is in this field that I commend this work by two barristers – Margaret Parrish and Michael Gregory.

To the majority the ownership and occupation of land is seen as a privilege. So it is, but it is a privilege coupled with responsibility. The mere ownership of land carries with it duties and obligations to house and maintain tenants or employees. Tenants owe their landlords good husbandry and reasonable returns; they owe their employees housing and continued prosperity. All concerned with agricultural land owe the public stewardship of it, limited access to it and as little interference from it as possible. Public authorities have a duty to safeguard agricultural land whilst inevitably encroaching upon it in the common good. The land itself can be of a deceptive nature for it has a speculative value that can be a liability. It may cover minerals that conflict with its agricultural potential; it may give rise to liability for its visitors; it may support visiting game. It may be criss-crossed by wayleaves and watercourses; preserved, protected and cocooned with planning restrictions. It may give rise to smells, nuisances and annoyance. Above all it is subject to the weather.

This book does not aim to duplicate the specialist legal textbooks on the many individual topics it spans. Rather it succeeds in collating the essential elements of the many problems facing the owners and occupiers of agricultural land today. It does not set out to replace specialist advice but it succeeds in presenting simply the essential law that will enable farmers to resolve many of their day-to-day problems on their own and without feeling out-manoeuvred by the increasing weight of legislation. The better informed that owners and occupiers of agricultural land are about their rights and obligations, the less threatened they will feel.

The authors, Michael Gregory and Margaret Parrish, have dedicated their working lives to the Country Landowners' Association and could not be better qualified to produce a work of this nature.

Sir Henry Plumb, DL, MEP
President, National Farmers Union 1970–79
President, European Parliament
President, International Federation of Agricultural Producers
Member of European Parliament for the Cotswolds
Leader of European Democratic Group

Preface to First Edition

'Ignorance of the law is no excuse' is the first truth every citizen is taught at the parental knee – or so judges and Ministers of the Crown would have us believe. This adage *is* a truth as a point of law. As a point of fact, of course, nobody can know more than a fraction of their legal rights, let alone their obligations. Hence the flood of questions we perpetually get in the Legal Department of the Country Landowners' Association, where we have worked together for twenty years. 'Can they do that to me?' 'Can I get compensation?' 'How do I get out of this fix?' The tangles with the law that beset farmers and owners are therefore familiar to us. Their problems are legion. Year in and year out some fifty thousand acres of farmland are lost for development, mostly under some form of official compulsion. Hundreds of miles of roads, pipes and cables are pushed through farms; ever-growing numbers look to the countryside for their playground; and Parliament churns out three thousand pages, or more, of legislation, while courts, tribunals and arbitrators in thousands of cases set about interpreting the mass of statute and common law.

The aim of this book is to collect together in one volume a summary of the laws that mostly concern landowners and farmers. We have concentrated on those which in our experience cause most bother and most queries, and we have sought to bring out the practical as well as the legal solutions. Whilst aiming to set out these laws, as far as possible, with the clarity the layman requires (though some are extraordinarily complex), we have at the same time included the references his professional adviser and the student may need in order to make the best use of this work as a reference book.

As with any wide-ranging book of this kind, new laws are being introduced to Parliament as we go to press and others are mooted. We have tried to forewarn about these from the best information available at the time of writing.

We acknowledge with gratitude our indebtedness to the enthusiasm and great skill of the publishers of this work, especially Richard Miles and Janet Hawkins who could not have been more helpful and who have the knack of jockeying you over obstacles in good time without you ever feeling the spur.

Preface to Second Edition

Since the first edition in 1980, it has become fashionable for legislators to make countryside laws, the agricultural holdings legislation has been totally refurbished and privatisation has become the mode. New laws, court decisions, repeals and overrulings are so numerous that this work has had to be totally revised, only a minority of its pages escaping the moving finger.

Chapter 1
Employment

Abbreviations in this Chapter:
'1978 Act' – Employment Protection (Consolidation) Act 1978.

Introduction

During the last twenty years, a number of controversial and complicated statutes regulating employment of labour have been passed by Parliament. Most of them are now consolidated in the Employment Protection (Consolidation) Act 1978. They require employers to give employees statements of terms of employment. They provide for compensation to be paid to employees who are unfairly dismissed, and for redundancy payments to be paid to workers made redundant. As a result of this legislation, the employment of workers on farms and estates is a much more onerous undertaking than it was before.

Contracts of employment

ENGAGING A WORKER

A farmer who proposes to engage a person to work on his farm can either enter into a contract of employment with a suitable employee, or he can have the work done by an independent self-employed contractor. An employee will be protected by the Employment Protection legislation. An independent contractor will not be so protected. However, an agreement to do work under contract must be a bona fide arrangement and not a contract of employment in disguise.

When engaging an employee or a contract worker, a farmer must avoid committing an offence under the Sex Discrimination Act 1975, that is he must not discriminate against women, or for that matter against men. However, where he is engaging an employee the Act will not apply unless he is employing more than five persons. Discrimination can arise in advertisements for jobs, in terms offered to women, or by refusal or failure to offer a job to a woman.

There are similar provisions in the Race Relations Act 1976, to prevent discrimination in employment of employees, or contract workers. The Act applies however small the numbers of employees.

A prospective employee is not bound to disclose to an employer convictions which have become 'spent' as a result of the Rehabilitation of Offenders Act 1974. The Act does not apply to sentences of imprisonment exceeding thirty months, and convictions are 'spent' only after periods laid down in the Act.

THE STATEMENT OF TERMS OF EMPLOYMENT

Generally a written statement of the terms of his employment must be given to an employee not later than thirteen weeks after the employment begins. Self-employed contractors are not entitled to a statement of terms of employment. There are a number of other exceptions which do not concern the farmer, but the following points should be noted.

Part-time employees. They need not be given a written statement if they normally work less than sixteen hours a week. However employees who have worked for eight or more hours a week but less than sixteen hours a week will be entitled to a statement if they have worked for five years for the same employer. Employees who work for less than eight hours a week are not entitled to a written statement.

Husband or wife of employer. No written statement need be given where a husband employs his wife, or vice versa.

Employees with written contracts. They need not be given a written statement provided the contract covers the statutory terms which have to be included in a written statement. Generally farm workers, estate maintenance workers, clerical staff, gardeners, gamekeepers and domestic staff will be entitled to a written statement of terms.

Failure to provide a written statement. There is no direct penalty for failure to provide a statement. An employer cannot be sent to jail or fined for not doing so. However, an employee who has not been given a written statement can ask for a reference to an industrial tribunal.

A wise employer will comply with the law and give the employee a written statement of terms. If the terms are clearly set out it should be much easier to decide whether an employee who is later dismissed has been dismissed for a good reason.

Particulars in the statement of terms. These may seem formidable, but actually they cover basic matters which any employee would expect to be told about. They are as follows:

(a) Salary; wages; rates of pay, including overtime and piece work rates.
(b) Times when wages or salary are paid, that is whether they are paid weekly, monthly or quarterly. Every employee has a right to be given an itemised pay statement in writing, setting out the gross amount of wages or salary, the amount and purpose of deductions and the net amount of wages and salary (Employment Protection (Consolidation) Act 1978, s. 8).
(c) Terms and conditions relating to hours of work, including normal working hours. Where hours of work are flexible or there are no set hours this should be stated.
(d) The title of the worker's job should be stated. Some farm workers are employed for special work, for example as a dairyman, pigkeeper, shepherd, tractor driver, but are expected to do other farm work occasionally. If that is the case, it should be made clear in the statement of terms.
(e) Terms and conditions relating to holidays, holiday pay, provisions for sick pay, injury, pensions and pension schemes. The current Agricultural Wages Order regulates holidays, holiday pay and sickness pay for farm workers. In the case of other workers, the employer should make clear what holidays the worker is entitled to, and whether provision will be made for pay during sickness, and if so, for how long. The Statutory Sick Pay Scheme introduced in the Social Security Act and recently extended, makes provision for employers to pay sick pay for a maximum of twenty-eight weeks in the year, and to deduct the cost from National Insurance contributions. These payments apply to agricultural workers as well as other workers, and notes have been issued by the Ministry of Agriculture to explain how sickness payments under the Agricultural Wages Order relate to payments under the Statutory Sick Pay Scheme. A pension scheme is usually attractive to an employee, and the employer would no doubt refer to any scheme he has to offer.
(f) Length of notice for terminating employment. The statutory periods for an employer dismissing an employee are one week's notice if the employee has worked continuously for the employer for four weeks or more, rising to two weeks for two years' continuous employment, three weeks for three years' and so on, until after twelve years' continuous employment an

employee is entitled to twelve weeks' notice. The parties can agree longer periods of notice but they cannot agree to shorter periods. An employee is only required to give an employer one week's notice however long his period of employment, but he may agree to give a longer period. Employers and employees can waive their right to notice. There is a common law right to terminate employment without notice if the behaviour of the other party justifies it, for example in case of serious misconduct.

(g) Information about grievance procedure, telling the employee to whom he should apply if he has a grievance about his employment, and how the matter will be dealt with. The procedure can be elaborate in a large establishment, but where there are only a few employees, notice of grievances in writing given to the agent, foreman or employer should suffice. Information should also be given about disciplinary rules (other than those relating to health and safety at work).

It is not necessary to set out all this information in the statement of terms itself, provided a document or notice containing the information is readily available to the employee. Thus the current Agricultural Wages Order can be posted up in a farm building or estate office. A booklet on sick pay schemes and pensions could be made available in a similar way.

Written information must be kept up to date, whether it is set out in a statement of terms or made available in other ways.

Redundancy

Increased mechanisation and other labour-saving inventions have led to a reduction in the farm labour force. Some farm workers may be made redundant, while others are not replaced when they retire. Workers who are made redundant are entitled to redundancy payments under employment laws. Any farmer may find himself liable to make a redundancy payment to a farm worker, maintenance worker, gardener, or domestic servant. However, a worker cannot claim redundancy payment unless he has worked for 104 weeks for one employer. Part-time workers working less than sixteen hours per week cannot claim, unless they have worked for eight hours or more, for five years or more. Other workers who do *not* qualify for payments are:

(a) Employees over sixty-five years old (men) and sixty years old (women)
(b) Certain fixed-term contract employees.
(c) Husbands or wives of employers.

(d) Domestic servants who are close relatives of the employer.
(e) Self-employed persons.

It should not be difficult to decide whether a worker has been made redundant. A worker is dismissed for redundancy where the employer no longer requires an employee to do a particular kind of work. For example, a farmer who sells his dairy herd will dismiss his herdsman for redundancy. If he then employs a tractor driver to work additional arable land, that will not affect the redundancy of the dairyman. If, however, the farmer dismisses a tractor driver and employs another tractor driver to take his place there is no redundancy. If an older man is dismissed for unfitness and replaced by a younger man, there is no redundancy.

A worker who gives notice to his employer is not usually entitled to a redundancy payment because he has not been dismissed. The burden of proving dismissal rests upon the employee. If he has been dismissed, there is a presumption that he was dismissed for redundancy, though it is open to the employer to prove that dismissal was for some other reason, for example, unfitness.

WHEN REDUNDANCY PAYMENTS ARE NOT PAYABLE
If an employee who has been dismissed for redundancy is offered further employment by the employer on the same terms as before, and *he accepts that offer*, the employee will not be entitled to a redundancy payment. An offer can be made orally or in writing, but it is advisable to make an offer in writing to avoid uncertainty and argument. An offer must be made before the notice of dismissal expires, *and* the new contract must start not later than four weeks after the end of the old contract. If the employee refuses the offer he will not get a redundancy payment unless he has reasonable grounds for his refusal.

If an employee is offered work by the same employer on different terms or in a different place and *he accepts that offer*, he will not be entitled to a redundancy payment. The offer can be made orally or in writing, but it is advisable to make the offer in writing. It must be made before the notice of dismissal expires *and* the new contract must start not later than four weeks after the end of the old contract. At one time employees were reluctant to try a new job in case they lost their right to claim a redundancy payment as a result of leaving the new job because they found it unsuitable. In 1975 trial periods were introduced to avoid penalising workers willling to try a new job. The employee is allowed a trial period of four weeks in the new job to see whether or not he likes it. If he finds it is not suitable he can give notice and will be treated as though he had been dismissed on the date when the old job ended. However, if a worker on trial gives notice unreasonably he will not get his redundancy payment. If he gives notice on reasonable grounds, he will get a redundancy payment.

A worker who unreasonably rejects the offer of a new job, without giving it a trial, will not get a redundancy payment. If he does accept the new job and continues working at it, he will not get a redundancy payment but his old job will count with his new job as continuous service so that if later he is made redundant he will have a payment based on employment in both jobs.

RE-ALLOCATION OF DUTIES

Farmers who have engaged workers as 'general farm workers' should not have any difficulty in re-allocating duties on a reorganisation of the work of the farm. Difficulties can arise in reorganisation. In *Kendall* v. *Linfield Co. Ltd* [1966] I.T.R. 550, an employee was engaged partly on general garage duties but chiefly on driving workers to a mushroom farm. He was told that after a certain date he would not be required to do general garage duties, but he would be required to continue driving workers to the farm, and also to work on the farm. He refused to accept the change, gave notice, and claimed for redundancy. He failed; it was held that he had not been made redundant.

DISMISSAL FOR MISCONDUCT

An employee who is properly dismissed for misconduct will not qualify for a redundancy payment, and that is so whether the employee has been dismissed with or without notice. The employee in *Button* v. *Sheerness & District Economical Co-operative Society Ltd* had worked in the electrical department, which was being reorganised. It was conceded by the employers that the department was in a condition of redundancy. After Button had been dismissed he was not replaced and the work he had done was put out to contract. The immediate cause of Button's dismissal on grounds of industrial misconduct was his refusal to do a piece of work which he thought inappropriate for an electrician. The employers claimed successfully that Button was dismissed for misconduct, not for redundancy.

CHANGE IN OWNERSHIP OF BUSINESS

Where a farm changes hands because there is a grant of new tenancy to a new tenant or a tenanted farm is taken in hand, or an owner-occupied farm is sold, there is a change in the ownership of the farm business (*Lloyd* v. *Brassey* [1969] 1 All E.R. 382). The Transfer of Undertakings Regulations

1981 introduced new requirements for redundancy where employees were made redundant solely because a business had changed hands. The provisions are difficult to apply to farms, but briefly the position is that if there is a change in the ownership of a farm business as described above, and workers are made redundant by virtue of that change in ownership and immediately before it takes place, the new owner of the business automatically becomes liable for the contracts of employment of existing employees. If he decides to make them redundant, he will be liable to pay redundancy payments based on their years of employment with the previous employer as well as with him. There are exceptions to the rule that the new employer must take over the contracts of employment entered into by the previous employer. If the employer who is giving up his business can show that he has an economic, technical or organisational reason for dismissing a worker, he can fairly dismiss him, and if dismissal is for redundancy he will be liable for paying a redundancy payment.

There is no change of ownership of a business where a private dwelling house and garden change hands, assuming that the house is not part of a business or run as a business. Consequently the vendor would be liable to make redundancy payments to domestic servants, and the purchaser would have no liability, even if he takes on the domestic servants.

DEATH OF AN EMPLOYER

If a farm business ceases as the result of the death of an employer, then his personal representatives will be liable to make redundancy payments to the employees of the deceased employer. However, in practice the personal representatives will want to carry on the farm business, at least for a time, and if they do so and they renew the contracts of employment or re-engage employees under new contracts and the renewal or re-engagement takes effect within eight weeks of the death of the employer, a redundancy payment will not then be payable. If, later on, the workers are made redundant, then the personal representatives would be liable to make a redundancy payment.

EMPLOYEES WHO LEAVE BEFORE THEIR NOTICE EXPIRES

An employee who has been dismissed for redundancy may wish to leave before his period of notice expires. This is understandable, as he may want to take a new job which has been offered to him. Such a worker may not wish to be penalised by loss of his redundancy payment. He need not lose it. He should give his employer the statutory notice of one week, or a longer notice if this is required under contract. If the employer does not object to the worker leaving he will still be entitled to his redundancy payment. If the employer objects, he should serve notice on the employee requiring him to withdraw his notice and also warning him that if he fails to do so, his claim for redundancy payment will be contested. The employee might decide to ignore this request and leave just the same. If the employer then refuses to make a redundancy payment, the employee has a right to apply to an Industrial Tribunal to decide whether or not he is entitled to such a payment. In order to take advantage of these provisions the employee's notice to the employer must be given with the period of notice the employer is obliged to give him (that is, under statute or contract) not within a period of notice voluntarily given (*Lobb* v. *Bright Son & Co. (Clerkenwell) Ltd* [1966] I.T.R. 566).

UNFAIR SELECTION FOR REDUNDANCY

Where economies are being made in a farm or estate, more than one employee may have to be made redundant. The choice may not be easy. In businesses employing a lot of labour there is probably a 'first in last out' rule, or there may be a customary arrangement to that effect. On farms it is probably better not to have any rule. Such a rule can easily be applied for example on the railways, but where a farm employs one diaryman, one shepherd, one tractor driver and two general farm workers, the rule would be very difficult to apply.

An employer must not dismiss an employee for an inadmissible reason (for example, because the employee takes part in trade union activities). If there is an agreed procedure for selection for redundancy it should be followed.

THE REDUNDANCY PAYMENT

Payments depend on the length of an employee's continuous employment, up to a maximum of twenty years' employment. The following points should however be noted:

(a) Service before the employee's eighteenth birthday does not count.

(b) Years of service before the last twenty years do not count.

(c) Scales of payment increase for each year of employment between forty-one and sixty-four years of age. Scales are one half a week's pay for each year of employment between eighteen and twenty-two years old; one week's pay for each year of employment between twenty-two and forty-one years of age, and one-and-a-half weeks' pay for each year of employment between forty-one and sixty-five years of age.

(d) A person who is made redundant after reaching retirement will not be entitled to a redundancy payment.

(e) As a rule one week's pay for the purpose of calculating a redundancy payment is the employee's current earnings for his normal weekly working hours.

The Department of Employment's handbook on the *Redundancy Payments Scheme* includes a ready reckoner for calculating redundancy payments. A copy of the booklet can be obtained free from the Department's offices. Any employer proposing to make redundancies is advised to get a copy of it, and to ask for the forms for getting rebates from the Redundancy Payments Fund.

REBATES

Owing to the amendments made by the Wages Act 1986, redundancy rebates are payable only to employers with less than ten employees (s. 104A, 1978 Act, s. 27, Wages Act 1986).

Rebates from the Redundancy Payments Fund may be claimed by employers who have made redundancy payments, provided they were legally liable to make such payments. The rebate rate is 35 per cent at present. An employer must give the redundant employee a written statement showing how the redundancy payment has been calculated, and this information must be sent to the Department of Employment when an employer makes a claim for a rebate. There is an official form for this purpose, and copies may be obtained from any of the Department's Redundancy Payments Offices. An employer who fails to provide an employee with written information may be fined. The official form of notice of dismissal is RP1. An employee who has received a redundancy payment from his employers should sign an official receipt form (RP3) and that form should be submitted with the employer's claim for rebate (RP2) to the Redundancy Payments Office. Rebate must be claimed within six months of the date on which redundancy payment was made to the employee. Employees will usually claim for redundancy at the date of dismissal, but a claim must in any case be made within six months from the termination of his employment. Employees do not have to pay tax on redundancy payments. Contributions to the Redundancy Fund by an employer are allowable for tax purposes as business expenses and the employer's share of the redundancy payment is similarly allowable.

CONSULTATIONS WITH TRADE UNIONS ABOUT PROPOSED REDUNDANCIES

Employers proposing to make workers redundant are required to consult recognised trade unions about redundancies. This rule does not apply to short-term employees such as seasonal workers. The union must be one which is recognised by the employers for the purposes of collective bargaining. The fact that a farmer pays the agricultural wage laid down in the Agricultural Wages Order does not amount to recognition by an employer of those unions involved in the fixing of the statutory minimum wage. The farmer pays that wage because the statutory order forbids him to pay less. He has not as an employer bargained with any union in respect of his employees. It seems that few farmers recognise a trade union for collective bargaining purposes. Those who do should consult the union in question about any proposed redundancies. Minimum times for consultation are laid down for redundancies of ten or more employees made within thirty days (thirty days) and 100 or more employees within ninety days (ninety days). Farm staffs are small, but some farms or estates may be obliged to make ten or more persons redundant within a short period. If an employer fails to consult a recognised trade union, that union can make a complaint to an Industrial Tribunal, and the Tribunal may make a protective award, which means that the employer will have to pay wages for a protected period, for example, ninety days where 100 or more employees have been made redundant, thirty days where thirty or more have been made redundant, or twenty-eight days in any other case. Complaints about failure to consult must be made within three months of dismissal. The burden of proving recognition is on the union. Recognition need not involve some formal act by the employer. It could be inferred from his conduct, and that of the union. In *Transport & General Workers' Union* v. *Dyer* (1977) 12 I.T.R. 113, the limited and unwilling contact which Mr Dyer had with union officials was held *not* to amount to recognition. In *Joshua Lulson and Brothers* v. *U.S.D.A.W.* [1978] 1 R.L.R. 120, where an employer had consulted a trade union about allocation of duties, security, and discipline, had allowed the union to put up notices about wages agreed by the Joint Industrial Council, and to collect union dues on the premises, the Company was held to have recognised the union.

NOTICE OF REDUNDANCIES TO THE SECRETARY OF STATE

In addition to consulting recognised trade unions about redundancies an employer must notify the Secretary of State about redundancies.

Advance written notice of redundancies of more than ten employees to be dismissed within thirty days must be notified to the Secretary of State in writing. Notice should be given thirty days before the first dismissal takes effect. For dismissals of 100 or more employees within ninety days, advance notice of ninety days is required: this provision is unlikely to be of interest to farmers.

Notices of redundancies to the Secretary of State should not be confused with notices to the local Redundancy Payments Office for the purpose of claiming rebates.

INSOLVENT EMPLOYERS: GUARANTEE PAYMENTS

Where an employer cannot make a redundancy payment because he is insolvent, then subject to satisfactory proof being given to the Department of Employment, redundancy payments will be made from the Redundancy Payments Fund. The Department will then try to recover the money from the employers as an ordinary unsecured creditor. The Department of Employment advises that an employer who admits liability for redundancy payments, but is unable to pay them, should explain his problem to the nearest employment office of the Employment Service Agency and be ready to send a statement of account or a written statement from an accountant or solicitor setting out his financial position. The Department also advises that legal representatives of deceased employers who expect delays in the settlement of the estate should explain the position to the nearest employment office for reference to the specialist office of the Department.

In the case of insolvent employers, the full amount of the rebate will be credited to the employer, and the Department will seek to recover only the amount less rebate. However where an employer is solvent, but fails to make a redundancy payment which is due, the Department will disallow the whole or part of the rebate.

The employer has a right of appeal to an Industrial Tribunal against refusal or reduction of rebate. The Tribunal can restore the rebate, or it can order a bigger reduction.

TIME LIMIT FOR CLAIMS

As a rule redundancy payments will be made at the time of dismissal, but an employer may fail to make a payment either because he is insolvent or for some other reason. An employee has six months from the date of termination of employment in which to make a claim; it should be made in writing. After the expiry of the six-month period any liability by the employer to make a payment will cease, if no claim has been made in writing.

If a claim in writing has been made within the six-month period, but refused, the employee has a further six months in which to make a claim to an Industrial Tribunal.

Any dispute about a right to a redundancy payment, or the amount of such a payment, may be referred to an industrial tribunal. A tribunal consists of a legally qualified chairman and two other members. Tribunals sit in different parts of the country. There is a right of appeal from a Tribunal on a point of law, to the Employment Appeal Tribunal. An employer may represent himself before the Tribunal, or he may be legally represented, or he may be represented by some other person, for example his agent, farm manager, or official of an employers' union or federation. A leaflet on Industrial Tribunal Procedure is available from the Department of Employment.

An employee who has been dismissed for redundancy, and who has worked continuously for the same employer for at least two years, is entitled to *reasonable* time off during his period of notice in order to look for another job, or to arrange for training for another job.

Unfair dismissals

Employment protection legislation includes provisions to protect employees against unfair dismissal by employers. The publicity given to some cases has led many employers to believe that they cannot dismiss an employee at all, or if they do he will invariably take the employer to an Industrial Tribunal and be awarded large sums by way of compensation. Neither of these beliefs is true. It is possible to dismiss an employee for good reasons. In cases taken to Industrial Tribunals the employer wins in two-thirds of those cases.

Unfair dismissal provisions apply to persons employed under a contract of service or a contract of apprenticeship. They do *not* apply to self-employed persons. They *do* apply to persons who work for at least sixteen hours per week for one employer. Unfair dismissal provisions apply only where a worker has worked for at least two years for his employer when his employment began after June 1985. Employees taken on before that date qualify after one year's employment, except in cases where the employer qualifies as a small business, in which case the qualifying period is two years. Generally any person employed in agriculture or forestry, or as a gamekeeper, stud groom, gardener, chauffeur or domestic worker, or as an estate worker or farm or estate secretary will be protected by the unfair dismissal provisions if he or she has worked for two years or more for his or her employer, and normally works sixteen hours or more per week. Part-time workers are not covered unless they have worked for between eight to sixteen hours per week for the same employer for five years.

Unfair dismissal provisions apply even where there are less than four employees.

EMPLOYEES NOT PROTECTED AGAINST UNFAIR DISMISSAL

There are a number of exclusions which do not concern farmers, but the following should be noted:

(a) Employees who reach the age of sixty-five (men) or sixty (women) before their employment terminates.
(b) An employee who is the husband or wife of the employer.

MEANING OF DISMISSAL

Dismissal usually means the termination of employment by the *employer*, with or without notice, but it can mean termination of a contract of employment by an employee, with or without notice, where the employer's conduct justified such termination. That is known as 'constructive dismissal'. It has given rise to claims by ex-employees for compensation. It has been laid down by the Court of Appeal that an employee has the right to treat himself as discharged from his contractual obligations only where the employer has been guilty of conduct which goes to the root of the contract of employment, or which shows that the employer no longer intends to be bound by one or more of the essential terms of the contract (*Western Excavating (E.E.C.) Ltd* v. *Sharp* [1978] 1 All E.R. 713).

The following cases have been held *not* to be constructive dismissal: *Devon County Council* v. *Cook* (1977) 12 I.T.R. 347 (employee leaving in anticipation of long term plan for redundancy); *Phillips* v. *Glendale Cabinet Co.* [1977] 1 R.L.R. 188 (employee resigning after being demoted following frequent complaints about persistent lateness at work); *Express Lift Co.* v. *Bowles* [1977] 1 R.L.R. 99 (employee leaving after refusing to work in another part of the country, although it was a term of his contract that he should work where directed by the employer). The following cases have *been* held to amount to constructive dismissal: *Wetherall (Bond St. W.1)* v. *Lynn* [1978] I.C.R. 205 (employer undermining authority of stock controller by criticising him in front of junior staff); *Associated Tyre Specialists (Eastern)*

v. *Waterhouse* [1977] I.C.R. 218 (employer failing to give support to supervisor in his dealings with other employees).

NOTICE OF DISMISSAL

Notice need not be given in writing, but it is necessary for an employer to give a written statement of reasons for dismissal if asked by an employee to do so, provided the employee has worked for six months for the employer. However, it is advisable in all cases to give written reasons for dismissal. It can be done in a letter making it quite clear to the employee what the reason for dismissal is. The worker is entitled to know why he is being dismissed, for example whether for redundancy, inefficiency or sickness.

TERMINATION OF CONTRACT OF EMPLOYMENT

Unless he is dismissed for serious misconduct, a worker is entitled to the statutory or a contractual period of notice (see p. 3). Generally a contract will terminate when the notice of dismissal expires. However, it sometimes happens that an employee is dismissed and given wages in lieu of notice. In that case the date of termination will generally be the date on which the employee last worked for the employer. However, for cetain purposes, the date of termination will be the date on which the contract would have terminated had the appropriate notice been given (Employment Protection (Consolidation) Act 1978, s. 55(5)).

COMPLAINT OF UNFAIR DISMISSAL

Complaints of unfair dismissal can be made by an employee to an Industrial Tribunal. A complaint can be made as soon as an employee has been given notice of dismissal by his employer, or at any time before the contract ends, or within three months after the effective date of termination of the contract. Industrial Tribunals have a discretionary power to accept complaints made out of time where they consider that it was not reasonably practicable for the complaint to be made earlier.

CONCILIATION

An employee who has made a complaint to an Industrial Tribunal should state on his application form whether he wishes to be re-instated, or whether he would prefer to receive compensation. A copy of the form will be sent to the employer and to A.C.A.S. (Advisory, Conciliation and Arbitration Service). The employer has the right to send a reply to the Tribunal refuting the allegations made against him by the employee. The employee and A.C.A.S. will get a copy of that reply. If so requested by the employer and employee A.C.A.S. will try to settle the dispute. Attempts at reconciliation can continue right up to the date of the Tribunal hearing. A hearing can be postponed if it looks as though a settlement will be reached. Information given by the parties to an A.C.A.S. conciliation officer in the course of his duty is confidential and must not be divulged to an Industrial Tribunal without the consent of the person who gave it.

WHAT THE TRIBUNAL MUST DECIDE

An Industrial Tribunal hearing an unfair dismissal complaint must be satisfied:

(a) That the employee has been dismissed.
(b) That he is not excluded from making a complaint (for example, because he has not worked for the employer for the qualifying period).
(c) That the complaint is not out of time.

The *employer* must satisfy the Tribunal that the reason for dismissing the employee was fair (for example, the employee was dismissed for inefficiency, unfitness, redundancy, or unsatisfactory conduct, or some other substantial reason). The Tribunal then has to decide whether the employer acted reasonably or unreasonably in treating it as a sufficient reason for dismissing the employee. The question has to be decided in accordance with equity and the substantial merits of the case.

Where an employee has been dismissed for redundancy, the Tribunal may hold that there has been unfair selection for redundancy and that the employee was unfairly dismissed. To avoid such a finding an employer should not select an employee for redundancy for an inadmissible reason (for example, because the employee takes part in trade union activities). An employer should not select an employee for redundancy in contravention of an agreed procedure or customary arrangement, such as 'first in last out'. If there is an agreed procedure or customary arrangement it should be followed.

RE-INSTATEMENT AND RE-ENGAGEMENT

One of the remedies for unfair dismissal is an order for re-instatement or re-engagement. A Tribunal has powers to make such an order if the employee wishes to be re-instated or re-engaged. Although an order can be made, an employer cannot be compelled to take the employee back, but if he fails to comply with an order he will be required to pay additional compensation to the employee.

Re-instatement means that the employer must treat the employee in every way as though he had not been dismissed.

Re-engagement means that the employee must be taken back into comparable or other suitable employment.

In the case of *re-instatement* the Tribunal must consider whether the worker wishes to be re-instated, whether it is practicable for the employer to re-instate him, and if the worker contributed to his own dismissal, whether it would be just to order re-instatement. In considering whether to order re-engagement instead of re-instatement the same rule applies.

If an employer who has dismissed an employee has replaced him with another employee, that fact must be disregarded by the Tribunal in deciding whether or not re-instatement or re-engagement is practicable unless the employer can show that it was essential to engage a replacement, or that the employer waited a reasonable time without having heard from the dismissed employee that he wished to be re-instated or re-engaged.

ENFORCEMENT OF ORDERS FOR RE-INSTATEMENT OR RE-ENGAGEMENT

If an employer takes a worker back, but the terms of the order are not fully complied with, the Tribunal may award compensation to the employee to take account of the loss suffered. If an employer refused to take a worker back, the Tribunal must award compensation for unfair dismissal to include an additional sum for the employer's failure to comply with the order.

COMPENSATION FOR UNFAIR DISMISSAL

If a Tribunal has found that an employee has been unfairly dismissed but has decided not to make an order for re-instatement or re-engagement, the Tribunal must award an unfair dismissal payment, which is made up of a basic award and a compensatory award.

Basic award. This is the same as the employee would have been entitled to if he had been made redundant and could claim a redundancy payment. As a rule there will be a minimum basic award of two weeks' pay. Calculation of the basic award is based on the employee's period of service with the employer. The amount of one week's pay for each year of employment is limited by statute, and the limit can be varied by statutory order. Not more than twenty years' employment can be taken into account. As in the case of redundancy payments, the amount of the basic award is progressively reduced in the case of employees nearing retirement age.

Compensatory award. This part of the award is to cover expenses arising from dismissal, and any loss of benefits which the employee might reasonably have expected to enjoy but for dismissal, including expectation of redundancy payment, but an employee cannot be compensated twice under this head, that is, under the basic award and under the compensatory award.

There is a maximum figure for a compensatory award, which is subject to variation by statutory order.

The employee has the same duty to mitigate his loss as a person suing for damages at common law. He can do that by diligently attempting to find alternative employment. Failure to mitigate loss will result in a reduction of the compensatory award. The award can also be reduced if the employee contributed to his own dismissal.

When calculating loss suffered by the employee, the Tribunal will make reductions for payments made by the employer (for example, *ex gratia* payments), and for wages received in the employee's new job.

DEATH OF AN EMPLOYER

Where an employer dies after dismissing an employee, any complaint to an Industrial Tribunal made against him by the employee can be defended by the deceased employer's personal representative. Similarly, if an employee dies before he has made a complaint, or while proceedings are pending, a personal representative of the deceased employee may make a complaint or continue the proceedings.

PRACTICAL POINTS

The procedure for dismissing a worker worries many employers. There are no statutory rules of procedure, but there are Codes of Practice issued by A.C.A.S. giving guidance on disciplinary rules to be adopted by employers. There is no penalty for failing to observe the Code of Practice, but an Industrial Tribunal is entitled to take into account any provision of the Code which seems to them relevant. A Tribunal is unlikely to expect an employer on a farm employing a small staff to observe rules as eleborate as those applying to a large enterprise. However, where disciplinary rules have been adopted and made known to employees, they should be followed. A dismissal can be held to be unfair if an unfair procedure for dismissal is followed, even though the reasons for dismissal were reasonable.

An employee who stands to be dismissed for breach of disciplinary rules should be given an opportunity to state his case.

Where a worker is dismissed for inefficiency, the employer must show that the acts complained of were serious enough for dismissal.

It is advisable to give a written warning before dismissing an employee, particularly in the case of a long-standing employee. The warning should make clear to the employee why his work or conduct is unsatisfactory, and should state that if he fails to improve or behave satisfactorily he will be dismissed.

SICK WORKERS

Special care is required when dismissing workers on grounds of ill-health. Frequent absence due to sickness is a ground for dismissal particularly where the employee is an essential worker on a small staff (*Clark* v. *Coronel Ltd* (1972) 7 I.T.R. 208). It is advisable to discuss the question of the employee's health with him, and to ask him to produce medical evidence that he will become fit and remain fit in future for the job for which he is employed.

The following cases show the care required before making a decision to dismiss a sick worker. In *Spencer* v. *Paragon Wallpapers Ltd* (1976) 11 I.T.R. 294, Mr Spencer was first employed by the company in June 1974: fifteen months later he became ill and unable to work. By November of that year the company's work was increasing. It needed all its employees. As a result of inquiries it was found that Mr Spencer would not be fit for about four to six weeks. The company decided that it could not keep the job open for so long and dismissed him. He brought a complaint of unfair dismissal before an Industrial Tribunal and lost his case. He appealed, and the court dismissed the appeal. The court said that the Tribunal had considered the nature of the illness, the likely length of the continuing absence, the need of the employers to have done the work the employee was engaged to do, and the circumstances of the case. There was no ground for interfering with the Tribunal's decision. In another case, *Owen* v. *Funditor* [1976] I.C.R. 350, the court found there was not enough evidence of ill-health to justify dismissal. In that case the employee had worked for a company for twenty-seven years and had become Chief Engineer. He became seriously ill, and afterwards was given a less exacting job. He did the job satisfactorily until he became ill again. His employers decided to retire him at sixty years of age, but then dismissed him shortly before that time. The Industrial Tribunal said that the employers were wrong in failing to discuss their intentions with the employee, or to obtain medical evidence, but they decided that evidence of ill-health was sufficient to justify dismissal. The employee appealed and his appeal was allowed.

Chapter 2
Housing

Abbreviations in this Chapter:
'1985 Act' – Housing Act 1985.
'1976 Act' – Rent (Agriculture) Act 1976.
'1977 Act' – Rent Act 1977.

Introduction

There is an enormous amount of law relating to housing, but fortunately farmers need to be interested only in certain aspects of it. Before a house can be built planning permission must be obtained. That is dealt with in Chapter 6 on town and country planning. In the case of existing houses, the farmer may wish them to be occupied by farm workers, maintenance workers, or other members of his staff under service agreements. He may want to let them temporarily outside agriculture. He may decide to let them only for holidays. He may not be able to let them at all because they are unfit. He may wish to improve them with the aid of a grant if possible. He may own an old house which is so unfit that it ought to be demolished, at any rate in the opinion of the local authority. It may even be dangerous and likely to collapse onto the highway. The law applying in these situations is as described here.

New houses

At one time modest subsidies were available under the Housing Financial Provisions Acts for private owners who built houses for members of the rural population. That subsidy scheme has been wound up. As already stated, planning permission must be obtained before a new house can be built on a farm or elsewhere. Building regulations must also be complied with, and approval of plans must be applied for and obtained from the local housing authority (district council). The building regulations are made under the Public Health Acts. They regulate construction of buildings, materials, space, lighting, ventilation, insulation, dimensions of rooms for human habitation, height of buildings, water supply, foul and surface water drainage, fire prevention and other matters. (Planning permission does not exempt an applicant from obtaining building regulation approval.) The applicant is entitled to receive from the local authority within a prescribed period, a notice that plans for his house have been passed for building regulation purposes, or that they have been rejected specifying the defects.

If works are done in contravention of building regulations, they may be pulled down or removed by the local authority if the applicant fails to pull down or remove them when ordered by the local authority to do so.

Service cottages

It is customary to offer service cottages to farm workers, estate maintenance workers, and other employees on farms and agricultural estates. Agricultural tenancy agreements which include cottages usually contain covenants by the tenant that he will not let such cottages, but will permit them to be occupied by his employees under service agreements. Where cottages are occupied under service agreements by full-time farm workers they will usually be protected by the Rent (Agriculture) Act 1976. Other workers (for example, estate maintenance workers, gardeners, gamekeepers) are not protected by that Act, but they cannot be compelled to vacate a cottage except under a county court order for possession which the owner will be able to obtain.

The Rent (Agriculture) Act 1976 came into force on 1 January 1977. Occupiers protected by the Act are entitled to a statutory tenancy as soon as their protected occupation of the cottage ceases, that is as soon as their right to occupy under their contract of employment ceases. If the owner wants to recover possession of the cottage for an incoming farm worker, he will have to apply to a local housing authority to rehouse the outgoing worker. If he does not want the cottage for an incoming farm worker he will not be able, in most cases, to recover possession of the cottage.

Service occupation agreements

Where a worker is to live in a farm or estate cottage as a term of his contract of employment, it is advisable to give him a written service agreement, stating that the house is to be occupied by him rent and rate free, or subject to the permitted statutory deduction under the Agricultural Wages Order, where that is appropriate. He should not be required under the agreement to undertake tenant's liabilities, but he should be required to keep the interior of the cottage clean and the garden tidy. He should agree that he is under an obligation to reside in the cottage for the purpose only of the better or more convenient discharge of his duty, and to occupy it as a residence for himself or his family only. Some owners will want to add further requirements, for example, that the occupier shall not keep animals or birds on the premises. Some occupiers like to do their own interior decorations, the owner supplying the materials, and there is no reason why they should not be allowed to do so, if the owner is agreeable.

As far as farm workers' cottages are concerned, the permitted statutory deduction from wages for the benefit of a cottage is fixed by the current Agriculture Wages Board Order, and is subject to revision when wages are revised. Deductions greater than the statutory deduction can be authorised by an Agricultural Wages Committee on application made by the owner. A statutory deduction from wages is not rent, and rent books are not required for service occupation agreements.

Many owners do not make any deduction at all. Others would like to charge a rent, but it can be demonstrated that only the tax collector would benefit if that were done.

PROTECTED OCCUPATION OF FARM WORKERS

Farm workers who are *not* protected by the Rent (Agriculture) Act 1976 will enjoy the limited protection of the Protection from Eviction Act 1977. Under that provision a worker has six months' security of tenure as from the date when his contractual right to occupy the cottage under a service agreement ceases. That will usually be the date when his contract of employment ends. The owner has a right to apply to a county court for a possession order within that six-month period if he urgently needs the house for another worker. The court may make a possession order within the six-month period but must suspend the order unless satisfied that suitable alternative accommodation is available to the cottage occupier, or that the cottage is urgently required in the interests of agricultural efficiency, or that greater hardship would be caused by the suspension of the order than by its execution, or that the cottage occupier has been guilty of misconduct or nuisance.

A farm worker who has only worked for six months in agriculture would be protected under the 1977 Act, but would not be protected under the 1976 Act.

Farm workers (including forestry workers) protected under the 1976 Act enjoy protection similar to Rent Act security. Protection applies to workers who have worked for two years in agriculture (or more exactly ninety-one out of the last 104 weeks) anywhere in the E.E.C. They must be full-time workers in agriculture (thirty-five hours per week) but there are special provisions for disabled workers. There is no qualifying period for occupation of a cottage.

The qualifying worker must occupy a house owned by his employer, *or* a house which his employer has arranged with the owner to be occupied by the employee. He must occupy it as a condition of his employment in agriculture. Once he has qualified for protection, he will not lose that protection (for example, because the owner sells the house, or he ceases to work in agriculture, by retiring or changing his job). The Act applies even where a qualifying worker rents a cottage at less than two-thirds the appropriate rateable value.

A qualifying farm worker who occupies under a service agreement (or tenancy at a rent less than two-thirds the appropriate rateable value) is called a 'protected occupier'. If he dies while a protected occupier, his widow can succeed him as 'protected occupier', or if the farm worker is a woman her husband can succeed her. If there is no surviving spouse, another member of the family can succeed instead, but there can only be one succession.

When a protected occupation ends and the contractual right to occupy the cottage ceases, a statutory tenancy will at once arise. Usually the contractual right to occupy will cease when the contract of employment ceases. That will usually be when a notice of dismissal expires, or the worker's notice to his employer expires, or when a worker dies. In cases where a worker enjoys a tenancy at less than two-thirds the appropriate rateable value, the tenancy may expire at some other date, following a notice to quit.

In the majority of cases a protected occupancy will terminate when the contract of employment expires. However the worker should be reminded, in writing, of the date on which his contractual right to occupy the cottage ceases; and where the cottage is required for an incoming worker, he should be notified that he will be required to vacate on that date. In the case of a retired worker, the owner may not wish him to vacate, but he should notify him of the date when his contractual right to occupy the cottage ceases.

If a worker who has become a statutory tenant dies, the widow or widower, as the case may be, can succeed to the statutory tenancy. If there is no surviving spouse, another member of the family living with the statutory tenant at the time of death can succeed instead. There can only be one succession.

A statutory tenancy will arise on termination of a protected occupancy, even if the worker himself gives notice to terminate his contract of employment.

EXEMPTIONS

A statutory tenancy cannot arise where the *immediate* landlord is the Crown, Duchy of Lancaster, Duchy of Cornwall, or a Government Department. The Act does not apply to Forestry Commission tied cottages, or Ministry of Agriculture tied cottages. Other exempt bodies are local authorities, New Towns Commission, Housing Corporation, Development Corporation under the New Towns Act 1965, or a housing trust which is a charity under the Charities Act 1960, and housing associations subject to certain conditions.

Recovery of possession of protected farm cottages

SUITABLE ALTERNATIVE ACCOMMODATION

An owner who wishes to recover possession of a farm cottage occupied by a protected occupier or statutory tenant, cannot obtain a county court order on the ground that he wants the cottage for an incoming worker. He can only get an order on one or more of the grounds set out in Schedule 4 to the 1976 Act. Most of these grounds are discretionary. The most important are Cases I and II, where which empower a county court to grant an order where suitable alternative accommodation is provided by the housing authority, or someone else (for example the owner). Thus if a housing authority offers accommodation and the occupier unreasonably refuses it, the court can make a possession order against him. This provision is a useful backstop in those few cases where occupiers are unduly fussy about council house accommodation offered to them. Some owners have been obliged to apply for possession orders in such cases.

BREACH OF COVENANT (CASE III)

An order may be obtained if a tenant fails to pay his rent, or is in breach of any obligation of his tenancy agreement. The terms of a statutory tenancy under the 1976 Act are set out in Schedule 5 to the Act. Since tenants who are genuinely unable to pay the rent can get a rent allowance from the local authority, there should not be many cases where a tenant cannot pay the rent (for further information on rent matters see p. 30).

NUISANCES (CASE IV)

An order may be obtained where a tenant or his lodger or a member of his household commits acts of nuisance or annoyance to adjoining owners, or is convicted of using a house for immoral or illegal purposes. Thus a drunken or excessively noisy tenant who seriously annoyed his neighbours might be got out on a county court order under this case. A man living with a woman to whom he was not married would not be using the house for an immoral purpose, and could not be got out under Case IV.

ACTS OF WASTE AND DAMAGE (CASES V AND VI)

A house may deteriorate as a result of acts of waste or neglect by a tenant, his lodger or a member of his household. Waste means acts such as pulling down or removing parts of the house, such as windows, doors, parts of the wainscoting, or internal dividing walls. A tenant's housekeeping standards may be deplorable, but it would not follow that he was guilty of acts of waste or neglect so as to justify an application for an order under Case IV.

Few farm cottages are furnished by the owner. If they are and the occupier damages the furniture, an order for possession may be obtained under Case VI.

TENANT SERVING NOTICE TO QUIT (CASE VII)

A tenant may serve notice to quit on the owner, who then advertises the house for sale and enters into a contract of sale with a purchaser. The tenant may refuse to vacate. That would give the landlord ground for applying for a possession order.

ASSIGNMENT OR SUBLETTING (CASE VIII)

It is a condition of a statutory tenancy, under Schedule 5 of the 1976 Act, that the tenant shall not assign, sublet, or part with possession of the dwellinghouse or any part of it. If a tenant is in breach of this condition the owner can apply for a possession order under Case VIII.

OWNER-OCCUPATION BY LANDLORD (CASE IX)

An owner may want to live in a farm cottage himself, or he may want it for a member of his family who is getting married. He can apply for a possession order on that ground provided he did not purchase the house after 12 April 1976.

TENANT SUBLETTING AT AN EXCESSIVE RENT

Under the terms of his *contractual* tenancy or occupancy a tenant may be allowed to sublet. If he is not he would be in breach of covenant if he did sublet. However, where he is allowed to sublet he must not abuse his position by charging an excessive rent. If he does the owner can apply for a possession order.

CASES WHERE COURT MUST GRANT A POSSESSION ORDER

Owner-occupier's house. It is unlikely that an owner-occupier would want to leave his house temporarily and allow it to be occupied as a service house for a farm worker, though he might perhaps allow a farm manager to occupy it under the terms of his contract of employment in agriculture. In the rare cases where an owner intends to do that, he should first serve notice under Case XI of Schedule 4, that is before the licence or tenancy begins. He will then be able to recover possession of the house when he wants it again for his own occupation.

Retirement home. It is possible that a farmer who has bought a house for his retirement would allow it to be used as a service house for a farm worker until such time as he needs it. If he does he should serve on the prospective occupier or tenant before the service agreement or tenancy begins, a notice under Case XII of Schedule 4 of the 1976 Act. That will ensure that when he wants the house for his retirement he will be able to recover possession of it.

Overcrowding. This is a ground for a mandatory order for possession. The house would have to be overcrowded as defined in the Housing Act 1985, s. 324.

Application to local authority to rehouse (1976 Act, s.27)

In practice there are unlikely to be many cases where an owner will apply for a County court order for possession. In most cases he will be able to apply to a local authority to rehouse his outgoing farm worker, because he wants the house for an incoming farm worker. However, the authority is only obliged to rehouse the outgoer where an application is made by the occupier of the agricultural land. Thus a contractor who does not occupy land will not be able to apply.

The authority will not be obliged to rehouse the outgoer unless he is a qualifying agricultural worker, and the house is required for another agricultural worker. Thus if the house is required for a carpenter or a gardener, the authority will not be obliged to rehouse. If the house is occupied by a housekeeper, the authority will not be obliged to rehouse her if the house is wanted for a farm worker, because the housekeeper's service occupancy is not protected under the 1976 Act.

If the outgoing farm worker has a rent-protected tenancy granted to him by his employer, the housing authority is obliged to rehouse him, if the house is wanted for another farm worker.

To sum up, an application must be made by the occupier of the agricultural land. The house must be occupied by a farm worker, who is a protected occupier, statutory tenant, or a Rent Act tenant, and it must be required for an incoming farm worker. The owner must show that he has no other suitable accommodation available, and that the house is needed in the interests of agricultural efficiency.

APPLICATION FORM FOR REHOUSING FARM WORKER

A form should be obtained from the local authority. The applicant will be asked whether he has other accommodation which could be used for rehousing the worker, and why it could not be used for that purpose. There are questions on the form designed to find out whether the occupier is protected by the Act. The owner is asked by what date he needs vacant possession of the cottage. Finally, he is asked whether he wishes an Agricultural Dwelling House Advisory Committee to advise on agricultural need and urgency. It is open to the owner to apply direct to the Chairman of the Agricultural Wages Committee to set up an A.D.H.A.C. to advise, or the local authority can make the application. The owner, the cottage occupier, and the local authority each have a right to obtain the advice of an A.D.H.A.C. Generally, an owner would be advised to make an application himself to the Chairman of the Agricultural Wages Committee.

When a local authority receives from the owner an application to rehouse the occupier, it must notify the occupier within seven days of receipt of the application that it has been made.

Agricultural dwelling house advisory committees

Each Committee consists of a chairman, one employer representative and one employee representative. The Chairman of the Agricultural Wages Committee for the area selects a Chairman for an A.D.H.A.C. from a panel of persons approved by the Ministry of Agriculture. Guidelines for A.D.H.A.C.s have been issued by the Ministry giving very detailed advice on procedure. As a rule A.D.H.A.C.s should deliver their advice not later than twenty-eight days from the request for that advice. Details of arrangements for a hearing are sent to the parties by the Secretary to the A.D.H.A.C. A tenant farmer is sent an extra copy for his landlord. A farmer may appear personally or be represented by his agent or solicitor. The Committee is concerned solely with agricultural need and urgency. It will be helped by an appraisal of the farm made by A.D.A.S.

Where confidential information may be disclosed by the owner or the cottage occupier, the parties may be heard separately.

An A.D.H.A.C. must inform the local authority of the advice it has given. This is done on a form designed for the purpose, and a copy must be sent to the cottage occupier and the applicant. (Copies of the A.D.A.S. appraisal are also given to the cottage occupier and the applicant by the A.D.H.A.C.)

AGRICULTURAL NEED AND URGENCY

The applicant must prove both need and urgency. If a worker is being made redundant he will find this impossible as a rule, though if a specialised worker (for example, shepherd) is being made redundant, he may be able to show need for a general farm worker instead. It is more difficult to show need in the case of a cottage for a tractor driver for example, than it is for a herdsman, or some horticultural workers needed to supervise heated glasshouses. In the case of tractor drivers or general workers, it is advisable to apply to the local job centre to find out whether there are any workers living locally who could fill the vacancy satisfactorily without requiring a service cottage. If there are no such workers available, the employer will be able to inform the A.D.H.A.C. of the position, and thus improve his case for agricultural need and urgency.

LOCAL AUTHORITY'S DUTY AND POWERS

Although a local authority has to take full account of advice given by an A.D.H.A.C. on agricultural need and urgency for rehousing a farm worker, it is for the local authority to decide whether or not to rehouse the outgoing farm worker.

The local authority must notify the applicant and the service occupier of its decision, stating what action it proposes to take, or if it does not propose to take any action, the reasons for its decision. Authorities should notify the parties of their decision within three months of receiving the application, or if the advice of an A.D.H.A.C. is sought, within two months of receipt of that advice.

An authority is obliged to use its best endeavours to rehouse an outgoing farm worker in case of agricultural need. If it fails to do so, the applicant can sue the authority for damages for breach of statutory duty. So far there have been no cases under the Rent (Agricultural) Act 1976 where an applicant has bought such an action, though there have been cases under similar provisions in other statutes. They demonstrate that it is difficult to sue a local authority successfully for breach of a statutory duty of the kind described.

Local authorities have been advised on the legal and practical aspects of their duties by the Department of the Environment in their Circular 122/76. Authorities have been advised that owners should not be expected to offer outgoing farm workers a house kept available for a replacement worker, or a seasonal worker, or which is bona fide let for holidays, or which is being kept for a worker who is due to retire. An owner should not be expected to find alternative accommodation which is not controlled by him. A house which has been let temporarily outside agriculture under special provisions in the Rent Acts (see now Rent Act 1977, Schedule 15 Case 16) could be required for rehousing an outgoing farm worker, though that is unlikely, because the temporary tenant would no doubt have to be rehoused by the local authority.

Local authorities have been advised that applicants need not show evidence of an actual or conditional contract of employment with the incoming worker. That is because farmers may be unable to attract an incoming worker without a firm offer of a service cottage.

Rents

Owners who are waiting to recover possession of service cottages, or who do not expect to be able to recover possession because the cottage is not required for the time being for a farm worker, will probably want to charge the occupier a rent *after* his service occupation terminates. In most cases there will not be a 'fair rent' already fixed by the Rent Officer and registered; therefore, the owner will *not* be able to charge a fair rent when the service occupation comes to an end. However, until a fair rent is registered, a rent can be charged. There are three types of rent provided for under the 1976 Act. They are as follows:

(a) An agreed rent (s.11).
(b) A provisional rent (s.12).
(c) A registered rent (s.14).

AGREED RENT (s. 11)

The term 'agreed rent' is a bit of a trap, because it is not open to an owner to agree any rent he likes with an occupier. An agreed rent cannot exceed the registered rent if one has been registered, and it cannot exceed the provisional rent if there has not been a fair rent registered. The provisional rent is one-and-a-half times the current rateable value to which the landlords' rates can be added. Thus if there is no fair rent registered, any agreed rent will be low. There seems to be no point in agreeing a rent, unless it is intended that a pensioner should be charged only a nominal rent. Since rent allowances are available from local authorities, there does not seem to be any point in charging even a pensioner a nominal rent. If landlords' rates are to be recovered notice must be served on the occupier to that effect, and rates can be recovered even if it is agreed that no rent shall be paid.

PROVISIONAL RENT (s. 12)

Usually an owner will want to charge a provisional rent as soon as the service occupation ceases. He cannot charge such a rent until the contractual right to occupy under the service agreement ceases, but he can serve an advance notice on the occupier that a provisional rent will be charged as from the date when the service occupancy ceases. A provisional rent is one-and-a-half times the current rateable value to which landlord's rates can be added. A notice should be served on the occupier under the 1976 Act, s. 12 explaining clearly how the provisional rent is calculated and stating the date from which it is to be charged. The earliest date on which a notice can take effect is four weeks before service of the notice. This should be noted by owners who delay serving a notice for some weeks after service occupancy has ended. There is no prescribed form of notice, but the notice can be in the form of a letter. Statutory tenants should be supplied with a leaflet about the local authority's rate and rent allowance scheme, and a rent book, as they are deemed to be weekly tenants. There is a prescribed form of notice to be fixed in the rent books. The notice was not prescribed until five years after the Rent (Agriculture) Act 1977 came into force.

REGISTERED RENTS

It will often not be worth having a rent registered because as a rule local authorities have been rehousing outgoing workers within a reasonable time. However, if an owner wishes to have a rent registered under the 1976 Act, he should make an application in the prescribed form as set out in the Rent (Agriculture) (Rent Registration) Regulations 1978. There is a special part of the register for registering rents occupied by ex-farm workers as statutory tenants under the Act. So far there is no prescribed form of notice of increase of rent to a fair rent under the Act.

Where a rent has been agreed, the agreement will have to be terminated by at least four weeks' notice in writing before the fair rent can be charged.

Where a provisional rent is being charged, and a fair rent is later registered, a notice of increase must be served on the tenant specifying the amount of the registered rent, and the date from which the notice is to take effect. There is no phasing of an increase to a fair rent in the case of a first registration of a fair rent. Notice of increase to a fair rent cannot take effect earlier than four weeks before the service of the notice.

Terms of the statutory tenancy

These terms are set out in the 1976 Act, Schedule 5 and may be varied by agreement between the parties subject to certain limits. Owners of houses where statutory tenants are likely to remain in occupation for some time, often ask whether they should enter into a written tenancy agreement with the tenant. There is a danger that if a new agreement is entered into with an ex-employee, it could be construed as a grant of an ordinary rent-protected tenancy. It is not necessary to enter into a written agreement when the terms are already set out in the statute. However, an owner could refer the statutory tenant to the statutory terms, and could supply the tenant with a summary of them, together with any variations which have been agreed between the parties. It should be made clear to the tenant that the terms under which he occupies are the statutory terms in the Rent (Agriculture) Act 1976.

The statutory terms are briefly as follows:

(a) The tenants must observe and shall be entitled to the benefit of all the terms of the original contract (usually a service occupancy).

(b) If the original contract was a licence (for example, service occupancy) the tenant will be a weekly tenant.

(c) If the original contract was a licence, the tenant will enjoy the benefit of an implied covenant for quiet enjoyment, and he will be under an obligation to use the premises in a tenant-like manner.

(d) If the landlord has been providing certain non-contractual facilities for the tenant (for example water from an estate supply), the landlord will be obliged to supply them if they are the only convenient supply.

(e) The landlord's repairing liabilities are as laid down in s. 11 of the

Landlord and Tenant Act 1985, replacing s. 32 of the Housing Act 1961. He must be allowed reasonable access to the premises to carry out repairs.

(f) The tenant can only use the house as a private dwellinghouse and he must not assign, sublet or part with possession of it, unless he was lawfully doing so before the statutory tenancy began. In the case of a service occupancy, it is unlikely that assignment or subletting would be permitted under the contract.

(g) The statutory tenant must be allowed reasonable access to the house. In practice he may have been allowed access to the house by a number of different ways over the farm, while he was in employment, but these would not necessarily be rights granted under the service agreement. Consequently he would not be entitled to them under the terms of the statutory tenancy, unless they were rights expressly granted to him under the service agreement. There are provisions in the Schedule for having a right of access permanently or temporarily stopped up, as long as an alternative is provided.

(h) A statutory tenant who wishes to vacate is required to give not less than four weeks' notice to quit, even if his original contract was a service occupancy, or even if he held under a tenancy which did not require him to give notice to quit before giving up possession.

(i) Landlord's rates (including water rates) can be recovered from the tenant including those cases where a rent is agreed, or it is agreed that no rent is payable. Notice must be served on the tenant stating the date from which landlord's rates can be recovered. The date must be not earlier than four weeks *before* the service of the notice.

Farm workers protected under the Rent Act 1977

Some owners let cottages to some of their farm workers under rent-protected tenancies. Since these workers are already enjoying protected tenancies under the Rent Act 1977, they are not entitled to protection under the Rent (Agriculture) Act 1976. However, such workers cannot be got out of their cottages by a county court order made under the Rent Act 1977, Schedule 15 Case 8 which was the situation before the 1976 Act came into operation. An application to rehouse such workers can be made to the local authority (see p. 27).

Under Case 8, a landlord who has let a house under a rent-protected tenancy to a worker employed by him, as a condition of a contract of employment, can apply to the county court for a possession order if he wants the house for another whole-time employee. A court has a discretionary power to make such an order. If, however, the tenant is a farm worker who has worked for two years in agriculture and has been let the cottage under his contract of employment, the court will not have power to make a possession order under Case 8.

Rent Act 1977

As a result of the Rent Act 1974, the rent protection code was applied to furnished lettings as well as to unfurnished lettings. Owners who used to let furnished for residential purposes have been discouraged from letting in that way, and have found other ways of letting, for example for holidays. Furnished lettings generally have been subject to full rent protection since 14 August 1974, except for certain lettings of parts of houses where the landlord is living.

LETTINGS OF SURPLUS FARM COTTAGES

Since 1965, it has been possible to let surplus farm cottages temporarily outside agriculture, and to recover possession when (but only when) the cottage in question is required for occupation by a person employed or to be employed by the landlord in agriculture. If a letting is made under the Rent Act 1977, Schedule 15 Case 16 whether furnished or unfurnished the landlord will be able to recover possession of the house for a farm worker. In order to comply with the terms of Case 16 the house must not be let under that Case to a person who is or at any time was employed by the landlord under a contract of employment in agriculture, or to a widow of such a person. Before the commencement of the tenancy and before the tenant enters into occupation the tenant must be given a notice in writing telling him that possession may be recovered when the house is wanted for an agricultural worker. If it becomes necessary to apply for a county court order for a possession, the court must be satisfied that the house is required for a person employed or to be employed by the landlord in agriculture. If the provisions of Case 16 are complied with, the court must make an order. In order to take advantage of Case 16, it is only necessary that the cottage should at some time have been a tied farm cottage occupied by a farm worker under his contract of employment. The provisions for letting surplus *farmhouses* and recovering possession when they are required again for agricultural purposes are more limited.

LETTING OF SURPLUS FARMHOUSES

Since 1970 it has been possible to let surplus farmhouses temporarily outside agriculture, but originally possession could only be recovered, if at all, within five years. The five-year limit on recovery no longer applies. However, possession can only be recovered if the house is required for someone who is going to run the farm (for example the owner, occupier, farm manager, etc.), or for a farm employee. The provisions are now contained in the Rent Act 1977, Schedule 15 Case 18.

There are special provisions for letting farmhouses which are surplus as a result of amalgamation schemes approved under the Agriculture Act 1967. These are now contained in the Rent Act 1977, Schedule 15 Case 17.

Owners who propose to let a surplus farmhouse outside agriculture should note that possession can only be recovered if the house is required for agricultural purposes. The following points should also be noted:

(a) The last occupier (or his widow) of the farmhouse before it is let outside agriculture, must have been the person responsible for running the farm.

(b) The letting must *not* be to a person who is or was at any time responsible for running the farm in question, or his widow, or a person who is or was employed in agriculture by the landlord. Owners of surplus farmhouses should not let them to an ex-farm tenant or his widow, or to a farm worker or ex-farm worker or his widow, if he hopes to recover possession under Case 18.

(c) The owner must serve a written notice on the prospective tenant before the commencement of the tenancy, telling him that possession may be recovered where the house is required for agricultural purposes. It is advisable that such a notice should be served before the tenant enters into occupation.

(d) If it becomes necessary to apply for a county court order, the owner must be able to satisfy the court that he wants the house for occupation by a person responsible or to be responsible for the control of the farm, or that he wants it for a farm worker. If the terms of Case 18 are complied with, the court must grant a possession order.

HOLIDAY LETTINGS

Holiday lettings have never been protected under the Rent Acts, and they are not protected now. No special form of agreement is necessary, but suitable forms can be purchased from law stationers. Holiday lettings will normally be furnished lettings. The owner can charge a market rent while letting for holidays. Owners who do not want cottages normally let for holidays to be left empty during the winter, and would like to let temporarily during the winter months, can take advantage of the provisions of the Rent Act 1977, Schedule 15 Case 13. If the terms of that Case are complied with an owner can be sure of recovering possession at the end of the winter or out-of-season letting. The out-of-season letting will be a regulated letting, and the following conditions must be complied with:

(a) Notice in writing must be served on the prospective tenant before the tenancy begins, telling him that possession can be recovered at the end of the tenancy.
(b) The winter let must be for a fixed term not exceeding eight months.
(c) The house must have been let for holidays at some time within the twelve months ending with the date the winter let began.

If the owner has to apply for an order for possession, he does *not* have to satisfy the court that he intends to use the house again for holidays. He must show that he has complied with the conditions of Case 13. If he has done that the court must grant an order for possession.

LETTING OF RETIREMENT HOME

An owner who has acquired a house for his retirement may allow it to be occupied under a service agreement by a farm manager. If he does he should first serve a notice under the Rent (Agriculture) Act 1976, Schedule 4 Case XII as already stated above. If he wishes to let it at a rent, outside agriculture, which is more likely, he would be advised to do so under the Rent Act 1977, Schedule 15 Case 12, otherwise he may not be able to recover possession when he needs the house on his retirement. In order to take advantage of Case 12 the owner must intend to occupy the house as his residence when he retires from regular employment. Before he lets the house, the owner should serve on the prospective tenant a notice in writing telling him that possession may be recovered under Case 12. It is advisable to ensure that such a notice is served before the prospective tenant enters into occupation. If the owner has to apply for a county court order when he wants the house, the court will have to be satisfied that he has retired from regular employment and requires the house as residence. If the owner has died, an application for a possession order can still be made if the house is required for a member of his family who was living with him at the time of his death, or his successor in title wants to live in the house or dispose of it with vacant possession.

Even if a notice in writing was not served on the prospective tenant at the appropriate time, the court may still make an order if he thinks it is just and equitable to do so.

LETTINGS OF HOMES BY OWNER-OCCUPIERS

There are special provisions in the Rent Act 1977, Schedule 15 Case 11, to enable an owner-occupier who is leaving his home for a time, for example for service abroad, to let it under a regulated tenancy and recover possession when he returns. This provision is really intended to enable businessmen, service men, diplomats and similar people to let their homes when on a tour of duty abroad, instead of leaving them empty. Farmers will probably not make much use of this provision, but the position is as follows: an owner-occupier can let his home under Case 11, subject to a notice being served on the tenant before the commencement of the tenancy, telling the tenant that possession may be recovered under that Case. If it is necessary to apply to the court for a possession order, the court will want to be satisfied that the house is required as a residence for the owner-occupier. In certain cases after an owner-occupant's death, possession may be recovered for a member of his family or a successor in title. The owner-occupier will not have to prove that his requirement is reasonable, but only that he wants and genuinely intends to occupy the house as a residence (*Kennealy* v. *Dunne* [1977] 2 All E.R. 10 CA). One of two co-owners is entitled to recover possession for his or her occupation (*Tilling* v. *Whiteman* [1979] 1 All E.R. 737).

LETTINGS TO STUDENTS

In the countryside near university towns there may be a demand from students for cottages to let. Lettings to students, whether they are furnished or unfurnished lettings, are protected by the Rent Acts, unless the tenancy is granted to them by an educational institution (Rent Act 1977, s. 8). It is unwise to let dwellings direct to students. Although most of them will leave the district when their course of education is finished, some may decide to stay on and claim rent-protected tenancies.

OWNER-OCCUPIER LETTING OFF PART OF HIS HOUSE

An owner who lives in his own house can let off part of it as a separate dwelling in such a way that he will be able to get the tenant out at the end of the tenancy. He can let furnished or unfurnished for a fixed term (for example, two years), and at the end of the term, the letting will terminate automatically. There will be no security of tenure. The owner could also let unfurnished or furnished under a periodic tenancy, but if he does the tenant will be protected to some extent, because he cannot be evicted without a court order. (Rent Act 1977, ss. 20, 103, 104 as amended by the Housing Act 1980, s. 69).

Tenancies granted by residential landlords will become protected if at any time a person who does not live on the permises becomes the landlord. Special provisions apply where the landlord's interests vest in trustees or there is a change in the ownership of the house (Rent Act 1977, Schedule 2, s. 12).

Shorthold tenancies

The Housing Act 1980, introduced a new kind of tenancy called the shorthold tenancy. Such a tenancy must be for a fixed term of at least one year but not more than five years. Before the tenancy commences a notice in the prescribed form must be served on the prospective tenant telling him that the tenancy is a shorthold tenancy, and may be terminated by the landlord at the end of the shorthold term. It is advisable also to enter into a written shorthold tenancy agreement reciting that a notice in the prescribed form has been served. Outside London, it is not necessary to have a rent registered before letting shorthold. A rent may be agreed between the landlord and the tenant. However, the tenancy is a regulated tenancy and it is open to the tenant to apply to have a rent registered even after one has been agreed.

The procedure for terminating a shorthold tenancy is unusual. Generally a fixed-term tenancy expires by effluxion of time. In the case of a shorthold tenancy, the landlord is obliged to serve at any time in the last three months of the term, a notice of at least three months telling the tenant that at the end of that three months he intends to apply to a county court for a possession order. When that notice expires, he has a further three months in which to apply to the county court for an order. If he fails to carry out this procedure, the tenant gets a further year's security because the Act prevents the landlord from serving another notice until the anniversary of the last three months of the contractual term.

SECURITY OF TENURE: REGULATED TENANCIES

Except in the special cases described above it is almost impossible to get a rent-protected tenant to vacate a house, and applications for court orders for possession can only be made on grounds set out in the Rent Act 1977, Schedule 15 or where suitable alternative accommodation is available to the tenant. Except in the special cases described above, the court is not bound to grant a possession order, but it may do so at its discretion. Grounds for possession are: breach of contract including non-payment of rent; nuisance and annoyance to adjoining occupiers; acts of waste, or negligence by the tenant leading to deterioration of the premises; ill-treatment of the landlord's furniture resulting in deterioration; tenant giving notice to quit and landlord contracting to sell in reliance on that notice; landlord requiring the house for himself or a member of his family to live in (an application cannot be made on this ground if the landlord purchased the house after 23 March 1965 in the case of most regulated tenancies; the dwellinghouse let at a rent as a tied cottage being required by the landlord for another whole-time employee (this provision does not apply to cottages let to full-time farm workers who have worked two years in agriculture – if it did it would enable the provisions of the Rent (Agriculture) Act 1976 to be avoided); and the tenant assigning or subletting the whole of a house without the landlord's consent, or subletting part of a house at an excessive rent, that is, rent in excess of that permitted under the Rent Acts.

An owner who thinks he has grounds for recovering for possession should instruct his solicitor to take the steps necessary for an application for a county court order for possession. If the tenancy is still a contractual tenancy, that tenancy will have to be terminated by at least four weeks' notice in writing. (In the case of a fixed-term tenancy, the tenancy would expire at the end of the term.) Where a contractual tenancy has come to an end, and the tenancy has become a statutory tenancy, a notice to quit need not be served, because the statutory tenancy will be ended if the court makes an order for possession.

RENTS OF REGULATED TENANTS

Regulated tenancies in the country are tenancies of houses with rateable values not exceeding £750, as at 1 April 1973. Since the Rent Acts now apply to furnished tenancies, a regulated tenancy may be furnished or unfurnished. Many tenancies granted after 5 July 1957 were then not protected, but are now regulated tenancies. Rent for regulated tenancies are *not* calculated by reference to gross values or rateable values. The may have been agreed between the parties or fixed by the Rent Officer at a 'fair rent'.

Unfit houses: repairs and improvements

Standards of fitness for human habitation are laid down in the Housing Act 1985, s. 604. It is an implied condition that any small house let under a tenancy is at the commencement of the tenancy, fit for human habitation, and it will be kept fit by the landlord during the tenancy. This implied condition also applies to houses occupied by farm workers under service agreements.

If a local authority is satisfied that any house is unfit for human habitation and *could be made fit at reasonable expense*, they should serve a repairs notice under the Housing Act 1985, s. 189 on the person having control of the house. The notice must specify the works to be done to make the house fit and the time allowed for doing them, which must be at least three weeks.

If a local authority is satisfied that a house which is not unfit for human habitation needs substantial repairs to bring it up to a reasonable standard they may serve a notice on the person having control of the house, requiring him to do the works specified.

If in either of the above cases the works are not done, the local authority can do them in default and recover their reasonable expenses plus interest from the date of the demand.

There is a right of appeal against a repairs notice to the county court under the 1985 Act, s. 191. If a Judge finds that a house cannot be made fit at reasonable expense, the local authority can purchase the house by agreement or compulsorily. If they purchase compulsorily they must carry out all the works specified in their own notice.

HOUSE BEYOND REPAIR AT REASONABLE COST

It may happen that an old house which is unfit for human habitation is believed to be not capable of being made fit at reasonable cost. In such cases a local authority has powers to serve on the person having control of the house a 'notice of time and place' under the Housing Act 1985, s. 264. Such a notice should not be ignored. It is the first step in a procedure which could lead to a demolition order. The purpose of a 'notice of time and place' is to get the owner to make an offer to the local authority about the future use of the house, or the carrying out of works. If the owner intends to make an offer he should do so without delay. The local authority can accept an undertaking from the owner that he will carry out works to make the house fit, or that he will not allow the house to be used for human habitation until it has been made fit. If there is a tenant in the house he can be compelled to vacate even if he is protected under the Rent Acts, if there is an undertaking not to use it for human habitation. If a house is used for human habitation in contravention of an undertaking, the penalty is a fine, and further fines for every day on which the offence continues.

An owner who cannot repair a house would be advised to make an undertaking that it will not be used for human habitation until made fit. He may be able to sell the house to someone who is prepared to make it fit, if he cannot afford to do the work himself. If an owner does nothing, or he makes an undertaking which he does not honour, the local authority will take steps to make a demolition order, or in certain cases, a closing order, or they may purchase the house. If a house is listed under the Planning Acts as a building of architectural or historical interest, a demolition order cannot be served, but a closing order can be made. If a house is semi-detached or in a terrace a demolition order would be unsuitable and a closing order can be made instead.

DEMOLITION ORDERS AND CLOSING ORDERS

When a local authority has decided to make a demolition order or a closing order, notice must be served in the prescribed form on the owner of the house and other interested persons. There is a right of appeal to the county court against any of these orders or notices. They should not be ignored. The effect of an appeal is to suspend the effect of the order or notice until the case is heard and decided. The court may confirm the order, or quash it, or vary it, or accept such undertakings from the owner as might have been accepted by the local authority. If no appeal is made, the order or notice will take effect after twenty-one days from the date of service.

When a demolition order becomes operative, the house must be vacated on a specified date not less than twenty-eight days after the operative date, and the house must be demolished within six weeks from the date by which the house is to be vacated. If the owner does not demolish the house within the time allowed, the local authority may enter and do the work in default and recover their reasonable expenses after giving credit for any amount from sale of the materials.

Even if a demolition order had become operative, all is not lost. There is an opportunity for the owner or someone else (for example, a prospective purchaser) to put to the local authority proposals for works of reconstruction, enlargement or improvement of a house. If satisfactory proposals are made and accepted by the local authority, they may extend the demolition period to allow the owner or a third party an opportunity to carry out the works (1985 Act, s. 274).

There is also a further opportunity for an owner of a house subject to a demolition order, which has become operative. The owner, or some other person who has an interest in the house, may submit to the local authority proposals for the use of the house for a purpose other than human habitation and if the authority accepts the proposal, they may determine the demolition order and substitute a closing order (Housing Act 1985, s. 275).

Owners clearly have several opportunities to avoid the making-or-taking effect of a demolition order.

COMPULSORY IMPROVEMENTS

A tenant of a house which lacks one or more of the standard amenities (for example a bathroom) can make a complaint to a local authority about the lack of amenities, with the object of getting the authority to serve an improvement notice on the owner, requiring him to provide the amenities needed to bring the house up to standard (Housing Act 1985, s. 209). A complaint can be made whether or not the house is in a state of disrepair. A farm worker occupying a farm cottage under a service agreement can make a complaint to a local authority under this section.

The authority must be satisfied that the house in question is capable of being improved at reasonable expense. The owner is allowed an opportunity of making representations to the authority after having received its provisional notice. The authority must satisfy itself that the dwelling ought to be improved. Generally, local authorities are reluctant to use compulsory powers for improvements. They will prefer to encourage owners to carry out improvements voluntarily with the aid of grants (which are also available if an improvement order is made). However, if an improvement notice is made there is a right of appeal within six weeks from service of the order, to the county court, on one or more of seven grounds (1985 Act, s. 217). The first and probably most important ground of appeal is that it is not practicable to comply with the requirements of the improvement notice at reasonable expense. It is also possible to appeal on the ground that the works specified are unreasonable in character or extent.

Where an improvement notice becomes operative it must be complied with, and grants and loans are available from the housing authority for provision of standard amenities provided under such a notice. If the work is not done, the authority may enter and do the work in default, and recover their reasonable expenses, plus interest from the date of the demand.

Where a landlord of an agricultural holding carries out improvements to a house on the holding under an improvement notice, he will be entitled to increase the rent of the holding under the Agricultural Holdings Act 1986, s. 13 as though the improvement had been made at the request of the tenant (see p. 50).

If a farm tenant carries out improvement works under an improvement notice, the improvement will qualify as a Seventh Schedule (para. 9) improvement under the Agricultural Holdings Act 1986, even though the landlord has not given his written consent to the improvement.

An owner of a house subject to an improvement notice can require the local authority to purchase it (1985 Act, s. 227).

INSANITARY OR DANGEROUS HOUSES

Where a house is in a dangerous or dilapidated condition, or it is insanitary, there are statutory powers in the Public Health Acts to enable a public health authority to deal with it. Those Acts also contain powers for requiring the owner of a house to provide a food store (Public Health Act 1961, s. 32), though a food store is not a standard amenity qualifying for grant under the Housing Acts.

Grants for repair and improvement of unfit houses

Grants for improvement of unfit substandard houses have been available during the post-war period under a series of Housing Acts. The Housing Acts 1974 amended by the Housing Act 1980 and now consolidated in the Housing Act 1985 introduced a new code for payment of housing grants. There are four types of grant available, but only the first two are likely to be of interest to farmers. They are:

(a) Improvement grant (formerly known as 'discretionary' grant). It is payable for the provision of a dwelling by *conversion*, or for the *improvement* of a dwelling, and for associated works of repair and replacement. It is a discretionary grant. Whether or not it is made depends on the discretion of the local authority.
(b) Intermediate grant. This grant is payable for the provision of standard amenities (for example, bath or shower in bathroom, hot and cold water supply, etc.) and for associated works of repair.
(c) Special grant. This grant is payable for the improvement of houses in multiple occupation by the provision of standard amenities.
(d) Repairs grant. This grant is payable for works of repair or replacement to houses in housing action areas, or general improvement areas, carried out independently of improvement works.

POST-1961 BUILDINGS AND DWELLINGS

Improvement grants will not generally be paid for provision of a dwelling by *conversion* of a post-October 1961 building, nor will improvement grants be paid for improvement or repair of a post-October 1961 dwelling.

APPLICATION FOR GRANT

Anyone who is thinking about applying for a grant would be advised to discuss the matter first with the local authority's housing department. In any case a form of application has to be obtained from the local authority, and it will require the applicant to give particulars of the work and estimate of the costs. If an improvement grant is applied for, the dwelling must be up to standard on completion of the works. This may, and probably will, mean that additional work has to be done. In some cases local authorities may require ceiling heights to be increased and windows enlarged to comply with the standard of fitness. Where conversion of a building for a dwelling – or substantial extension of an existing dwelling – is proposed, planning permission will be required (see Chapter 6, on town and country planning).

An applicant for grant must be the freehold owner or a lessee for a term of years with at least five years to run or a tenant protected by statute, for example under the Rent Acts.

It must be clearly understood that an application for grant must be made and approved before works are begun. It is only in very exceptional cases that an authority will approve an application for grant where works have already begun.

IMPROVEMENT GRANTS

Improvement grants are payable for works for provision of a dwelling by conversion of a house or other building, or for works for the improvement of a dwelling. In both cases these include any work of repair or replacement needed to bring the dwelling up to standard. An application for grant must not be approved unless the local authority is satisfied that on completion of the works, the dwelling will be of the required standard. A dwelling is up to standard if it is provided with all the standard amenities, is in reasonable repair, and conforms with requirements about construction, physical condition, and provision of services and amenities as laid down from time to time by the Government. As a rule the dwelling must be likely to provide satisfactory housing accommodation for thirty years.

Improvement grants will not be paid to owner-occupiers where the rateable value of the dwelling exceeds a prescribed limit. This restriction does not apply in the case of other grants.

Since improvement grants are discretionary, applicants may well be disappointed. Where an application is approved, the local authority has to decide what is the amount of the expenses properly incurred for the execution of the improvement works, and they must notify the applicant of the amount. The grant eventually paid is based on it. Not more than 50 per cent of the estimated expense can be allowed for works of repair and replacement. When the amount of improvement grant has been fixed, the applicant must be notified.

INTERMEDIATE GRANT

The purpose of these grants is to help provide houses with standard amenities, which are as follows:

> A fixed bath or shower; a hot- and cold-water supply at a fixed bath or shower: a wash hand basin; a hot- and cold-water supply at a wash hand basin: a sink; a hot- and cold-water supply at a sink: a water closet.

Intermediate grants are mandatory but a local housing authority must not approve an application for a grant unless they are satisfied that on completion of the works, the dwelling will be fit for human habitation.

Works of repair and replacement needed in order to bring the house up to standard will qualify for grant. However, the local authority must assess separately the proper expenses for works to provide the standard amenities, and works for repair and replacement, and must notify the applicant of the amounts.

REPAIRS GRANTS

These grants are payable in certain cases, for repairs which are not associated with improvement or conversion of a dwelling. They are payable only for works of a substantial or structural character, and only for old dwellings as defined by an order made by the Secretary of State. Outside a housing action area an application for a repairs grant may only be approved if the house is below a specified rateable value. A grant must not be made unless on completion of works the dwelling will be in a reasonable state of repair.

GRANT CONDITIONS

It has been a feature of housing grants that certain conditions were imposed for a period of years after grant-aided works have been completed. Grant conditions currently imposed are a condition as to owner-occupation, a condition as to availability for letting, and conditions about provision of information. In certain cases additional conditions about letting may be imposed.

OWNER-OCCUPIED HOUSES

During the first year after completion of grant-aided works the house must be occupied as a residence exclusively by the applicant or a member of his family. For the next four years when it is not occupied by the applicant or a member of his family, it must be let or available for letting as a residence, and not for holiday letting. Any letting must be to persons outside the family.

HOUSES FOR LETTING

Where a house is improved with grant for purposes of letting, the house must be available for letting during the five-year grant condition period, as a residence, and not for holidays, or it may be occupied as a tied farm cottage.

INFORMATION ABOUT OCCUPATION

A local authority is entitled within the five-year condition period to require an applicant to whom grant has been paid to fill in and sign a certificate with information about the occupation of the dwelling. Where a house is let, a tenant may be required to provide the owner with the information needed to fill-in the certificate to be sent to the local authority.

REPAYMENT OF GRANT

Where there is a breach of grant condition, the local authority may demand that the owner of the dwelling shall repay the grant at once. However, the authority is not bound to demand repayment of all or any of the grant.

It is open to an owner to repay grant voluntarily, if he wishes to be freed of the grant conditions.

REFUSAL OF GRANT

If a local authority refuses to make a grant or makes a grant less than the maximum, they must give the applicant a statement in writing of their reasons for doing so.

PAYMENT OF GRANT

Grant may be paid after completion of the works, or by instalments as the work progresses, and the balance after completion of the works. Grant will only be paid if work is done to the satisfaction of the local authority.

Chapter 3
Landlord and Tenant

Abbreviations in this Chapter:
'1986 Act' – Agricultural Holdings Act 1986

Agricultural holdings

Farming is a long-term business. If he is to farm well a farm tenant must be able to plan ahead and to invest in the present and the future with confidence that he will have reasonable security of possession. The law recognises this. The policy of the agricultural holdings laws is to give a farm tenant security at least during his lifetime, but should the tenancy end before or at his death there will then be a fair reckoning. A system of succession to tenancies by close relatives, in suitable cases, on the death or retirement of tenants, is included.

The code of law governing the relationship between landlord and tenant has recently been put together in one consolidating Act, the Agricultural Holdings Act 1986, after a comprehensive revision in 1984. Important Regulations are made from time to time to deal with details.

WHAT IS AN AGRICULTURAL HOLDING?

The legal code regulating the relationship between landlord and tenant applies to lettings of 'agricultural holdings'. As these laws affect the freedom of contract between the parties (for example as to security of tenure and family succession) it is essential to know whether what is let is an agricultural holding at law. To get the answer a number of definitions in the 1986 Act have to be jig-sawed together (in ss. 1 and 96). When this is done it appears the ingredients of an agricultural holding are these:

(a) There must be a contract of tenancy to let land for use as agricultural land.
(b) The land must be used for a trade or business.

(c) The letting to the tenant must not be 'during his continuance in any office, appointment or employment held under the landlord'.

'Agriculture' is not exactly defined. The 1986 Act says it 'includes horticulture, fruit growing, seed growing, dairy farming and livestock breeding and keeping, the use of land as grazing land, meadow land, osier land, market gardens and nursery grounds, and the use of land for woodlands where that use is ancillary to the farming of land for other agricultural purposes' (s. 96).

Grazing non-agricultural animals by way of business is using land for agriculture (*Rutherford* v. *Maurer* [1961] 2 All E.R. 755 – riding horses). Buildings included in the letting will be part of the agricultural holding. Where land is let for both agricultural and non-agricultural uses it will be either wholly an agricultural holding or not at all. If the actual or contemplated use of the land at the time of the contract and subsequently is predominantly agricultural it will all be an agricultural holding (s. 1(2); *Howkins* v. *Jardine* [1951] 1 All E.R. 320). A non-agricultural tenancy will not become agricultural by a change of use contrary to the contract, unless the landlord agreed to, or acquiesced in, the change (s. 1(3)).

The terms of the tenancy

The rights and obligations of the parties are in the first place decided by the tenancy agreement. Although the tenancy agreement is the first word it is not always the last because of statutory intervention on the freedom of contract of the parties. The Act intervenes in the following ways.

(a) *Getting a written agreement.* If there is no written agreement, or if there is one but it does not contain one or more of a list of items set out in the First Schedule of the 1986 Act, either party may refer the terms of the tenancy to arbitration (1986 Act, s. 6). The arbitrator's job is to provide a written agreement containing the terms the parties have agreed and including all the items in the First Schedule (except for any inconsistent with what the parties have agreed). The First Schedule items are the basic bones of any properly drawn agreement, dealing with such things as the identification of the parties and the holding, the rent, repairing duties, covenants in the event of fire damage, landlord's power of entry for breach of tenancy and a prohibition against assignment, subletting or parting with possession without consent. Before demanding an arbitration the other party must be requested to enter into a written agreement containing the First Schedule items. The arbitrator may vary the rent if he thinks it fair to do so on account of any change he makes in the tenancy terms (s. 6(3)).

(b) *Permanent pasture*. The 1986 Act allows either landlord or tenant to go to arbitration to seek to have the tenancy agreement modified as regards the amount of land required to be maintained as permanent pasture 'in order to secure the full and efficient farming of the holding' (s. 14 as amended by the Agriculture Act 1958). This is rarely, if ever, done nowadays.

(c) *Repairs and insurance*. As explained below, Regulations supply 'model clauses' setting out the duties for the maintenance and insurance of the fixed equipment (pp. 51–52).

(d) *Freedom of cropping*. No matter what the tenancy agreement says the tenant has, by s. 15 of the 1986 Act, 'without incurring any penalty, forfeiture or liability', the following rights:

(i) to dispose of the produce of the holding, other than manure, provided he makes suitable and adequate provision to return to the holding the full equivalent manurial value; and
(ii) to practise any system he likes of cropping the arable land, provided he protects the holding from injury or deterioration.

An important qualification is that this right does not apply in the last year of the tenancy or in any period after the tenant has given or received notice to quit. In that period he must not sell or remove from the holding any manure, compost, hay, or straw or any roots grown for consumption on the holding, without the landlord's consent.

(e) *Security of tenure*. The Acts provide an elaborate scheme of security of tenure for tenants described below (pp. 55–66). A test case has established that you cannot contract out of this security of tenure (*Johnson* v. *Moreton* [1978] 3 All E.R. 37 (HL)).

(f) *Rent*. The 1986 Act provides for rent reviews by arbitration as described below (pp. 49–51).

(g) *Compensation and improvements*. The golden rule is that the parties can only contract out of sections dealing with compensation for tenants where the section expressly allows it. There are special rules about the tenant's right to do improvements. These topics are dealt with below (pp. 52–55).

The rent

The rent at the beginning of the tenancy is for the parties to agree and it can be changed at any time by agreement. The 1986 Act lays down a scheme enabling rent reviews to take place every three years if either party desires. The landlord or the tenant may demand an arbitration to fix the 'rent properly payable' for the holding, provided the rent change sought will not take effect during the first three years of the tenancy, or before three years have elapsed since the rent was last changed, or directed by an arbitrator to stay unchanged (1986 Act, s. 12 and Schedule 2).

TIMING THE ARBITRATION DEMAND

Somewhat confusing wording in the Act means in effect the arbitrator's award will take effect on the next term date but one after service of the arbitration demand (the Act unhappily calls this 'the termination date'). The 'term date' is the anniversary of the beginning of the tenancy – frequently a quarter day such as Michaelmas (29 September) or Lady Day (25 March). Timing the arbitration demand is therefore all-important for the party seeking the rent change. If a term date is looming up he will want to serve the demand before it. The arbitrator, however, assesses what the proper rent was at the date of the reference to arbitration, which will always be at least one year before it takes effect.

REVISION BY AGREEMENT

Usually no arbitrator is appointed because the parties agree a new rent, but any party seeking a rent review is advised to serve an arbitration demand as a safeguard, even if he believes it can be negotiated by agreement.

THE 'RENT PROPERLY PAYABLE'

The rent arbitrator's task is to fix 'the rent properly payable in respect of the holding'. A new and wordy formula for assessing it was introduced in 1984. It is now in the 1986 Act Schedule 2. For the most part it spells out what rent arbitrators have always done. The main features of the rent formula are that the rent arbitrator must:

(a) Fix 'the rent at which the holding might reasonably be expected to be let by a prudent and willing landlord to a prudent and willing tenant'.

(b) *Taking into account*

(i) 'All relevant factors';
(ii) The terms of the tenancy;
(iii) The character, situation and locality of the holding;
(iv) The productive capacity and related earning capacity of the holding with the fixed equipment and other facilities on it, assuming 'a competent tenant practising a system of farming suitable to the holding'; and
(v) Rents of comparable holdings let on similar terms, including tendered rents likely to become payable.

(c) *Disregarding*

(i) In evidence about *comparables* (if any), any element in the rent due to 'appreciable scarcity' of such holdings available for letting or any element due to the tenant (or tenderer) having the convenience of other land close by, or any allowance or reduction made for charging a premium.
   Note: These factors are not required to be disregarded in respect of the subject holding.
(ii) Certain tenant's improvements and high farming, grant-aided landlord's improvements, the fact that the tenant is a sitting tenant, and any disrepair or deterioration of the holding.

APPOINTMENT OF ARBITRATOR
The parties can choose an arbitrator by agreement, or either party can ask the President of the Royal Institution of Chartered Surveyors (RICS) to appoint one from a panel set up by the Lord Chancellor. It is important for the party seeking the rent arbitration that a new rent should be agreed before the 'termination date' (that is, the next term date but one after the arbitration demand), or an arbitrator is appointed by agreement, or an application is made to the RICS before that date to appoint an arbitrator. Otherwise the arbitration demand lapses (1986 Act, s. 12(3)) and it will be necessary to start all over again.

RENT INCREASE FOR LANDLORD'S IMPROVEMENTS
Where the landlord carries out improvements on the holding 'at the request of, or in agreement with, the tenant' (or under some statutory provisions which rarely apply) he is entitled to increase the rent, regardless of the 'three years' rule' mentioned above, provided he gives the tenant written notice within six months from the completion of the improvement (1986 Act, s. 13). The increase is to be 'by an amount equal to the increase in the rental value of the holding attributable to the carrying out of the improvement' but if the

landlord gets grant aid the rent increase shall be 'reduced proportionately'. Any dispute is to be settled by arbitration.

Repairs and insurance

It is for the parties to agree in their tenancy agreement what their respective obligations will be as regards the maintenance and insurance of the holding. There are, however, two lots of Regulations (Agriculture (Maintenance, Repair and Insurance of Fixed Equipment) Regulations 1948 and 1973) containing 'model repair clauses'. These are deemed to be incorporated in every agricultural tenancy 'except insofar as they would impose on one of the parties to an agreement in writing a liability which under the agreement is imposed on the other' (1986 Act, s. 7). Both Regulations give a comprehensive code, the 1973 Regulations repeating most of the 1948 code but brushing it up and extending it. Copies are obtainable from Government bookshops.

If there is no written agreement, the 1973 Regulations will apply in full. It is common for written tenancy agreements to adopt the current 'model clauses' entirely. The existence of two sets causes complications. Although the 1948 Regulations were revoked by the 1973 Regulations the older code still applies to some older tenancies, the newer applies to others and in yet others there is a mixture of the two, depending on the wording of the agreement. The golden rule is that if there is conflict between the statutory 'model clauses' and the tenancy agreement, the tenancy agreement prevails.

The Regulations are too long and detailed to outline here (it is planned to bring out new Regulations in 1987). In broad terms the scheme of both codes is to make the landlord responsible for repairs and replacements to main structures of buildings, water mains, sewage disposal systems and reservoirs and to insure the buildings against loss or damage by fire. The tenant's obligations are 'except in so far as such liabilities fall to be undertaken by the landlord ... to repair and to keep and leave clean and in good tenantable repair, order and condition' most other items of fixed equipment on the holding including such things as hedges, ditches, roads and ponds.

Certain liabilities are shared. Both sides are released from any liability for obsolete or redundant items or work rendered impossible by subsidence or blocking of outfalls which are not under their control.

An important feature of the 1973 Regulations (not in the 1948 version) is to make the landlord responsible for replacing items which become worn out and incapable of further repair (subject to exceptions).

ENFORCEMENT OF REPAIRING LIABILITIES

Both Regulations allow a party, on the failure of the other to do his repairs, to carry them out himself and to recover the reasonable cost from the other, provided one month has elapsed after sending a written request to the other to do the repairs.

The landlord has also a heavier-handed, but more complex, sanction of serving a notice to remedy breaches of tenancy. Failure to comply with it may result in a notice to quit which may or may not lead to eviction as described below (pp. 61–62).

TENANCIES DEPARTING FROM THE STATUTORY CLAUSES

Where the written agreement 'effects substantial modifications in the operation of the model clauses' (for example, a full repairing lease) it is open to either the landlord or tenant to go to arbitration seeking to bring the tenancy in line with the Regulations (1986 Act, s. 8). The arbitrator has a discretion whether to vary the tenancy. If he does he may also vary the rent accordingly (1986 Act, s. 8(4)).

Improvements

For the most part it is open to the parties to agree whether any improvement should be done on the holding and who should carry it out. The initial cost might by agreement fall to the landlord, or the tenant or might be shared. It is important to note that if a grant is sought the work should not be started before the Ministry of Agriculture give the starting signal because it is too late to apply for a grant once the work has started.

We have seen above (p. 50) that if the landlord undertakes an improvement with his tenant's agreement, the rent may be increased under the 1986 Act, s. 13.

IMPROVEMENTS BY THE TENANT

The important consideration here is compensation. In short:

(a) The tenant will be entitled to compensation for certain classes of improvements carried out by him, whether or not he obtained consent to do them.
(b) For a further class of improvements he will not be entitled to compensation unless he first obtained his landlord's written consent.
(c) For yet another class of improvements he will require either his

landlord's consent or approval of the Agricultural Land Tribunal in lieu.

In all cases the compensation, where payable, will be payable by the landlord at the end of the tenancy.

The different classes of improvements are listed in Schedules to the 1986 Act. Only an outline can be given here.

(a) *No consent needed.* The tenant will be entitled to compensation for any improvements he does listed in the Eighth Schedule of the 1986 Act. For the most part these are acts of good husbandry and the tenant is compensated for leaving behind some benefit from them at the end of the tenancy. The Eighth Schedule may be amended by Orders from time to time. The calculation of the compensation for each item in the Schedule is dealt with by Agriculture (Calculation of Value for Compensation) Regulations. New Regulations come out quite often. It is usual for each side to employ a valuer who specialises in 'tenant-right' valuation.

(b) *Landlord's consent required.* A tenant carrying out any improvement listed in Part I of the Seventh Schedule to the 1986 Act (see Appendix A below) will not be entitled to compensation unless the landlord's written consent is first obtained. If the landlord gives consent he can attach conditions to it. It will be seen in Appendix A that these items are of a somewhat specialised kind. The measure of compensation is:

> an amount equal to the increase attributable to the improvement in the value of the agricultural holding as a holding, having regard to the character and situation of the holding and the average requirements of tenants reasonably skilled in husbandry (1986 Act, s. 66(1)).

It is quite common for the parties to agree a value at the time of the improvement and to write it off by decreasing steps over an agreed number of years.

(c) *Consent of landlord or Tribunal required.* For improvements listed in Part II of the Seventh Schedule of the 1986 Act (see Appendix A below) the tenant will require the landlord's consent if he is to be entitled to compensation, or, if the consent is refused or is given with conditions the tenant does not like, the tenant may apply to the Agricultural Land Tribunal for its approval. Should the Tribunal give its approval the landlord may elect to carry out the improvement himself, or otherwise the approval will count as the landlord's consent. The Tribunal may attach conditions to its approval. The rules and procedures are set out in the 1986 Act, s. 67. The measure of compensation is the same as for improvements under Part I of the Seventh Schedule quoted in (b) above (s. 66).

TENANT'S RIGHT TO REMOVE FIXTURES

Certain fixtures and buildings for which the tenant is not entitled to compensation, installed by him on the holding, remain his property and may be removed by him, provided they were not installed under a tenancy obligation. Before removing them, however, the tenant must have paid his rent, fulfilled his other tenancy duties and given his landlord the opportunity to purchase them. The rules and procedures are to be found in the 1986 Act, s. 10.

Compensation at the end of the tenancy

DISTURBANCE COMPENSATION

In addition to any compensation the tenant may be entitled to at the end of the tenancy for improvements and 'tenant right matters' explained above, he will normally be entitled to disturbance compensation unless the tenancy was surrendered or the tenancy ended under Cases C, D, E, F or G (bad husbandry, breaches of tenancy, insolvency or death, see pp. 59–60 below). Disturbance compensation is usually equal to one year's rent. In some cases, where extra expense on quitting is incurred it may be up to two years' rent. Additional compensation of a further four years' rent may be claimed where the landlord is recovering possession for a non-agricultural purpose. For the precise rules see 1986 Act, ss. 60 and 61, with some special cases in s. 62 (early resumption) and s. 63 (sub-tenancies, and quitting part only of a holding). See also warning for landlords on p. 59 below.

HIGH FARMING

The 1986 Act allows claims for high farming (s. 70) but they have been almost unknown.

MILK QUOTA

The Agriculture Act 1986 provides for compensation to be paid by the landlord to the tenant at the end of the tenancy in respect of milk quota if it was allocated to the tenant in relation to the holding, or if the tenancy is a succession tenancy granted after 2 April 1984. For the complicated manner of assessment see the 1986 Act s. 13 and Schedule 1.

An E.E.C. Outgoers' Scheme is in preparation by which producers will be compensated for giving up milk production on their land. In the case of tenanted land, the proposal is that the tenant will need the landlord's consent to enter the scheme, but consent may not be unreasonably withheld. Compensation will be shared between the tenant and the landowner. United Kingdom Regulations, as well as E.E.C. Regulations, will be made to implement the scheme.

LANDLORD'S COMPENSATION

The landlord is entitled to compensation from the tenant for any 'dilapidation or deterioration of, or damage to, any part of the holding or anything in or on the holding caused by non-fulfilment by the tenant of his responsibilities to farm in accordance with the rules of good husbandry'. The amount is to be the cost of making good as at the date of quitting but shall not exceed the diminution in the value of the landlord's reversion (1986 Act, s. 71). If the neglect is so bad that the general value of the holding has been reduced, the landlord may claim for the decrease in value (s. 72).

SETTLING CLAIMS

The 1986 Act lays down strict time limits for making the claims and provides for settlement of disputed claims by arbitration (see the sections cited and s. 83).

Game damage

Where the tenant has not the right to kill game and he suffers game damage, s. 20 of the 1986 Act makes provision for compensation during the tenancy, as explained in Chapter 13.

Security of tenure

Freedom of contract is largely displaced by statutory protection for the tenant in the realms of security of tenure. Security of tenure is achieved by the 1986 Act giving tenants a measure of protection against notices to quit and by securing that as far as possible contracts to occupy farmland become ultimately (if not in the first place) tenancies subject to notice to quit (namely, yearly tenancies). The Act also includes laws to provide possible succession to tenancies by 'close relatives' on the death or retirement of tenants.

It is essential for landowners to note there is no contracting out of statutory security of tenure. An elaborate attempt to do so was held by the House of Lords to be unenforceable in *Johnson* v. *Moreton* [1978] 3 All E.R. 37. Landowners must be circumspect about what might seem to be 'gentlemen's agreements' for the occupation of farmland for limited periods. Such agreements might well give the occupier security of tenure for life as has happened with casual agreements made over the garden gate.

We shall first examine agreements which do not start as yearly tenancies and then go on to deal with notices to quit under yearly tenancies.

AGREEMENTS FOR LESS THAN FROM YEAR TO YEAR

The effect of the 1986 Act s. 2 is to convert, by statutory magic, certain agreements less than yearly tenancies, into protected yearly tenancies 'with the necessary modifications'. The section is a snare, for it is only too easy for landowners to get caught unwittingly.

Subject to the exceptions mentioned below, the conversion into a protected tenancy occurs, in the mystical wording of the section, where:

'(a) any land is let to a person for use as agricultural land for an interest less than a tenancy from year to year, or
(b) a person is granted a licence to occupy land for use as agricultural land, if the circumstances are such that if his interest were a tenancy from year to year he would in respect of that land be the tenant of an agricultural holding.'

The exceptions, where the conversion does not take place are agreements approved by the Minister of Agriculture and grazing or mowing agreements for less than a year (explained below), and lettings or licences by anyone whose own interest is less than a yearly tenancy and has not itself been converted by the magic of the section.

From the considerable case law interpreting the section the following points emerge:

(a) *A tenancy for one year*, no more or less, is less than a tenancy from year to year and therefore converted by the section to a protected tenancy (see *Lower* v. *Sorrell* [1963] 1 Q.B. 384).
(b) *Only agreements enforceable at law can be converted* by s. 2 magic (*Goldsack* v. *Shore* [1950] 1 All E.R. 276). A gratuitous licence may not be an enforceable contract, though absence of rent is not necessarily decisive (*Verrall* v. *Farnes* [1966] 2 All E.R. 808).

(c) *Unless the occupier has exclusive possession the arrangement cannot be converted to a yearly tenancy* by s. 2 magic (*Bahamas International Trust Co. Ltd* v. *Threadgold* [1974] 3 All E.R. 881).

FIXED TERM OF TWO OR MORE YEARS

A tenancy for a fixed term of two or more years does not end automatically at the end of the fixed term, but (again by the touch of the statutory wand) continues as a tenancy from year to year until ended by notice to quit (1986 Act, s. 3). A notice to quit may be served 'not less than one year nor more than two years before the date fixed for the expiration of the term', or at any time after the tenancy has become a yearly tenancy, but the tenant will have the protection against notices to quit described below (pp. 58–59). The tenancy will not, however continue in this way if the tenant dies during the fixed term (s. 4).

APPROVED SHORT-TERM TENANCIES

Provision is made for fixed-term tenancies to end automatically at the end of the fixed term if they are for not less than two and not more than five years and before the grant of tenancy the parties agree the provision will apply to it, and they jointly apply to the Minister in writing for his approval and get it. The written agreement must indicate that s.3 of the 1986 Act does not apply to it (1986 Act, s. 5).

FIXED TERM OF MORE THAN ONE YEAR BUT LESS THAN TWO

Protection is therefore given to tenants for terms up to and including one year and for terms of two years or more. Oddly, this leaves a gap in the statutory protection for fixed terms of more than one year but less than two years, due to a strange drafting oversight (confirmed by *Gladstone* v. *Bower* [1960] 2 Q.B. 384, eighteen months' tenancy not protected – see below p. 68.

TENANCIES FROM YEAR TO YEAR

A tenancy from year to year (commonly called a yearly tenancy) carries on until a notice to quit ends it at the end of a year of the tenancy (that is, on a term date) or until the tenant surrenders the tenancy back to the landlord. It is also possible in special circumstances, involving court proceedings, for a yearly tenancy to be ended by forfeiture, provided the tenancy agreement provides for it, but it is beyond the range of this book to go into the law of forfeiture which is rarely used in agricultural tenancies.

Tenants of agricultural holdings are given security and landlords are given safeguards by the statutory rules for notices to quit.

Notices to quit

LENGTH OF NOTICE

The general rule is that at least twelve months' notice to quit must be given, expiring at a term date (see p. 49 for meaning) of the tenancy (1986 Act, s. 25). There are exceptions to this rule (to be found in s. 25). Briefly, a shorter notice may be served in the following cases (among others rarely occuring):

(a) The tenant's insolvency.
(b) The tenancy agreement validly containing a clause for resumption of the whole or part of the holding for a non-agricultural purpose.
(c) Notice to a sub-tenant.
(d) The Tribunal or arbitrator specifying a date for the end of the tenancy upon issuing a certificate of bad husbandry (s. 25(4)), or upon the tenant failing to comply with a notice to do work (Agricultural Holdings (Arbitration on Notices) Order 1978, S.I. 1978 No. 257 arts. 7 and 14 as amended. The Regulations may be replaced before printing of this book is completed).
(e) a tenant can serve a short notice (at least 6 months) after a rent increase award (s. 25 (3)).

COUNTER-NOTICES

The tenant's main protection is his right to serve a counter-notice to a notice to quit. He is entitled to do this to all notices to quit except those served for one or more of the special reasons sometimes known as 'deadly sins' (or, more technically, Cases A to H in Schedule 3 of the 1986 Act, described below). When the tenant is entitled to and does service a counter-notice on the landlord within one month of service of the notice to quit, the notice to quit will not operate unless the landlord obtains the consent of the Agricultural Land Tribunal (s. 26).

Trap for tenants. Tenants are warned they must get the counter-notice in within one month. There is no way of getting an extension of time.

The Tribunal may give consent to the operation of the landlord's notice to quit if he applies within one month of the counter-notice and proves one or more of special statutory grounds (1986 Act, s. 27). In brief the grounds are that he requires possession:

(a) In the interests of good husbandry; or

(b) Sound estate management; or

(c) To carry out agricultural research, education etc; or

(d) For statutory allotments; or

(e) Because greater hardship would be caused by withholding than by giving consent to the notice to quit; or

(f) For certain non-agricultural uses of the holding not within Case B (see below), the most likely being private forestry.

Even if the landlord proves grounds he still may not be granted consent because the Tribunal are required to withhold consent 'if in all the circumstances it appears to them that a fair and reasonable landlord would not insist on possession'.

Trap for landlords. It should be noted that all notices to quit should state the landlord's grounds for requiring possession. If no ground is stated the landlord will be liable to pay the tenant, if he quits, additional compensation equal to four times the rent, no matter what the ground for possession (1986 Act, ss. 60 and 61).

CASES WHERE NO COUNTER-NOTICE ALLOWED

In the cases where the tenant has no right to counter-notice (the 'deadly sins') the notice to quit will take effect with no Tribunal involvement. However, the tenant is allowed to challenge by arbitration whether the ground stated in the notice to quit in fact exists in Cases B, D, or E below (Agricultural Holdings (Arbitration on Notices) order 1978, S.I. 1978 No. 257 as amended – due to be replaced).

In brief the 'deadly sins' (Cases A to H of 1986 Act, Schedule 3) are:

(a) *Case A   Retirement from smallholding.* The tenant attained age 65, suitable alternative accommodation available and the tenancy agreement expressly subject to this Case.

(b) *Case B   Planning permission.* The land required for a non-agricultural use for which planning permission has been obtained or is not needed (but not for N.C.B. opencasting where restoration to agriculture or forestry stipulated).

(c) *Case C   Bad husbandry certificate.* A certificate of bad husbandry issued by the Agricultural Land Tribunal and notice to quit served within 6 months.

(d) *Case D   Notices to remedy breaches of tenancy.* This contains two grounds:

(i) Failure of the tenant to comply with a notice requiring him to pay overdue rent within two months.
(ii) Failure by the tenant to comply within a reasonable time with a notice to remedy a breach of tenancy capable of being remedied.

These grounds are explained more fully below.

(e) *Case E   Irremediable breach of tenancy.* The landlord's interest 'materially prejudiced' by a breach of tenancy not capable of being remedied.

(f) *Case F   Tenant's insolvency.*

(g) *Case G   Death of tenant.* Death of 'the sole (or sole surviving) tenant' provided the notice to quit is served within 3 months of receiving written notification of the death, or an application for succession tenancy. The notice to quit will end the tenancy but a close relative might be granted succession to the tenancy under the family succession laws described below pp. 62–67).

(h) *Case H   Minister's amalgamation scheme.* The Minister of Agriculture or Secretary of State for Wales requiring the land for an amalgamation scheme. This only applies if the tenancy agreement foreshadowed the possibility of recovery for amalgamation.

In each of Cases A to G the notice to quit must state the statutory reason for possession.

NOTICE TO PAY OVERDUE RENT
It should be noted the first ground in Case D is *not* that the rent is two months overdue. When rent is overdue the landlord is allowed to serve a notice requiring the tenant to pay it within two months. If the tenant fails to pay it within two months the ground under Case D is established. The notice to pay must be in the form prescribed by S.I. 1984 No. 1308. These Regulations may be replaced before the printing of this book is completed.

Trap for tenants. The two-month period under the notice to pay the rent is the very last chance for the tenant. If he fails no subsequent payment by the tenant will remove the landlord's right to possession even if the rent is paid after the two months have expired but before notice to quit is served (*Stoneman* v. *Brown* [1973] 2 all E.R. 225).

NOTICES TO REMEDY BREACHES OF TENANCY

The law about notices to remedy has got rather complex. Rules are laid down for notices to remedy and special rules for notices to do work. The importance of them is that a notice not complying with the rules is invalid and a subsequent notice to quit based on non-compliance may also be invalid.

RULES FOR ALL NOTICES TO REMEDY

(a) The notice must be in a prescribed form (1986 Act, Schedule 3, para. 10). Forms are prescribed with notes attached in the Agricultural Holdings (Forms of Notice to Pay Rent or to Remedy) Regulations 1984: (the current Regulations, S.I. 1984 No. 1308 are due to be replaced). The notes are part of the forms and must be included.

(b) The notice must give the tenant a reasonable time to comply with all the items in the notice (*Wykes* v. *Davis* [1975] 1 All E.R. 399).

ADDITIONAL RULES FOR NOTICES TO DO WORK

(a) *A valid notice cannot be served within twelve months of a previous notice to do work* unless the previous notice was withdrawn with the tenant's written agreement (1986 Act, Schedule 3, para 10).

(b) *Less than six months shall not be a reasonable period for doing any item of work* (Schedule 3, para. 10).

(c) *On receiving the notice the tenant may go to arbitration* on any question arising under it, such as challenging his liability to do any of the work. He may also invite an arbitrator to exercise his powers to delete any 'unnecessary or unjustified' items in the notice, or to substitute 'a different method or material' for any specified in the notice if he is satisfied that undue difficulty or expense is involved.

These arbitration rights are set out in the Agricultural Holdings (Arbitration on Notices) Order 1978 (S.I. 1978 No. 257). The Order should be studied by anyone concerned for the detailed rules, time limits, etc.

It should be noted that by modifying the notice the arbitrator does not modify the tenancy obligations of the tenant and so the landlord could pursue any other remedies open to him and the tenant may have to meet a dilapidations claim at the end of the tenancy if he does not do the work as required by the tenancy agreement.

(d) *Right to counter-notice*: if, and only if, a notice to quit under Case D is for failure to comply with a *notice to do work*, the tenant can serve a counter-notice within one month. The notice to quit will then not take effect unless the Agricultural Land Tribunal consents to its operation. The Tribunal's task on this occasion is to decide whether a fair and reasonable landlord would insist on possession. If after the counter-notice the tenant goes to arbitration to test the reason given in the notice to quit, the counter notice is nullified but should the arbitrator uphold the notice to quit the tenant can counter-notice again within one month from the delivery of the award (1986 Act, s. 28).

Succession Tenancies

The laws enabling close relatives of tenants to obtain succession tenancies were revised in 1984. They no longer apply to 'new tenancies' (starting after 12 July 1984) but a new scheme for retirement successions was added to the existing one for succession on the death of a tenant. Unfortunately the laws were made more complex. They are now to be found in Part IV of the 1986 Act, and Schedule 6.

OUTLINE OF THE LAWS

It is beyond the scope of this book to set out the whole complex code for succession tenancies. The main features are outlined. There is no automatic right of succession. The scheme is that when 'a sole (or sole surviving) tenant of an agricultural holding' dies, certain near relatives or 'treated' children of the deceased may apply within three months of the death to the Agricultural Land Tribunal for a direction entitling them to follow as tenant of the deceased's holding. One such near relative can be nominated to apply for a succession tenancy during the tenant's lifetime, once he reaches age 65. Before an applicant can succeed, the Tribunal must be satisfied that he or she is both eligible and suitable for succession and they must also consider any case put forward by the landlord for recovering possession. There can be only two successions to a holding under the scheme. The succession laws apply to tenancies granted before 12 July 1984, and succession tenancies stemming from them, but it is open to the parties to agree in later tenancies that the succession laws shall apply (s. 34). The rules concerning succession on the death of a tenant will be considered first, and then the special rules for retirement successions.

Even for pre-12 July 1984 tenancies there are exceptions from the succession laws.

EXCEPTIONS
There are instances where no application for succession may be made. They are listed in ss. 36, 37, and 38. They look complicated but what it amounts to is there can be no claim to succession:

(a) Where there have already been two successions under the Act (s. 37).
(b) Where the deceased had no security of tenure at the time of his death (s. 36(2) (b) and s.38(1)–(3)).
(c) Where the deceased's tenancy was for a fixed term with more than twenty-seven months still to run (s. 36(2)).
(d) Where the holding is a statutory smallholding or one under certain ex-servicemen's charitable trusts (s. 38(4) and (5)).

WHO IS AN 'ELIGIBLE PERSON'?
There are three eligibility hurdles to be surmounted to qualify for family succession. They are found in the definitions of 'eligible person' and 'close relative' (ss. 36 and 35(2)). They are:

(a) *The applicant must be within the qualifying degrees of kindred* to the deceased tenant, namely wife, brother, sister, child or 'treated child'. A 'treated child' is a person 'who in the case of any marriage to which the deceased was at any time a party, was treated by the deceased as a child of the family in relation to that marriage'.
(b) *Deriving livelihood from the holding:* the applicant must, for at least five out of the last seven years of the deceased's life, have derived his only or principal source of livelihood from his agricultural work on the holding or on an agricultural unit of which the holding forms a part. Up to three years on a full-time course at an establishment of further education in any subject, will count towards the qualifying five years (Schedule 6, para. 2). In the case of the deceased's widow, the agricultural work of the deceased will count as hers (s. 36(4)).
    The livelihood rule is not an absolute rule, because s. 41 provides that if the rule if not fully satisfied, but is satisfied to a 'material extent', the

Tribunal may treat the applicant as qualifying under the rule if they consider it fair and reasonable to do so.

(c) *Occupiers of commercial units*: the applicant must not be the occupier of a commercial unit of agricultural land.

'Commercial unit' is defined to mean 'a unit of agricultural land which is capable, when farmed under competent management, of producing a net annual income of an amount not less than the aggregate of the average annual earnings of two full-time, male agricultural workers aged twenty or over' (Schedule 6, para. 3). Whether a unit is commercial can largely be calculated by rule of thumb as the Minister of Agriculture periodically publishes average agricultural earnings and also makes Unit of Production Orders annually to enable the net annual income for various kinds of farming enterprises to be assessed (see Schedule 6, para. 4).

The 6th Schedule also specifies rules for determining whether a joint occupier (for example a partner) has a sufficient legal interest or share in a commercial unit to be disqualified for succession (paras. 6 & 7) and counts occupation by a spouse, or by a company controlled by the applicant or spouse, as occupation by the applicant.

No multiple successions. Further, an applicant may not succeed to more than one commercial unit under these laws (see Schedule 6, para. 8 and the procedures in s. 42).

Timing the application. An application to the Tribunal for succession must be made 'within the period of three months beginning with the day after the date of death' (s. 39), on prescribed Form I.

SUITABILITY

Where the Tribunal are satisfied an applicant is eligible they must then go on to decide whether he is also 'a suitable person to become the tenant of the holding' (s. 39(2)). If there is more than one eligible applicant then (unless one must be given preference because of designation in the will, or the landlord agrees to a joint tenancy) the Tribunal must decide which is the more or most suitable (s. 39(6)).

In deciding on suitability the Tribunal must 'have regard to all relevant matters', including the extent of the applicant's training and experience in agriculture, his age, health and financial standing and also the views (if any) stated by the landlord on his suitability (s. 39(8)).

THE LANDLORD'S CASE

The landlord should serve notice to quit within the three month period required by Case G (see above p. 60). If an application is made for family succession, he is entitled to reply (on prescribed Form IR) disputing the applicant's eligibility or suitability. He may also apply for consent to the operation of his notice to quit (on Form 2, to which the applicant may reply on Form 2R). Consent may be given on any of the grounds in s. 27 (see pp. 58–59 above), but if a ground is proved there will still be the 'fair and reasonable landlord' test under which the Tribunal may refuse consent. If consent is given to the notice to quit, or if the Tribunal determines the applicant not to be eligible or suitable, the family succession application must be dismissed (s. 44). If there is an eligible and suitable applicant and consent is not given to the notice to quit, the Tribunal must direct succession to the tenancy in favour of the applicant.

A trap-prescribed form. The prescribed forms must be used. At the time of writing they are in S.I. 1984 No. 1301, but they are expected to be changed by a new order in 1987.

A trap for landowners – voluntary agreements. As only two successions are allowed under the Act it is important for landowners that any succession taking place counts as one under the Act. A voluntary grant to an eligible person who has not applied for succession will not count. The close relative should apply under the Act, then, if after the time limit for applying for succession has elapsed, he is, or has become, 'the sole or sole remaining applicant' a voluntary grant of tenancy can be made under the Act without a hearing (s. 37(1)(b)). In these instances it is prudent to record the succession under the Act by a recital in the tenancy agreement.

THE NEW TENANCY

A tenancy directed by the Tribunal to a successful applicant will be a new tenancy on the same terms as the deceased's at the end of his tenancy (s. 47). However, whether or not the deceased had a covenant against assignment, subletting or parting with possession without the landlord's consent, the new tenancy will have such a covenant included by law (s. 47(3)). The new tenancy will start from the date on which the notice to quit ends the deceased's tenancy (or the equivalent date if no notice was served) (s. 45(1) and definition of relevant time in s. 46).

ARBITRATION OF TERMS

The terms of the new tenancy may be revised, because either the landlord or the successful applicant is entitled to demand an arbitration to review the terms and/or the rent (s. 48). The arbitrator may make any justifiable variations and in any event must include in the new tenancy:

(a) Payment of the usual 'ingoings' to the landlord.
(b) Payment over to the new tenant any compensation for dilapidations recovered by the landlord at the end of the deceased's tenancy in respect of any items the new tenant is required to make good.

If the tenancy terms are varied the arbitrator may adjust the rent accordingly (s. 48(6)).

A rent arbitration may be demanded no matter when there was a previous rent review. The arbitrator must fix 'the rent properly payable' in accordance with the formula in Schedule 2 (see p. 49 above).

SUCCESSION ON RETIREMENT OF TENANT
A succession counting as one of the two under the Act may take place by agreement during a tenant's lifetime. The Tribunal is not involved if there is an agreement between the landlord, the tenant and a relative of the tenant who is within the qualifying degrees of kindred (see p. 63 above) that the tenant retires from his tenancy and a new tenancy is granted to the relative or assigned to him or her (1986 Act, s. 37(2)). It is prudent to include in the new tenancy agreement or deed of assignment a recital evidencing it is a succession under the Act.

Retirement notice. In the absence of agreement a tenant from year to year of a tenancy which started before 12 July 1984, may, on or after reaching age 65 (earlier in the case of bodily or mental incapacity) serve on the landlord a retirement notice nominating one eligible close relative (s. 49). The nominated close relative may then apply to the Tribunal, within one month, for a succession tenancy (s. 50). The rules for eligibility and suitability, and the other rules are much the same as for applications on the death of a tenant (outlined above). If the Tribunal grants succession, the tenant will retire from his tenancy and the succession tenancy will begin during his lifetime.

Note the following special rules
(1) The tenant may serve only one retirement notice and nominate only one close relative (ss. 51(2) and 49(1)(b)).
(2) Nobody but the nominated person may apply for succession and a prescribed form must be used (s. 53(1) and (2)).

(3) As there is no notice to quit for the landlord to seek consent to, there is a 'greater hardship' test in every case (s. 53(8)).

(4) If the applicant fails, the tenancy continues and the applicant cannot apply again on the tenant's death (s. 57(4)).

Notices to quit. Somewhat complex rules about notices to quit are laid down in the 1986 Act (ss. 51(4) and (5) and 52). The principles involved are these. A notice to quit which is going to take effect (for example an 'incontestable' notice or one to which the Tribunal has given consent) cannot be defeated by the subsequent service of a retirement notice. Once a retirement notice has been served an 'incontestable' notice to quit may be validly served, provided it is given before the Tribunal hearing begins and the 'incontestable' ground existed before the retirement notice. Notices to quit based on Cases C and D will only prevail if the certificate of bad husbandry, or the notice to remedy or to pay rent was applied for, or given, before the retirement notice.

TIME LIMITS

Anyone concerned with a family succession case should watch the time limits laid down in the 1986 Act and the Regulations. The time limits for applying for succession, putting in replies, etc. are strict.

Unprotected occupation

We now outline certain kinds of occupation of farm land which do not get statutory security of tenure.

AGREEMENTS APPROVED BY THE MINISTER

If the prior approval of the Minister of Agriculture is given to a letting (less than a yearly tenancy) or licence to occpuy agricultural land it will end automatically at the end of the period specified in the agreement (1986 Act, s. 2). The same applies where a prospective landlord and tenant jointly apply for approval for a term of not less than two and not more than five years (s. 5). Approval is only given for good reasons within a policy adopted by M.A.F.F.

SHORT GRAZING AGREEMENTS

An agreement only for grazing or mowing (or both) 'during some specified period of the year' is not protected (1986 Act, s. 2(3)). This agreement must therefore be for less than a year. If it allows ploughing and re-seeding the agreement will not be within the grazing exemption (*Lory* v. *Brent B.C.* [1971] 1 All E.R. 1042) and, as buildings cannot be grazed or mowed they should not be included unless they are, for example, shelters 'purely ancillary' to the grazing (see *Avon C.C.* v. *Clothier* (1977) 242 E.G. 1048).

CONTRACTS OF ENGAGEMENT
The engagement of an agricultural contractor, or a manager is not protected if the landowner does not give exclusive possession of the land.

TENANCY FOR MORE THAN ONE YEAR AND LESS THAN TWO
We have seen above (p. 57) *Gladstone* v. *Bower* [1960] 2 Q.B. 384 confirmed such a tenancy is not protected by the 1986 Act. It should be noted the business tenancies code (Landlord and Tenant Act 1954 Part II) expressly excludes agricultural holdings. A fixed-term tenancy for, say, eighteen months or twenty-three months, will therefore end automatically at the end of the fixed term. No notice to quit should be served by the landlord and if the tenant is allowed to hold over he might well obtain statutory security of tenure.

PARTNERSHIPS
Where a farmer goes into partnership with the owner of the land he cannot claim this creates a protected tenancy by s. 2 magic (see p. 56) above and *Harrison-Broadley* v. *Smith* [1964] 1 All E.R. 867). It is open to a landowner to grant a tenancy of his land to himself and his parnter (*Rye* v. *Rye* [1962] A.C. 496) but in view of the decision in *Featherstone* v. *Staples* [1986] 2 All E.R. 461 (C.A.) and the joint and several liability of partners, landowners are advised to be circumspect about plunging in.

SHARE FARMING
There is no partnership or sharing of profits or losses between share farmers. Each retains his separate business. Inputs and gross output are shared. If no exclusive occupation is given by the landowner to a share farmer, the occupation will be governed by the Agreement with no statutory protection.

SUBTENANTS
The normal rule of law is that a subtenant cannot have a greater interest than his immediate landlord granting the subtenancy and so the subtenancy perishes with the tenancy above. The agricultural subtenant, however, has a degree of security of tenure, because the subtenancy will not end by reason

of the tenant above surrendering his tenancy or giving notice to quit to the landowner. Further, the subtenant will have the same rights as a full tenant to challenge a notice to quit by counter-notice, provided the tenant serving the notice to quit is not himself under notice from his own landlord. Where the intermediate tenant's tenancy is being ended by his landlord, then the subtenancy must perish with the head tenancy and the subtenant will have no right to counter-notice.

POSTSCRIPT

Milk–EEC Outgoers Scheme – Whilst going to press the EEC Outgoers scheme along the lines envisaged at pp. 54–55 above has been made and implemented by the milk (Community Outgoers Scheme) (England and Wales) Regulations 1986 (S.I. 1986 No. 1161).

Chapter 4
Rating

Abbreviations in this Chapter:
'1967 Act' – General Rate Act 1967.
'1971 Act' – Rating Act 1971.

Rating generally

A rate is in effect a form of local taxation on property. It is calculated by charging 'so much' in the pound of the rateable value of the property. Fortunately there are exceptions and reliefs from rating for most agricultural property.

The main Act to refer to for rating law is still the General Rate Act 1967, which when passed contained nearly all the statute law on rating, but there have been some additional laws since. The Rate Act 1984 provides for rate limitation and other details and the Local Government Planning and Land Act 1980 tinkers with the rate support grant. Neither Act is gone into here. The Government in a consultation paper 'Paying for Local Government' (1986, Cmnd 9714) has proposed fundamental changes in rating. Among other reforms, domestic rates would be replaced by a community charge paid by every resident adult.

The rateable unit is called the 'hereditament' and in each rating area the rateable hereditaments and their rateable values, assessed by valuation officers, are entered on a valuation list. Any 'person aggrieved' by an entry on the valuation list (including the rating authority) either because of the inclusion of a hereditament, or because of the rateable value put on it, may make a 'proposal' for the alteration of the list (1967 Act, s. 69). Often the solution can be negotiated by the occupier with the rating authority (if a deletion is sought) or the District Valuer (if value is challenged). If not, local valuation courts determine disputes, from which an appeal can be taken to the Lands Tribunal (s. 77).

Generally it is the occupier of the property who is liable to pay the rates, though in some cases, for convenience of collection, the owner is made liable, and also there is power to rate unoccupied premises (1967 Act, s. 17 amended by Local Government Act 1974). If rates are not paid the rating authority can (and usually will) take out a summons for the defaulter to appear before the magistrates, and they may issue a warrant to levy distress against the defaulter's goods and chattels for the amount of the unpaid rates plus costs (Part VI of 1967 Act).

Agricultural land and buildings are exempt from rating. Agricultural dwellings are not, but have special treatment.

Agricultural land

The 1967 Act states, 'No agricultural land or agricultural buildings shall be liable to be rated or be included in any valuation list or rate' (s. 26(1)). The Act defines 'agricultural land' to mean:

> any land used as arable meadow or pasture ground only, land used for a plantation or a wood or for the growth of saleable underwood, land exceeding 0.10 hectare used for the purpose of poultry farming, cottage gardens, nursery grounds, orchards or allotments, including allotment gardens within the meaning of the Allotments Act 1922, but does not include land occupied together with a house as a park, gardens (other than as aforesaid), pleasure grounds, or land kept or preserved mainly or exclusively for purposes of sport, or recreation, or land used as a racecourse.' (s. 26(3) amended by S.I. 1978 No. 318).

It also includes land occupied with and used solely in connection with the use of buildings exempt from rating by the 1967 Act and by the 1971 Act (dealt with below).

The Act goes on to define 'cottage garden' to mean 'a garden attached to a house occupied as a dwelling by a person of the labouring classes' (s. 26(3)).

Agricultural buildings

As seen above, the 1967 Act states plainly agricultural buildings shall not be rated, but until the 1971 Act a series of court decisions excluded from the rating relief certain intensive farm buildings. The 1971 Act amended the meaning of 'agricultural building' to bring into rating relief certain intensive buildings, and also bee-keeping buildings and buildings of corporate syndicates.

The basic definition of 'agricultural buildings' is 'buildings (other than dwellings) occupied together with agricultural land or being or forming part of a market garden, and in either case used solely in connection with agricultural operations thereon' (1967 Act, s. 26(4)). Breeding and rearing hunters is not an agricultural operation (*Evans* v. *Bailey* (1981) E.G.D. 730).

LIVESTOCK BUILDINGS

Even if they are not 'used solely in connection with agricultural operations' on the agricultural land as stated in the above definition, buildings for keeping or breeding livestock are, by the 1971 Act, exempt agricultural buildings provided:

(a) they are used solely for that purpose; or
(b) they are occupied with agricultural land and used in connection with agricultural operations on that land; and
(c) they are surrounded by or adjoin at least two hectares of agricultural land (1971 Act, s. 2).

ANCILLARY BUILDINGS

Any building (other than a dwelling) occupied together with one or more exempt livestock building(s), is itself exempt from rating, provided:

(a) it is used solely in connection with the operations carried on in the livestock building or buildings; or
(b) it is occupied also together with agricultural land and used also in connection with agricultural operations on that land, and that use together with its use in connection with the livestock building(s) is its sole use; and
(c) it is surrounded by or adjoins at least two hectares of agricultural land (1971 Act, s. 2).

Meaning of 'livestock'

'Livestock' in the 1971 Act is stated to 'include' any mammal or bird kept for the production of food or wool, or for the purpose of its use in the farming of land (s. 1(3)). Rating exemption will not therefore apply to stables for riding horses, or to buildings for keeping animals in wild life parks or zoos. Pasture racing stock is not an agricultural operation (*Hemens (VO)* v. *Whitsbury Farm and Stud Ltd* (1986) (*The Times*, 10 November 1986)). Game birds not raised for food but for release are not 'livestock' (*Cook* v. *Ross Poultry Ltd* [1982] R.A. 187).

FISH FARMS

Land and buildings used solely for, or in connection with, fish farming are exempt from rating, whether the fish are reared directly for food or for stocking fisheries (Local Government Planning and Land Act, 1980, s. 31).

As bees are unlikely to be interpreted as 'livestock', the 1971 Act makes special provision to exempt as an agricultural building any building (other than a dwelling) occupied by a person keeping bees, if it is used solely for that purpose and it is surrounded by or adjoins at least two hectares of agricultural land (s. 3).

SYNDICATES' BUILDINGS
The 1967 Act specially provides for buildings of farming syndicates to come into de-rating because the wording of the definition of 'agricultural building' had been interpreted as excluding a building occupied by a management committee for separate occupiers of agricultural land. Now, so long as the building is occupied by all the occupiers of the land it serves, or by persons appointed by them each of whom occupies some of the land, the agricultural building gets rating relief, provided there are not more than twenty-four occupiers of the land (joint occupiers counting as one) (s. 26(4)). The 1971 Act still had to fill a gap, however, because no account had been taken of incorporated associations or co-operatives. The 1971 Act came to the rescue (s. 4), but if the incorporated body's building is used in connection with agricultural operations on land occupied by a person who is not a member of the body, it will not qualify for exemption. Nor will there be exemption if there is but a single occupier of the building (*Prior* v. *Sovereign Chicken Ltd* [1984] 2 All E.R. 289 (CA)). A marketing society's auction hall was held not exempted from rating where a substantial quantity of the goods sold belonged to non-members (*Corser* v. *Gloucestershire Marketing Society Ltd* (*The Times,* 21 November 1980 (C.A.)).

Farmhouses and cottages

Agricultural dwellings do not get the agricultural rating exemption, but the special rules for assessing their rateable value usually, if not always, results in a lower valuation than would otherwise be the case.

WHAT DWELLINGS QUALIFY?
To qualify for this special form of assessment the dwelling must be:

(a) occupied in connection with agricultural land; and
(b) used as the dwelling of either:

(i) a person primarily engaged in carrying on or directing agricultural operations on that land; or

(ii) a person employed in agricultural operations on that land in the service of the occupier, and entitled to use the dwelling only so long as he is so employed (1967 Act, s. 26(2)).

Farmhouses, whether occupied by an owner-occupier or the farm tenant, therefore qualify, if farming the land is the primary occupation of the occupier. Where the occupier has another occupation the question as to which he is primarily engaged in does not turn on which gives him the more livelihood, but on which he spends the more time (*Scott* v. *Billet* (1956) 1 R.R.C. 29 – a barrister devoting more attention to farming than his practice held to be primarily engaged in farming although he made a loss at farming and a profit from his practice).

Tied cottages occupied by agricultural workers qualify, whether or not the occupier is a tenant of the cottage, so long as his right to occupy lasts only while he is employed as a worker on the employee's land.

THE VALUATION

While the agricultural dwelling is occupied and used as described in (a) and (b) above, the gross value for rating must 'be estimated by reference to the rent at which the house might reasonably be expected to be let from year to year if it could not be occupied and used otherwise' (1967 Act, s. 26(2)).

This notional restriction on the type of letting that must be assumed for the purposes of the assessment often results in a rateable value less than would be likely if the normal rule of assessment applied (see below) though each case must be considered on its merits.

Non-agricultural dwellings

'GROSS VALUE' AND 'NET ANNUAL VALUE'

The rateable value on which the rate is calculated is the 'net annual value'. In the case of houses the 'gross value' is required to be assessed, and from this a certain deduction, prescribed by order, must be made to reach the 'net annual value'.

'Gross value' is defined to mean 'the rent at which the hereditament might reasonably be expected to be let from year to year if the tenant undertook to pay all the usual tenant's rates and taxes and the landlord undertook to bear the cost of the repairs and insurance and the other expenses, if any, necessary to maintain the hereditament in a state to command that rent' (1967 Act, s. 19(6)).

This hypothetical rent a hypothetical tenant would pay may not be the same as the actual rent paid by the actual tenant where the premises are in fact let.

MANSION HOUSES

What if a house is a magnificent part of our heritage, but because it is so magnificent and because conditions today are not what they were (appalling cost of upkeep, lighting and heating, impossibility of keeping a fleet of servants, etc.) it is unlettable in the open market? What is the hypothetical rent of an unlettable house? A succession of cases has shown it is not an easy assessment to make and the answer is not a nil valuation.

The cases show that the Lands Tribunal will consider what the existing occupier, as the most likely tenant, would offer to an imaginary landlord:

> on the hypothesis that both are reasonable people, the landlord not being extortionate, the tenant not being under pressure, the dwelling being vacant and to let, not subject to any control, the landlord agreeing to do the repairs and pay the insurance, the tenant agreeing to pay the rates, the period not too short nor yet too long, simply from year to year.
> (The words are Lord Denning's in *R. v. Paddington Valuation Officer* (1965) R.A. 177 adopted in *Mills v. Peak* (1965) 11 R.R.C. 237 – (Bisterne House) and *Mullineaux v. Castle Howard Estate Co. Ltd* (1968) 14 R.R.C. 88 (Castle Howard)).

Not getting a clear answer to this inscrutable question, the Tribunal will consider the rateable values put on any comparable premises and do the best it can. This way Bisterne was assessed at £350 gross value (£266 net) in 1965 and Castle Howard at £300 gross value (£266 net) in 1967, to take just the two examples already cited.

Sporting rights

Sporting rights can be a rateable hereditament separate from the land. The 1967 Act states that 'any right of sporting (that is to say, any right of fowling, of shooting, of taking or killing game or rabbits, or of fishing) when severed from the occupation of the land on which the right is exercisable shall be liable to be assessed to rates ...' (s. 16(e)).

'SEVERED FROM THE OCCUPATION OF THE LAND'

This is the key rule. If the sporting rights are not at law severed they are not rateable. This benefits owners of shoots more than fisheries, because in the case of shoots the land over which the shooting takes place will normally be agricultural land also free from rating. A fishery is less likely to be counted as agricultural land and might be rated as land even though the fishing rights are not severed. If, for example, a fishery is rated as 'land covered by water' or as 'the bed of the River Slurpe' the rating will be upheld unless it be shown that the agricultural use (for example, drainage, watering cattle and improving pasture) predominates over the fishing use (as it did in *Watkins* v. *Hereford Assessment Committee* (1935) 154 L.T. 262, but not in *Clay and Clay* v. *Newbiggin* (1956) 1 R.R.C. 13 and *Garnett* v. *Wand* (1960) 7 R.R.C. 99).

The question whether the sporting rights are severed depends on somewhat artificial rules evolved from court decisions. Much turns on a technicality, namely whether there was a letting of the rights by deed (*Swayne* v. *Howells* [1927] K.B. 385) or whether the rights were reserved by the landlord out of a letting of the land (*Cleobury Mortimer R.D.C.* v. *Childe* [1933] 2 K.B. 368). A deed is a formal legal document signed, sealed and delivered. An unsealed tenancy agreement or licence is not therefore a deed.

Without going into all possible permutations the rules may be summarised like this:

(a) There is rating liability in these cases:

(i) Where the owner-occupier lets sporting rights by deed;
(ii) Where the landowner lets the land (whether or not by deed) and reserves the sporting rights. The reservation severs the sporting rights and they are then rateable whether or not he lets them;
(iii) Where the landowner lets the land with the sporting rights and the tenant then sublets the sporting rights by deed; and
(iv) Where the landowner lets the land with the sporting rights and the tenant then sublets the land reserving the sporting rights.

Where sporting rights are exercisable on non-agricultural land and they are severed from the occupation of the land and are not let and the owner receives rent from the land, the rights are not to be separately valued but the rateable value of the land is to be estimated as if the sporting rights were not severed (1967 Act, s. 19(1)).

(b) There is no rating liability in these cases:

(i) Where an owner-occupier keeps the sporting rights;
(ii) Where the owner-occupier lets the sporting rights not by deed;

(iii) Where the landowner lets the land with the sporting rights and the tenant retains them; and

(iv) Where the landowner lets the land with the sporting rights and the tenant sublets them not by deed.

The moral is, to avoid rating, the grant of fishing should be by a tenancy agreement *not* under seal (*Swayne* v. *Howells*, above) or by licence (*Whitby* v. *Warrington Angling Association* (1985) 276 E.G. 1169 (L.T.)).

ASSESSING THE RATEABLE VALUE

The net rateable value to be entered on the list for sporting rights is the estimated rent at which they might reasonably be expected to be let from year to year if the tenant undertook to pay all usual tenant's rates and taxes and to bear the cost of the repairs, insurance and other expenses, if any, necessary to maintain the hereditament in a state to command that rent.

Relevant factors will therefore include the quality and accessibility of the sporting rights, the demand in the area, the degree of interference from other users of the land or waters, whether the public have access and the cost of maintenance, bailiffing etc. The actual rent paid is not necessarily the net annual value (in *Olding* v. *Denman* (1951) 167 E.G. 633 the Lands Tribunal assessed the rateable value lower than the actual rent paid for the sporting rights).

RATING RELIEF FOR SPORTING RIGHTS

Where there is rating liability for any hereditament occupied by a charity and used wholly or mainly for charitable purposes, the charity is entitled to 50% rating relief (1967 Act, s. 40(1)).

A club, society or other organisation not established or conducted for profit may obtain relief at the discretion of the rating authority if it occupies a hereditament wholly or mainly for purposes of recreation (s. 40(5)). This does not avail a shooting or fishing syndicate or the individual landowner, but many angling clubs are given rating relief in varying degrees. It is a hit-or-miss affair, however, as it is left to the whim of the authority whether they should give relief, and also the extent of the relief if they decide to give it.

Readers may care to note that poverty is also a ground for claiming rating relief.

Chapter 5
Compulsory Acquisition of Land

Abbreviations in this Chapter:
'1961 Act' – Land Compensation Act 1961.
'1965 Act' – The Compulsory Purchase Act 1965.
'1973 Act' – Land Compensation Act 1973.
'1981 Act' – Acquisition of Land Act 1981
'C.P.O.' – Compulsory purchase order.

Bodies with compulsory powers

Compulsory powers are spread around widely nowadays – too widely the farming community will think – so widely that not only are they enjoyed by local authorities and departments of state, but also by quangos and even private companies. They can, however, only be exercised for purposes specifically authorised by statute and in accordance with set procedures. The owner and occupier of the land nearly always has a right to object and to be paid for any land or rights acquired from him.

Powers of acquisition

Broadly there are two kinds of compulsory powers:

(a) POWER TO ACQUIRE LAND OR RIGHTS COMPULSORILY WITHOUT FURTHER ADO
In these cases the acquiring authority can acquire without the need of a higher authority confirming a compulsory purchase order (C.P.O.).

Emergency powers. These have sometimes been conferred on Departments of State (usually only in wartime) allowing such acquisitions for the defence of the realm. The landowner or occupier cannot do much about it, but under the 'Crichel Down principle' (which is not law but has been accepted by all governments since the famous Ministerial statement in Parliament on 20 July 1954) the landowner, or his successors, should be given the first option to repurchase (at market value) if and when compulsorily acquired land becomes surplus to the State's requirements.

Private Acts. More commonly Private Acts of Parliament are sometimes passed authorising an authority to purchase a specific area of land for a specific purpose within a specified time. Again, once that Act is passed the landowner or occupier cannot do much about it, but in these instances there is the opportunity to petition against the Bill before it is passed.

(b) POWER TO MAKE A COMPULSORY PURCHASE ORDER NEEDING
CONFIRMATION
This is the usual case. The procedures will be examined further in this chapter. Although there are variations in detail, a general pattern is followed. The acquiring authority makes a C.P.O., there is an opportunity for objection and the order does not take effect unless confirmed by a higher authority (usually a Minister). In each case the Act conferring the powers should be looked at to see what procedures are laid down.

Uniform procedure

Odd procedures still exist under various Acts, but fortunately a uniform procedure is laid down by the Acquisition of Land Act 1981 which nowadays applies in most cases. It is common form for an Act giving compulsory powers to adopt the 1981 Act by cross-reference. An exception is the New Towns Act 1981 where the whole area for a new town is first designated after a public inquiry and thereafter rights to object to C.P.O.s within the area are curtailed. Much of the uniform procedural law is to be found in the Compulsory Purchase Act 1965 and Regulations made under it. Rules for compensation are found in the Land Compensation Acts 1961 and 1973 (see below p. 83–88).

An alternative procedure of acquisition by making vesting declarations is sometimes used, but is not dealt with in this book (see Compulsory Purchase (Vesting Declarations) Act 1981).

Making and serving the C.P.O

The form of the C.P.O. is prescribed by regulations (Compulsory Purchase of Land Regulations 1982, S.I. 1982 No. 6). The C.P.O. will state under which Act it is made, the purpose of acquisition and the time limit for objections. The land to be acquired will be identified and the names of the owner and occupiers given (if known). The order must be served on every owner and occupier except a tenant for a month or any period less than a month. As usual there are exceptions; the main two are:

(a) Service is not required in a new town designated area.
(b) Individual service may be dispensed with by the confirming Minister in cases of difficulty, in which case the C.P.O. may be addressed to 'the owners and any occupiers' (1981 Act, s. 6).

An advertisement of the C.P.O. must also be published in a local newspaper in two successive weeks stating where it may be examined and the time for objections (1981 Act, s. 11).

Objections

HIGH COURT CHALLENGE

If a C.P.O. is defective at law because it is ultra vires (the acquiring authority overreaching its powers) or there is a procedural defect, its validity may be challenged in the High Court within six weeks of its coming into operation.

RIGHT TO OBJECT

Landowners and occupiers entitled to be served with the C.P.O. are also entitled to object to it and (subject to special exceptions) to have the objection heard (1981 Act, s. 13). Others may also object, such as neighbouring landowners, 'environmentalists', and busy-bodies. They have no right to be heard at a hearing or inquiry (unless they would be entitled to compensation under the Land Compensation Act 1973), though it may be granted them. The C.P.O. and advertisements will state where objections are to be sent and the time limit for objecting. There may be no more than twenty-one days given for objecting, so if there is any doubt whether the acquisition is acceptable an objection should be submitted in time, even if no details can be given. It can always be withdrawn or supplemented later.

TRY TO NEGOTIATE

Parley between the two sides should always take place. They cannot expect to understand each other's problems without talks, and often a helpful degree of agreement can be reached. The chances of defeating the proposed acquisition are usually slender (though not always hopeless) but it is often possible for the owner to negotiate modifications or improvements to mitigate some of the disadvantages especially where land is severed. He should not hesitate to engage professional help. Professional fees reasonably incurred will be recoverable from (or paid by) the acquiring authority. Where only part of an owner's land is to be taken there will be accommodation works to negotiate, for example fencing, new accesses, underpasses beneath, or bridges over a road or railway – and possibly an alteration of the siting of the works, landscaping and a reduction of the land take. The owner of farmland should insist on the minimum interference with agriculture.

THE HEARING OR INQUIRY

If the owner, tenant or occupier objects to the C.P.O. in principle (believing there is no need for the works, or they are going in the wrong place) or if he has not been able to negotiate the modifications or accommodation works he requires, there will be a 'hearing' by an Inspector or a public local inquiry. However, if the objection is only about compensation, the objector is not entitled to a hearing or an inquiry because it is for the Lands Tribunal to settle compensation disputes (see below p. 88). There are certain special cases where the Secretary of State need not hold a hearing or inquiry, usually where the planning status for the development has already been fixed by previous procedures.

In practice the owner can choose whether to have an inquiry or a hearing (1981 Act, s. 13). A hearing is less formal, but a successful objector cannot be awarded costs.

INQUIRY PROCEDURES

The formal procedures at the inquiry are laid down in Regulations (S.I. 1976 No. 746 or No. 721). Those entitled to be heard must be given at least six weeks' notice of the inquiry and notices of it must be displayed on the land at least two weeks in advance (usually the Minister orders advertisements as well). At least four weeks beforehand the authority must furnish copies of their written reasons for the acquisition.

Owners and occupiers objecting must consider whether to be represented by counsel, or a solicitor or other professional person, and what – if any – expert evidence to call. Expense is a consideration here, because if the objection is unsuccessful costs would not be awarded (though fees incurred in negotiations should be recoverable as compensation). The objector may appear in person, if he thinks he has the necessary knowledge, wisdom and ability.

INSPECTION

It is advisable to ask the Inspector if he proposes to make a site inspection. Anyone entitled to be heard can require an inspection and has a right to be present.

THE DECISION

The Inspector does not make the decision whether to confirm the C.P.O. He writes a report to the Minister with a recommendation which may or may not be accepted. Owners and occupiers of the land are entitled to the Minister's decision letter and to a copy of the Inspector's report. Other objectors allowed to appear are advised to request at the inquiry that these documents are sent to them though they may only get the decision letter.

NEW ROADS

Roads are a special case. They present special difficulties both for the planners and for the landowners who do not want their land severed. The pattern of events is not always the same as the standard procedure described above and advisers will need to refer to the Highways Act 1980.

The important consideration for objectors is to get the objection in early enough, namely when road schemes are being settled. Once a motorway or other new road scheme has been established under the Highways Act, the scope for a landowner to achieve joy on objecting to a later C.P.O. is very limited, especially if there has already been a public inquiry into the scheme. Schemes will be publicised and owners and occupiers along the route (or within 100 yards of it) will be given direct notice. If they object they should state their grounds of objection (Highways Act 1980, Schedule 1, para. 18).

This is the stage for negotiation with the highway authority or Road Construction Unit. The landowners and occupiers cannot insist on a public inquiry (though local and other authorities can) but if there is a body of objection an inquiry is normally held.

NOTICE TO TREAT

Once a C.P.O. has been confirmed, but not before, the acquiring authority can serve notice to treat, which they will on all owners, tenants and mortgagees of the land. It must describe the land to be acquired, state that the authority is willing to treat for its purchase and to negotiate the compensation and require the recipient to disclose his exact interest in the land (1965 Act, s. 5). He will usually be required to return a claim form within twenty-one days. Once the purchase price has been agreed, or fixed by the Lands Tribunal in default of agreement, the acquiring authority can compel a conveyance of the land, by court order if necessary.

Withdrawal. If the authority withdraws a notice to treat, the owner usually does not mind, to say the least, but he may be left out of pocket. The Land Compensation Act 1961, s. 31, therefore allows him to claim for any loss or expense caused by the service and withdrawal of the notice to treat.

MINERAL CODE

Commonly minerals in the land will not be included in the C.P.O., but a statutory 'mining code' will be applied. If minerals are included they must be paid for, but if they are not included the mining code will apply a procedure under which the acquiring authority must be given notice before it is intended to extract minerals from a specified area of support under or near the acquired land. The authority can then either permit the extraction to go ahead, or stop it wholly or partly, in which case they must pay for the minerals sterilised.

Compensation

NO CONFISCATION

It is a fundamental principle enshrined in our law (sometimes disregarded by certain authorities) that land or interests in land are not to be confiscated in the exercise of statutory powers, unless the enabling legislation *expressly* permits it (*Central Control Board* v. *Cannon Brewery Co. Ltd* [1919] A.C. 744). They are to be paid for unless the Act says otherwise. Very rarely indeed does an Act say otherwise.

PAYMENTS ON COMPULSORY PURCHASE

There are many complexities in the laws for compensation, which will not be imposed upon the reader of this book. The main headings of compensation, explained further below, are the purchase price for the land or interest acquired; compensation for injurious affection to land not taken; 'disturbance' costs and fees; home loss and farm loss payments; and interest on compensation.

Much of the law will be found in the Land Compensation Acts 1961 and

1973 and the Compulsory Purchase Act 1965, but some important principles have also been established by decided cases.

PURCHASE PRICE

This is always payable (save in extremely exceptional cases which are unlikely to happen to the reader of this book) and in most cases it will be the open market price.

THE SIX PURCHASE RULES

Six statutory rules for assessing the payment have existed since 1919 (now in 1961 Act, s. 5), which can be summarised as follows:

(a) Rule 1. No allowance payable on account of the acquisition being compulsory;

(b) Rule 2. Subject to rules 3 to 6, the value of the land shall 'be taken to be the amount which the land if sold in the open market by a willing seller might be expected to realise';

(c) Rule 3. No account to be taken of the special suitability of the land for any purpose if the purpose could only be achieved by the exercise of statutory powers, or if the purpose is one for which there is no market apart from the special needs of a particular purchaser or the requirements of an authority with compulsory powers. (This complicated rule is explained in the leading case of *Pointe Gourde Quarrying & Transport Co. Ltd* v. *Sub-Intendent of Crown Lands* [1947] A.C. 565);

(d) Rule 4. Any increase in value due to unlawful or health-hazardous use of the land to be disregarded, for example, where the use is in contravention of planning law;

(e) Rule 5. The reasonable cost of equivalent re-instatement shall be paid (instead of market value) where the land is devoted to a purpose for which there is no general demand or market, provided it is genuinely intended to re-instate it elsewhere, for example, a hostel for redundant farmworkers;

(f) Rule 6. Disturbance compensation is payable, notwithstanding that the purchase price is paid under rule 2.

THREE MORE RULES

Three further rules in the 1961 Act (ss. 6, 7, 9 and First Schedule) can be summarised as follows:

(a) Effect of Schemes. Any increase or decrease in value of the land due to a statutory scheme must be disregarded. A 'scheme' may be, for example, the designation of a new town. This is sometimes called 'the Pointe Gourde principle' because it derived from the Pointe Gourde case (cited above). In over-simple terms it means in such cases you must assess what a private developer would have paid if there were no scheme;

(b) Betterment. If retained land is increased in value by the compulsory acquisition, the increase can be off-set against the purchase money;

(c) Blight. Any lowering in value caused by the compulsory acquisition plan is to be disregarded. It might be noted here that if part of a farm is acquired leaving the remainder unviable, the owner can require the authority to purchase the whole agricultural unit by serving a counter-notice (1973 Act, ss. 53; further laws on planning blight are in 1973 Act, ss. 70–81; Town and County Planning Act 1971, ss. 192–207; Local Government, Planning and Land Act 1980, s. 147).

CERTIFICATES OF ALTERNATIVE DEVELOPMENT

The market value of the land turns to a large extent on its planning status and what (if any) planning permissions could be obtained. This may be ascertained to an extent from the development plan for the area and any existing planning permissions. Where the planning potential is uncertain, it can be resolved by the owner, or the acquiring authority, applying to the planning authority to certify what development would be permitted if there were no compulsory acquisition. An appeal from the certification of alternative development can be made to the Secretary of State (see 1961 Act Part III).

Farm tenants are also to be compensated as explained below (p. 87).

INJURIOUS AFFECTION

Compensation for injurious affection is payable when only part of the owner's land is acquired and what is left is diminished in value as a result (see 1965 Act, s. 7). The typical case is severance of a farm by a new road. The claim is for 'damage' (in the legal sense of loss or injury) sustained by the owner through the severance or other injurious affection, and the effect of the whole of the works can be taken into account, not only works on the land acquired from the owner (1973 Act, s. 44). In practice the injurious affection is usually lessened by accommodation works such as fencing, underpasses or new accesses carried out by the authority.

WHERE NO LAND TAKEN

Owners of dwelling houses, business premises and farms can claim compensation for injurious affection caused by 'physical factors' from certain public works, even though none of their land is acquired for the works. The somewhat complex rules can be found in the 1973 Act Part I. The 'physical factors' are noise, vibration, smells, fumes, smoke, artificial lighting or the deposit on the land of any liquid or solid substance from qualifying works coming into use (or substantially altered) on or after 17 October 1969 which decreases the value of the claimant's interest in the land. The public works that qualify for such claims are 'any highway; any aerodrome; and any works or land (not being a highway or aerodrome) provided or used in the exercise of statutory powers'. 'Physical factors' caused by an aircraft arriving at or departing from an aerodrome count, but otherwise 'the source of the physical factors must be situated on or in the public works' causing the loss of value to the land.

DISTURBANCE

We have seen that rule 6 makes disturbance compensation additional to the purchase money. The principle, enunciated in the leading case of *Horn* v. *Sunderland Cpn* [1941] 2 K.B. 26 (C.A.), is the owner is to be left no worse off financially, and no better off, as a result of the compulsory acquisition. If he gets full development value for the land, therefore, he would not be entitled to additional disturbance compensation, but otherwise he must be compensated for the costs, losses and injury directly consequent on the acquisition.

WHAT CAN BE CLAIMED

The kinds of items of compensation are loss of farm profit during the dislocation caused by the loss of the land, removal costs, any loss due to forced sale of live and dead stock on a bad market, loss of business goodwill, and professional fees.

Professional fees. Fees reasonably incurred in the sale to the acquiring authority, in negotiating compensation and accommodation works and, where the claimant is displaced, in acquiring another property are recoverable. They may include fees of a solicitor, chartered surveyor and, if reasonable, the commission and expenses of more than one agent (*Harvey* v. *Crawley Development Cpn* [1957] 1 Q.B. 485). In the absence of an agreed fee the entitlement is to reasonable remuneration for the work involved. This will usually be a scale fee. The scale fee, however, will not always be adequate remuneration though some authorities refuse to pay more regardless of its adequacy in the circumstances. In such cases owners should beware of their adviser seeking to recover the balance from them.

FARM TENANTS

Tenants with security of tenure beyond the date of displacement will be entitled to compensation. If the farm tenancy is terminated by notice to quit they can claim under the Agricultural Holdings Act 1986, s. 60 one or two years' rent basic compensation, and additional compensation of four years' rent. Where there is no claim under these provisions, however, the tenant can claim for costs, losses and 'tenant right' (see p. 53 above), and also for the value of the unexpired term of the tenancy taking into account statutory security of tenure (see *Ministry of Transport* v. *Pettit* [1968] L.G.R. 449 as modified by 1973 Act, s. 48, and see 1973 Act, s. 37 for occupiers with an otherwise insufficient interest). He can choose whether the agricultural holdings code shall apply, or the compulsory purchase compensation laws (1973 Act, s. 59).

Where an acquiring authority allows the tenant to remain in occupation of all or part of the land under a licence after the acquisition, any benefit from the licence reducing his loss caused by disturbance will not reduce the compensation payable unless there is agreement to the contrary (*Wakerley* v. *St Edmundsbury B.C.* [1979] E.G.D. 576).

HOME LOSS AND FARM LOSS PAYMENTS

Home loss payment. This is in the nature of a 'sweetener' to soothe the anguish of an occupier forced out of his or her home by compulsory powers. The rules are to be found in the 1973 Act, ss. 29–33. To qualify the occupier (who may be an owner or tenant) must have occupied the dwelling as his only or principal residence for at least five years. The amount currently payable is three times the rateable value of the dwelling (minimum payment £150, maximum £1500, but there is power for the Secretary of State to vary the formula from time to time).

Two points to watch out for are:

(a) The claim must be made within six months of displacement.
(b) Occupiers should not vacate the dwelling before the C.P.O. is confirmed.

Farm loss payment. The purpose of this is to compensate for the lower farm profit to be expected in the early years on moving, because of a C.P.O., to an unfamiliar farm. The rules are to be found in the 1973 Act, ss. 34–6. Only an owner-occupier, or a tenant for a fixed term with three years still to run, can apply for the payment (a yearly tenant, or an owner temporarily allowed by the authority to stay on as a tenant will get the special compensation noted above). To qualify, the claimant must be displaced by the compulsory acquisition from the whole of his agricultural unit, and must begin to farm elsewhere within three years as the occupier of the whole of the newly acquired unit.

The 1973 Act, s. 35 deals with the amount of the payment, which is calculated on a formula based on the annual farming profit from the vacated unit averaged over three years. Reasonable professional fees reasonably incurred in preparing and negotiating the claim can be recovered. The claim must be made within one year of the beginning to farm the new unit.

INTEREST

On a compulsory acquisition interest is payable on the purchase money from the date of entry (Land Clauses Consolidation Act 1845, s. 85; 1965 Act, s. 11). The rate of interest is laid down in Regulations (under 1961 Act, s. 32) and in inflationary times is changed frequently. As to interest on other claims, the Lands Tribunal has power to order interest to run on its awards and the courts have power under the Law Reform (Miscellaneous Provisions) Act 1934. On farm loss payments interest is to run from the date the claim is submitted. As regards awards of interest by the Lands Tribunal, see *Weeks* v. *Thames Water Authority* (1980) 39 P&CR 208 and the note on p. 133 in Chapter 9.

SETTLEMENT OF DISPUTES

In the absence of agreement, either the claimant or the acquiring authority can refer the assessment of compensation to the Lands Tribunal for determination.

Chapter 6
Town and Country Planning

Abbreviations in this Chapter:
'1971 Act' – Town and Country Planning Act 1971.
'1960 Act' – Caravan Sites and Control of Development Act 1960.
'General Development Order' – Town and Country Planning General Development Order 1977.

Introduction

Agriculture is comparatively free from planning controls, but an owner of agricultural land who wishes to build a farmhouse or farm cottage is in the same position as anyone else outside agriculture. He must get planning permission to build. If, however, he wishes to put up a farm building, it will not usually be necessary for him to obtain planning permission, unless the building is very large, or he wants to put it near a trunk road or a classified road. Under the General Development Order there is deemed to be planning permission for farm buildings subject to certain limits. In some areas the planning authority may have made an Article 4 Direction under the General Development Order. If it has, planning permission may be required for farm buildings for which it would not otherwise be needed.

Farmhouses and cottages

Where planning permission is granted for the erection of a farm house or cottage, the planning authority usually imposes a condition restricting occupation to a member of the agricultural population or to persons employed or last employed in agriculture. Such a condition will not prevent the owner from selling the house but it will limit the market. Where a house was built many years ago, subject to an occupancy condition, and there is no longer a demand for houses for farm workers, it may be possible to get the condition removed. An application may be made to the planning authority for removal of the condition.

As a matter of policy, planning authorities are reluctant to grant permission for houses and cottages on farms, unless there are very strong reasons for putting them there. Planners prefer houses to be built in villages. If a house is allowed on a farm, a site related to existing farm buildings is favoured by the authorities. Farmers about to retire often find it difficult to get permission to build a house on the farm to retire into. It is probably better to apply for permission while the farmer is still actively farming and can show agricultural need for a house.

Agricultural buildings and works

The General Development Order provides that planning permission is deemed to have been granted for agricultural buildings on agricultural land having an area of more than one acre and comprised in an agricultural unit. However the deemed permission is subject to the following conditions:

(a) The ground area covered by the farm building must not exceed 465 square metres either on its own or together with other buildings within ninety metres of it, on the same farm, which have been erected within the previous two years;
(b) The building must not be more than twelve metres high or three metres high if it is within three kilometres of the perimeter of an aerodrome;
(c) The building must not be within twenty-five metres of the metalled portion of a trunk or classified road.

The Government proposes to introduce new restrictions on deemed planning permission for farm buildings, by amending the General Development Order.

Change of use of land or buildings

A material change of use of land or buildings may amount to development for which planning permission is required. As a rule the use of farmland as a caravan site will need planning permission. The use of farm buildings for storing building materials has been held to amount to a material change of use for which planning permission was required (*Trentham Ltd* v. *Gloucestershire C.C.* [1966] 1 All E.R. 701). It is not unusual for a farmer with spare storage space to be asked to let it for storing non-agricultural materials. If he agrees to do so, he may need planning permission for the change of use, and in addition the building may become rateable.

Where an unfit farm cottage was used for agricultural storage and then later was wanted for residential use again, it was held that the change from an agricultural store to a dwelling would be a material change of use (*McKellan* v. *Ministry of Housing and Local Government* [1966] E.G.D. 347).

Show jumping has become very popular in recent years. In the case of *Belmont Farms Ltd* v. *Minister of Housing and Local Government and Hendon B.C.* (1962) E.G.D. 543, it was held that the use of a farm for breeding and training horses for show jumping amounted to a material change of use.

Farm shops

Sales of produce direct from the farm often raise planning problems. Generally where produce grown on the farm is sold on the premises, planning permission is not required. However, it is not unusual for farm produce to be processed before sale, or for additional supplies to be brought in from outside. In these cases planning permission will be needed, because there is a material change of use. In several cases, the Secretary of State for the Environment has decided in planning appeals, that sales of meat from farm animals which have been slaughtered off the farm and then cut up and packed before being sold on the farm, amount to a material change of use. In the case of a shop which was part of a nursery garden it has been held that sale of imported fruit, such as oranges and lemons, amounted to a material change of use. Apart from sales in farm shops, produce may be sold from vending machines. In one case where eggs produced on a farm were sold by way of a machine set up by the roadside, that was held to be a material change of use for which planning permission was required.

Rubbish tipping

It is not unusual for farm land to be used for rubbish tipping. If the only object of tipping is to improve the land in order to make it suitable or better for agricultural use, the tipping is an agricultural work deemed to have planning permission under the General Development Order (*Hadley* v. *Dickman* (1979) 250 E.G.D. 568). However, it is a condition of such deemed permission that no refuse or waste material shall be brought on to the agricultural land from elsewhere. If it is to be brought in from elsewhere, planning permission will be required for the operation.

AGRICULTURAL RESERVOIRS

On the face of it, an agricultural reservoir would be permitted development, but where digging for the reservoir results in the removal of large amounts of minerals such as sand and gravel, planning permission will be needed, both for mineral extraction and making the reservoir (*West Bowers Farm Products* v. *Essex County Council* [1985] JPL 857).

Engineering operations

Engineering operations are included in the definition of development, though some minor operations are deemed to have planning permission under the General Development Order. For example, permission is not required for winning and working minerals on agricultural land where the materials are required for agricultural purposes such as fertilisation of the land, but excavations must not be made within 25m of a metalled portion of a trunk road or a classified road. It is a condition of permitted development that none of the minerals dug out of the agricultural land shall be moved outside the land from which they were extracted. They could however be moved to other farm land in the agricultural unit.

FISH PONDS FOR FISH FARMING

The General Development Order allows permitted development rights for fish farms where fish are reared for food. The business must be registered with M.A.F.F. or the Secretary of State for the purposes of the Diseases of Fish Act 1983. The permitted engineering operations for construction of fish ponds are subject to a number of conditions.

Minor operations not requiring permission

There are a number of minor operations which are deemed to have planning permission under the General Development Order. These include enlargement of a dwellinghouse within certain limits, and some developments within the curtilage of a dwellinghouse. Gates, walls and fences are permitted development provided they are not more than 1m high if abutting on to a road or two metres high elsewhere. Some tented camping sites are permitted development if used by members of approved organisations holding a certificate of exemption under the Public Health Act 1936. Use of land for a caravan site is permitted development in those cases where a site licence is not required under Schedule 1 to the Caravan Sites and Control of Development Act 1960 (see the section on caravans, below).

Article 4 directions

These have already been mentioned. Although there is deemed planning permission for operations listed in Schedule 1 to the General Development Order, there are cases where it is necessary to apply for permission to carry out those operations because the planning authority or the Secretary of State has made a direction to that effect under Article 4 of the Order. Thus, in an area where an order has been made, it could be necessary to apply for planning permission for all types of caravan sites, or for all farm buildings. Article 4 directions are most likely to be made in conservation areas, or coastal areas, or other areas specially subject to pressure from caravans or other types of development. Where an Article 4 direction applies and an application for planning permission has to be made, the usual application fee will not be payable. If permission is refused, compensation may be payable.

Applications for planning permission

If there is any doubt about whether planning permission is required for any particular operation, an application may be made to the planning authority for a decision as to whether or not it is required.

Anyone can apply for planning permission, whether he is the owner or occupier of the land or not. However, certain classes of proposed development have to be publicly advertised, for example sewage works, slaughterhouses and buildings for killing or plucking poultry. Where it is proposed to develop land occupied by a farm tenant, notice of application for planning permission has to be given to the tenant. (Where planning permission is granted for the development of agricultural land, the landlord can serve an incontestable notice to quit on the tenant under agricultural holdings legislation; see Chapter 3.)

A planning authority must give a decision on a planning application within two months (eight weeks) or an extended period agreed between the parties. If a decision is not given within that period, the applicant may appeal to the Secretary of State for the Environment as though the application had been refused. If planning permission is refused, as appeal may be made to the Secretary of State within six months from the date of decision.

The Local Government, Planning and Land Act 1980, introduced payment of fees for most types of planning application. However, there are a number of exemptions, including agricultural buildings, glasshouses and polythene tunnels. Where application is made for planning permission for an agricultural building the first 465 square metres of floor space do not count for the purposes of calculating fees. This means there is no fee for applications for 465 square metres or less floor space. Similar provisions apply to glass houses and polythene tunnels.

Appeals against refusal of planning permission

Notice of appeal must be given to the Secretary of State within six months of notice of decision. The period may be extended by the Secretary of State. The form of appeal provides for an agreement by the applicant to have the appeal decided by way of written representations instead of by a public local inquiry. The appeal form should be accompanied by the application for planning permission, together with any certificate or notice required (for example that notice of the application has been served on the agricultural tenant), plans and drawings, notice of the authority's decision if any, and any relevant correspondence with the planning authority. The advantage of a decision made on written representations is that it saves time. If the written procedure is followed, a letter giving the Secretary of State's decision will be sent to the applicant. If there is a public local inquiry, the Secretary of State's decision will be notified to the applicant, who is entitled to a copy of the inspector's report on written request. The Secretary of State must give proper and adequate reasons for his decision. He may make an order as to costs of the parties at any public local inquiry arranged by him or one of his inspectors.

Appeals to the High Court

There is no right of appeal against the decision of the Secretary of State on planning grounds, but there is a right of appeal on the ground that the decision was outside the powers of the 1971 Act or that the requirements of the statute have not been complied with. For example in *Fawcett Properties Ltd* v. *Bucks C.C.* [1961] A.C. 636, an applicant appealed to the court against a planning condition restricting occupation of a house to persons employed or last employed in agriculture, or their dependants. He claimed that it was beyond the powers of the planning authority under the Planning Acts to impose such a condition. He lost his case in the House of Lords.

Enforcement notices

Anyone who carries out development or makes a material change of use in breach of planning control is liable to have an enforcement notice served on him by the planning authority. Such a notice may be served on the owner and occupier and anyone else having an interest in the land which would be materially affected by the notice, for example a mortgagee. The notice must specify the matters which are said to amount to a breach of planning control, and the steps needed to remedy the breach. It must state the period (not less than twenty-eight days) at the end of which the notice will become effective. It must also state the period within which the breach must be remedied. When he is served with the notice, the owner or occupier may either comply with it, or appeal against it to the Secretary of State. If he decides to comply, the notice takes effect on the date specified in it. If he decides to appeal, the notice becomes effective when the appeal is dismissed or is withdrawn.

If an effective enforcement notice is not complied with, then as a general rule the owner or occupier can be prosecuted and fined. The authority can also enter the land and do the work in default, and recover their reasonable expenses.

If the notice requires a use of the premises to be discontinued, any person who uses the land or causes or permits it to be used in contravention of the notice, may be prosecuted and fined.

Owners and occupiers who have incurred expenses in complying with an order, or in re-imbursing the authority's reasonable expenses, may recover those expenses from the person who committed the breach of planning control.

APPEAL AGAINST AN ENFORCEMENT NOTICE

An appeal may be made to the Secretary of State at any time before the notice takes effect. The grounds of appeal are as follows:

(a) Planning permission ought to be granted for the development in question.

(b) The matters alleged in the notice do not amount to a breach of planning control.

(c) The breach of planning control alleged has not taken place.

(d) In appropriate cases, the four-year period for serving notice has elapsed.

(e) In other cases, the breach of planning control took place before the beginning of 1964.

(f) The enforcement notice was not served as required by the Act.

(g) The steps required to remedy the breach are excessive.

(h) The period allowed for complying with the notice is unreasonable.

An appeal should be made by way of notice to the Secretary of State, stating the grounds of appeal and the facts on which it is based. When the appeal has been decided, the Secretary of State must make directions to give effect to his decision. He may grant planning permission for the development that is the subject of the notice. Even if the applicant has not included ground (a) above in the appeal he is deemed to have made a planning application simply by virtue of his appeal against the enforcement notice. It should be noted that an appeal against an enforcement notice cannot be made after the notice has taken effect. It should therefore be made in good time. An appeal to the High Court from the Secretary of State's decision can be made on a point of law, or a case may be stated for the court.

STOP NOTICES

Until an enforcement notice takes effect, the development in question can be carried on. If there is an appeal, the notice does not take effect until the appeal is dismissed. In order to prevent developers continuing development during this period, authorities have been given powers to serve 'stop notices' to prohibit specified activities on the land from being carried out. A 'stop notice' can usually be served at any time before an enforcement notice takes effect. There is a twelve-month limit in certain cases. It may be served on any person who has an interest in the land, or anyone carrying out activities on the land. It operates personally against the person on whom it is served. It must state the date on which it is to take effect, which must be not earlier than three days nor later than twenty-eight days from the date it was first served. There is no procedure for an appeal against a stop notice, but compensation may be payable for loss arising from it.

CASES WHERE AN ENFORCEMENT NOTICE CANNOT BE SERVED

In certain cases an enforcement notice cannot be served, because the breach of planning control took place before 1 January 1964, or because the notice should have been served within four years from the time the breach took place, and the planning authority failed to serve it within the time required. It often happens that caravans were placed on land in breach of planning permission long before 1 January 1964, but enforcement action was not taken. In other cases there may have been building or engineering operations carried out where the planning authority should have served an enforcement notice within four years but failed to do so.

EXISTING USE RIGHTS

Where an enforcement notice cannot be served for the reasons stated above, the land is said to have existing use rights. One advantage of such rights is that the use may be intensified in the same way as a use which enjoys planning permission, and a change of use may be made to another use in the same class. However, it must be noted that existing use rights are not sufficient to enable a caravan site licence to be obtained now (see section on caravans, below). There are other disadvantages.

ESTABLISHED USE CERTIFICATES

It is possible under s. 94 of the 1971 Act and Article 22 of the General Development Order, to get an admission from the planning authority of existing use rights in certain cases, by applying for a certificate of established use. Application should be made to the district council as planning authority. Such certificates are useful for an appeal against an enforcement notice.

Compensation

Where a planning authority revokes or modifies a planning permission, compensation is payable for any abortive expenditure incurred by a person with an interest in the land, or for loss or damage suffered by such a person. Compensation is also payable where permission granted by a special or general development order has been withdrawn and it becomes necessary to apply for planning permission, which is either refused or granted subject to conditions (1971 Act, ss. 164, 165). However, in a case where an outline permission for agricultural cottages was later modified and made subject to condition restricting occupation to persons employed in agriculture, the

Lands Tribunal held that no compensation was payable (*Wilson* v. *West Sussex C.C.* (1962) 14 P. and C.R. 310).

Duration of planning permission

The general rule is that planning permission granted after April 1969 is subject to a condition that development must begin within five years from the date of grant of planning permission. Every outline planning permission granted after 19 April 1969 is subject to a condition that approval of detail must be applied for within three years from the date of grant, and development must be begun within five years of the grant, or within two years of the last approval of detail whichever is the later.

A renewal of permission may be applied for by letter before the time limit expires. Operations may be started by digging a trench, but if there is undue delay, the planning authority has powers to serve a completion notice stating that the work must be completed by a certain date not earlier than twelve months after the notice takes effect.

Buildings of architectural or historical interest

Buildings may be listed by the Secretary of State for the Environment, under the 1971 Act, s. 54 as being of special architectural or historical interest. Works done on listed buildings are subject to control under the 1971 Act. Written consent must be obtained from the local planning authority or the Secretary of State by anyone who proposes to carry out demolition works, or alterations or extensions, which would affect the special character of the building. In the case of demolition, notice must also be given to the Royal Commission on Historical Monuments. If work is done without consent, or in breach of condition of consent, the person who carries out the works, or causes them to be carried out, will be liable on summary conviction to three months' imprisonment, or a fine or both, or on conviction on indictment to twelve months' imprisonment or a fine or both.

There is no right of appeal against the listing of a building, but there is a right of appeal against the refusal of listed building consent, and there is a right to claim compensation for refusal of consent (1971 Act, s. 171).

PRESERVATION NOTICES
Buildings that are not listed, but which are of a special architectural or

historical interest, and are in danger of demolition or alteration, may be protected by a preservation notice served under the 1971 Act, s. 58. A building preservation notice comes into force as soon as it has been served on both the owner and occupier of the building, and remains in force for six months from the date when it is served. During the six month period, the building may be listed by the Secretary of State, or he will decide not to list it. If it is not listed, the building will cease to be protected when the preservation notice expires at the end of the six-month period. If the Secretary of State decides not to list the building, the owner can claim compensation under the 1971 Act, s. 173.

ENFORCEMENT OF LISTED BUILDING CONTROL

Control is enforced by way of notice served under the 1971 Act, s. 96 on the owner and occupier of the building. The notice must state the date on which it takes effect, and that must be a date not less than twenty-eight days after the service of the notice. There is a right of appeal to the Secretary of State against such a notice. One of the grounds of appeal is that listed building consent ought to be granted for the works, but there are several possible grounds of appeal. The effect of an appeal is to suspend the enforcement notice until the appeal is determined or withdrawn. When he decies an appeal, the Secretary of State may grant listed building consent for the works. The penalty for not complying with a listed building enforcement notice is a substantial fine, with further fines for each day on which the notice is not complied with.

The local planning authority also has powers to enter and do works in default, and to recover their reasonable expenses from the owner.

UNOCCUPIED LISTED BUILDINGS

Urgent works can be carried out on empty listed buildings by the local planning authority or the Secretary of State, after giving the owner not less than seven days' notice in writing of their intention to do so. The owner may be required to repay their expenses.

COMPULSORY ACQUISITION OF LISTED BUILDINGS IN NEED OF REPAIR

A local authority may be authorised by the Secretary of State to acquire compulsorily a building in need of repair, in order to preserve it. However, an authority must first serve on the owner of the building a repairs notice specifying the works needed to preserve the building, and the effect of the notice and the legal provisions for dealing with buildings in need of repair. The Acquisition of Land (Authorisation Procedure) Act 1981 applies to the compulsory acquisition. Compensation will be assessed on the basis that as a rule depreciation due to the listing is to be disregarded. Where a building has deliberately been left derelict, minimum compensation is payable (1971 Act, ss. 114–17).

Tree preservation orders

The preservation of trees is regulated by the 1971 Act. Tree preservation orders may be made by the local planning authority. Tree preservation orders may cover individual trees, groups of trees or woodlands. They may prohibit cutting down, lopping, topping, uprooting, wilful damage or destruction. Where trees subject to an order are cut down, lawfully or unlawfully, the landowner generally has a duty to replace them. Disputes as to the amount of compensation payable may be referred to the Lands Tribunal. They may secure replanting of woodlands. An order cannot apply to dead or dying trees which are dangerous or amount to a nuisance at law. Notice of the making of the order must be given to the owners and occupiers of the land, and objections may be made as provided in the regulations made under the Act. There are special provisions for land for which the Forestry Commission has made advances under the Forestry Act 1969, s. 4 or where there is a forestry dedication convenant in force.

The penalty for contravening a tree preservation order is a fine of £2000 or twice the value of the tree, whichever is the greater, and on indictment a fine which takes account of the financial gain resulting from the unlawful felling. Trees subject to a tree preservation order should be replaced if they are removed or destroyed in breach of the order.

In certain cases a provisional tree preservation order may be made. It will expire after six months unless confirmed by the local planning authority.

There are special provisions for protection of trees in conservation areas.

A tree preservation order may make provision for compensation for damage or expenditure caused or incurred by the refusal of consent to fell, top, lop or due to conditions restricting grant of consent.

Advertisements

The display of advertisements is controlled under the 1971 Act, s. 63 and regulations made under the Act. There are six classes of advertisement which are deemed to have planning permission provided they comply with the regulations. These include miscellaneous advertisements relating to the premises on which they are displayed, for example direction signs, business name-plates, or advertisements of a temporary nature, such as notices for sale of property or goods or livestock posted up on the land concerned. Certain advertisements are excepted from the regulations and for them no consent is needed. They include advertisements displayed on enclosed land not readily visible from outside or from a public right of way through the enclosure, and advertisements displayed on or in a vehicle normally moving on the highway.

Reference should be made to the Town and Country Planning (Control of Advertisement) Regulations 1984 for details.

Minerals

The extraction of minerals is development for which planning permission is usually needed, and application should be made for it in the usual way. Planning conditions may be imposed requiring the filling-in of pits and restoration of sites for agriculture or other purposes after extraction is completed. In other cases conditions may require landscaping of pits for fishing or other sports. Planning permission is not required for minerals workings on agricultural land for use for agricultural purposes on the land (General Development Order, Class VI) subject to the condition that no minerals extracted shall be moved to any place outside the land from which they were extracted. However they could be moved to land farmed within the same agricultural unit.

Caravans

The placing of caravans on farm land is a frequent cause of dispute with local planning authorities. Before 1960 it was necessary to get planning permission for a caravan site, and also to get a licence under the Public Health Act 1936, s. 269 but the law did not enable planning authorities to control caravans as they wished. To remedy the situation, the Caravan Sites and Control of Development Act 1960 was introduced, and it imposed a special licensing system for caravan sites. At the same time the planning laws relating to caravans were strengthened. It is important to note that the licensing provisions and the planning laws for caravans are interdependent, and that this is deliberate.

It is an offence for the occupier of land to cause or permit land occupied by him to be used as a caravan site, unless he holds a site licence under the Act of 1960. A caravan site means land on which a caravan is sited for human habitation, as distinct from a caravan which is simply parked empty. There are, however, a number of exemptions from licensing requirements and from planning permission.

Caravans within the curtilage of a house. There is no need to get planning permission or a site licence for a caravan situated within the curtilage of a dwellinghouse and used in a way which is incidental to the enjoyment of the house. A caravan used as a separate residence for a farm worker would not be exempt, but a caravan used for a domestic worker or a member of the family to sleep in would be exempt, where such persons live partly in the house and have their main meals there.

Caravan site for traveller with caravan. A site used for one or two nights by a person travelling with a caravan will be exempt from planning and licensing requirements, if it is used for not more than twenty-eight days in any twelve months. It can be used to allow only one caravan at any time to spend not more than two nights on the land. Thus a holiday maker could park his caravan for two nights on a farm, but the total number of days the farm could be used for that purpose would be twenty-eight days a year.

Five-acre sites. Where a site exceeds five acres, up to three caravans can be stationed on the land for human habitation at any one time, provided the site is not used for this purpose for more than twenty-eight days in the year.

Sites approved or supervised by exempt organisations. There are three types of exemptions for sites occupied and supervised or approved by organisations such as the Caravan Club and the Camping Club of Great Britain and Ireland. They are as follows.

(a) Sites occupied and supervised by exempt organisation and which are used for recreation and not permanent residence.
(b) Sites approved by exempt organisation on which up to five caravans are stationed for human habitation, and for which a certificate has been issued

by the organisation. The certificate may state that the site has been approved by the organisation for use by its members for recreation, but there is no express requirement that users of the site should be members of the organisation, nor that they should use it only for recreation. The certificate is issued to the occupier of the land.

(c) Sites used for meetings of exempt organisation, provided the meeting lasts not more than five days, and the site is supervised by the organisation.

Agriculture and forestry workers' sites. There is no need to get planning permission or a site licence for caravans for *seasonal* farm workers sited on the agricultural land where they are being employed and there is a similar exemption for forestry workers' sites. However, the workers must be seasonal workers.

Building and engineering workers' sites. Caravan sites for building or engineering workers are exempt from planning and licensing requirements even if they are on land adjoining the land on which the works are being carried out, provided that any planning permission required for the building or engineering works has been granted.

Travelling showmen's sites. There are not many travelling showmen left, but for any who are members of a certificated organisation, their sites are exempt from licensing if they are travelling on business or have gone into winter quarters between 1 October and 31 March. Sites for winter quarters are not exempt from planning permission.

PLANNING PERMISSION AND SITE LICENCES

If a site is exempt from site licensing it will usually be exempt from planning permission as well. Apart from the exemptions described above, planning permission must be obtained for caravan sites. A site licence cannot be obtained unless there is planning permission for the site. Generally if there is planning permission, a site licence will be granted by the local authority. Conditions in the licence must comply with any planning condition imposed.

Site licence conditions. Site licence conditions may specify the number of caravans on the site, type of caravans, siting, planting of trees, fire precautions and standards of sanitation. They may not require that rent should be agreed with the council, nor that Rent Act security should be given (*Chertsey U.D.C.* v. *Mixhams Properties Ltd* [1964] 2 All E.R. 627). A condition requiring a right of way to another site at the back has also been held to be invalid (*A. G.* v. *Maidstone R.D.S.* (1913) 226 E.G. 224). There is an appeal to a magistrates' court against conditions attached to a site licence, or against variations of those conditions, by the local authority.

Sites in existence in 1960. Owners of some of these sites have not obtained site licences and have consequently got into difficulties. The Caravan Sites Act 1960 made special provisions for sites already in existence. Some of them had express planning permission, while others had no planning permission but as the four-year period for serving an enforcement notice had expired, they had existing use rights. In other cases the four-year period had not expired and an enforcement notice could have been served.

In cases where existing sites had express planning permission, an occupier was entitled to a site licence as of right. In the other cases, an application for a site licence had to be made not later than 29 October 1960. The applications had to be referred to the local planning authority. Authorities were allowed six months in which to decide either to grant planning permission, or to take enforcement action, or where existing use rights were established they could make a discontinuance order.

Many occupiers of existing sites made their application before 29 October 1960, and their cases were decided in one or other of the ways described, but others failed to make their applications in the period allowed. They are liable to be prosecuted under the 1960 Act, s. 1 because they have not obtained a site licence, and they cannot get one without an express grant of planning permission. Existing use rights or deemed planning permission are not enough. If such a site occupier has existing use rights, an enforcement notice cannot be served on him, but he can be prosecuted for not having a site licence.

Sunday markets

Owners are sometimes asked by enterprising traders to let a parcel of agricultural land to them for the purpose of a Sunday market. Such markets may be an offence under the Shops Act 1950, and may contravene the planning laws, and legal advice should be sought before agreeing to such lettings.

The use of a piece of land as a market for not more than fourteen days in any calendar year is development for which permission is deemed to have been granted under the General Development Order (Class IV). However, it is open to a local planning authority to make an Article 4 direction to make it necessary to apply for planning permission for such use, and this has been done in Sunday market cases (*Thanet District Council* v. *Ninedrive Ltd* [1978] 1 All E.R. 703).

In another case in 1977, Melton Borough Council served an enforcement notice where a Sunday market was held on agricultural land without planning permission, and to some extent in contravention of the Shops Act 1950. The market was held to be a commercial undertaking and not a normal rural pursuit. The enforcement notice served by the local planning authority was unheld by the Secretary of State.

Chapter 7
Highways

Abbreviations in this Chapter:
'1980 Act' – Highways Act 1980.
'1981 Act' – Wildlife and Countryside Act 1981.

Introduction

The law relating to highways affects the farmer in many different ways. His farm may be situated near a motorway, a main road, or a narrow country lane with high banks eroded by heavy vehicles. Trees on his land may overhang the road, and his boundary ditches may run alongside the highway verges. His hedges may be damaged by salt and snow clearance in bad weather. Highway drainage water may drain onto his land in defined channels, or may overflow it in time of storm or flood. Vehicles may leave the road by accident and crash into his fences or stone walls causing damage. His animals may escape from his land onto the highway and cause injury to road users. His cattle lawfully driven along the road with reasonable care, may stray onto adjoining land through defective fences or open gates. His trees may fall across the road during gales. His ditches and drains may flood the road. Animals driven along the road may leave dung and mud behind them. Farm vehicles carrying manure and other materials may drop part of the load on the road. In addition there are all the problems which arise from the existence and use of public footpaths and bridleways.

What is a highway?

A highway has been defined as a piece of land over which every subject of the Crown may lawfully pass as of right. A way over which people may pass by licence only is not a highway. An occupation road laid out for the convenience of adjoining occupiers, or a customary churchway for the use of the inhabitants of a parish is not a highway. Although a highway is open to all members of the public as of right, it may not be open to the public for all purposes. Highways are usually classified under three heads:

(a) Public footpaths, which are restricted to the use of footpassengers.
(b) Public bridleways, which are restricted to the use of footpassengers and people riding or leading horses.
(c) Public cartways or carriageways, which are open to carts or carriages (including cars, lorries, etc.) as well as to footpassengers and horseriders.

The public are entitled to use any highway only for the purpose of passing and repassing. There is no right to loiter, or to picnic or camp, or search for treasure with or without metal detectors. There is a right to rest on it for a reasonable time only.

How are highways created?

Highways may be created by dedication, express or presumed, by the owner of the land, and by the acceptance of the dedication of the way by the public. They may also be created by statute, for example under the Enclosure Acts, Housing Acts, Town and Country Planning Acts, or the Highways Act 1980.

Express acts of dedication are very unusual. Dedication is usually presumed from public use of the way over a period of time, which amounts to evidence of dedication by the owner and acceptance by the public. The public user must be as of right and without interruption. Only a freehold owner can dedicate, and that includes a tenant for life under the Settled Land Act 1925. A tenant for a term of years cannot dedicate without the consent of the owner of the freehold. However, it has been held by the courts that where land has been occupied by a series of tenants during a long period of use by the public, the assent of the freeholder may be presumed.

Public paths may be created by agreement made between the owner and the highway authority under the Highways Act 1980, s. 25 or by an order made under s. 26 of that Act. Public path agreements may include conditions as to payments and other matters such as liability for repairs to stiles and gates.

Dedication of a way subject to existing rights

A way may be, and often is, dedicated subject to existing rights such as private rights of way, or the owner's right to maintain gates across a road, or a fence with a stile across a footpath. However a highway cannot be dedicated only for a limited time, nor for use by a limited part of the public.

A way may have been dedicated subject to the owner's right to plough it from time to time. If there is evidence that as far back as living memory goes there has been a right to plough, or to maintain gates or stiles across the way, it can be assumed that such a right is as old as the way itself, and that it was dedicated subject to those rights.

At common law there is no prescribed period of user which gives rise to a presumption of dedication. The existence of a public right of way may be proved even where the way has been used for less than twenty years (*Jones* v. *Bates* [1938] 2 All E.R. 237).

Under the Highways Act 1980, s. 31, it is provided that dedication will be presumed where the right has been enjoyed for twenty years. Thus for practical purposes, where a way has actually been enjoyed by the public as of right without interruption for a full period of twenty years, the way is deemed to have been dedicated as a highway, unless there is enough evidence to show that there was no intention during that period to dedicate it.

Anyone who wishes to prove that a way has been dedicated to the public under the 1980 Act, s. 31 must therefore show:

(a) That the way has been used for the last twenty years by the public.
(b) That is has been used as of right.
(c) That it has been used without interruption.

Where a way has been used under licence, with the permission of the owner, that is not user as of right; it is user by permission.

Use without interruption means without interruption at the hands of the owner. Interruption could consist of closing the way against all comers for at least one day every year, or in isolated acts of turning back people who were trying to use the way. These acts must be carried out by the owner or with his authority. They must be done with the intention of challenging the alleged public right. In *Lewis* v. *Thomas* [1950] 1 All E.R. 116, the owner tried to prevent the public using the way over property, which she owned. She claimed that on certain occasions a gate across the way had been locked. However, it was shown that the gate had only been locked to prevent cattle from straying into the cornfields. As there was no intention to interfere with the public right by means of a gate, the locking of the gate did not rebut a presumption of dedication.

How to rebut a presumption of dedication

In order to rebut a presumption, the owner must be prepared to prove:

(a) That use by the public was permissive only.
(b) That the use had been effectively interrupted or resisted.
(c) That there was no intention during the twenty-year period to dedicate.

NOTICES
In order to prove that he did not intend to dedicate, the owner may be able to show that he had put up notices on the way stating that it was a private road, or that he had closed the way for one day each year, or that he has lodged a notice with the highway authority under the Highways Act 1980, s. 31(6), or where a notice has been torn down, he has notified the highway authority that the way has not been dedicated.

Notices are not conclusive evidence, but it is difficult to prove an intention to dedicate where notices are put up and maintained by the owner. They should be so placed that they clearly describe the passage along a defined way.

Repairs by a highway authority

The fact that a highway authority has never repaired a road may be evidence that it is not a highway, though there are highways which a highway authority is not obliged to repair. If repairs have been carried out by a highway authority, this suggests that the way may be a highway, but it is not conclusive evidence that the way is a highway.

Highways laid out under Enclosure Acts

Where a highway has been laid out under an Enclosure Act, there should be a description of the way in the Award made under the Act, and the ways should be shown on the plan attached to the Award. Such Awards are not easy to trace, but reference can be made to the County Archivist. If the Award is not lodged with the Archives, the archivist may know where it is to be found.

Ownership of a highway

What rights are left to the owner of the soil when a way has been dedicated as a highway? The ownership of the soil under the highway is not affected, and the owner is entitled to use it in any way which is not inconsistent with the public right of passage. At common law the owner's consent would have to be obtained by anyone who wished to lay pipes under a highway or to put poles into it. However, such works are nowadays done under statutory powers which exempt the operators from having to get the owner's consent.

The owner of land adjoining a highway has a right of access to any part of his land from the highway (*Marshall* v. *Blackpool Corporation* [1935] A.C. 16). The right is a private right. There is no right to pass over land owned by someone else in order to gain access to the highway, though such a right may be acquired. It should be noted that the creation of new means of access onto a highway is subject to Town and Country laws. In cases where roads have been made under statute, the highway authority may have acquired the land on which the road is made, either by agreement with the owner or by compulsory purchase. In such cases the owner will not retain ownership of the subsoil.

Repair and maintenance of highways

Generally it is the highway authority's duty to repair and maintain highways, whether they are public carriageways or public footpaths. However, there are highways which are repairable by private individuals (for example under Enclosure Acts), and there are highways which nobody is liable to repair, for example highways dedicated after 1835, which have not been formally adopted under the procedure laid down in the Highways Act of that year and now contained in the Highways Act 1980, s. 37. In some cases roads which were maintainable by the highway authority are no longer maintained by them, because their repair has been declared unnecessary by a magistrates' court under the Highways Act 1980, s. 47. (This section does not apply to footpaths and bridleways.) There are cases where a farmer may believe that a lane is maintainable by the highway authority, but the authority denies liability. There is a procedure for enforcement for liability to maintain a highway, provided of course that such a liability can be shown. It is in the Highways Act 1980, s. 56. An application can be made to the Crown court or, where liability is admitted by the highway authority, to the magistrates' court.

The duty to repair and maintain continues for as long as the highway exists. If a highway falls into the sea, or is extinguished or stopped up under statute, the liability to repair will cease.

DUTY TO REPAIR. HOW FAR DOES IT GO?

It is sometimes difficult to decide what has to be repaired as part of the highway. There may be retaining walls which may or may not be part of the highway. The wall may belong to a private individual, but the public may have acquired a right of support for the highway. In such a case he would not be obliged to repair the wall which would be repairable as part of the highway.

A ditch running alongside the highway may be a farmer's ditch made on his land by the owner to drain his land. The ditch would not be part of the highway. On the other hand the ditch may have been made on the highway by the highway authority for the purpose of draining the highway, and would be part of the highway and maintainable as such.

In the case of a public carriageway, the highway authority has a duty to maintain the surface in a condition safe and fit for the ordinary traffic which uses the road. As an exception to this rule, a highway authority is not required to provide a hard surface for a road used as a public path, which has been reclassified as a byway open to all traffic. If traffic increases, the road must be made and kept fit for the increased traffic. Sometimes large heavy vehicles use narrow lanes not fit for carrying them. It is possible for the use of roads to be restricted to vehicles below a certain weight, under regulations made under the Road Traffic Acts.

As far as public paths are concerned, generally it is the duty of the highway authority to see that the paths are kept clear and in a condition reasonably fit for use as a footpath or bridleway as the case may be. There is no obligation to provide a hard surface. The highway authority may require the owner or occupier of adjoining land to cut back vegetation overhanging the path from his land, but he cannot be required to maintain the surface of the path, save in those exceptional cases where a private individual has a legal liability to maintain.

The highway authority's duty to maintain a public path was the subject of a Court of Appeal decision in *Hereford and Worcester C.C.* v. *Newman* [1975] 2 All E.R. 673. Mr Newman applied to a magistrates' court under the Highways Act 1959, s. 59(4) for an order requiring the County Council to put a public path in good repair. One path had a seven-foot-high hedge across it. Another was crossed by a barbed-wire fence. When the case got to the Court of Appeal, that court held that the path could only be out of repair if the surface was defective or disturbed in some way. An act of obstruction that made a path unusable did not make it out of repair. The mere removal of an obstruction was not of itself a repair. A fence was an obstruction, but vegetation growing in the path interfered with the surface and caused the path to be out of repair. (See now Highways Act 1980, s. 56).

Highway nuisances

A highway nuisance has been defined as a wrongful act or omission on or near a highway, which prevents the public from passing along the highway freely, safely and conveniently. A fence blocking a public path is a highway nuisance. Other examples are a dangerous animal at large near a public path, a load of manure dumped on a highway, and an overhanging tree which interferes with a public right of passage.

OVERHANGING TREES

Trees and shrubs overhanging a highway from adjoining land are a common form of highway nuisance, and the highway authority has powers to deal with such nuisances under the Highways Act 1980, s. 154. A notice under that section is served on the owner or occupier of the land requiring him to cut back the vegetation within fourteen days. A person aggrieved by such a notice has a right of appeal to a magistrates' court. If an owner or occupier fails to cut back the vegetation the authority may do the work in default and recover their reasonable expenses. A notice under s. 154 may be served with respect to a public road, bridleway or footpath.

DANGEROUS TREES NEAR ROADS OR PUBLIC PATHS

A highway authority has power to require the owner of dangerous trees, shrubs or hedges, or the occupier of the land, to cut and fell those which are dead, diseased, damaged, or insecurely rooted, if they are likely to cause danger by falling onto the road or path. A person aggrieved by a notice to cut or fell served under the Highways Act 1980, s. 154(3) has a right of appeal to a magistrates' court.

TREES FALLEN ACROSS THE HIGHWAY

Trees beside a highway may be blown down across roads in gales. Highway authorities have powers to remove such trees and will usually do so promptly where a main or secondary road is blocked by the tree. Occupiers of farmland who were prepared to remove their own trees fallen over the road were often resentful when the highway authority removed trees without first giving them an opportunity to do so, and then sent in a bill to cover their costs, which often seemed too high. Under s. 150 of the 1980 Act, a highway authority has powers to recover its reasonable costs for removal of fallen trees from the highway, except where the owner can show that he took reasonable care to secure that the tree did not cause or contribute to the obstruction (see *Williams* v. *Devon County Council* (1966) 65 L.G.R. 119). The owner of trees who has them regularly inspected to ensure that they are secure would not be liable to pay the highway authority's expenses of removal where a healthy safe tree nevertheless falls over a highway in a gale. (See further Chapter 12.) It is advisable to insure against risk of damage by trees falling on the highway. In *Quinn* v. *Scott* [1965] 2 All E.R. 588, owner occupiers were held liable in negligence for injury to a road user damaged by a tree which fell across a road.

BARBED WIRE

A barbed-wire fence alongside a highway may amount to a highway nuisance. If members of the public using the path are likely to wander into the barbed wire, bearing in mind that the path may be used at night, the fence will amount to a nuisance. As well as being a nuisance at common law, a barbed-wire fence can be the subject of a statutory notice under the Highways Act 1980, s. 164. The occupier of the land may be required to remove the fence within a specified time, and if he fails to do so, a complaint may be made to a magistrates' court for the making of an abatement order. If the order is not complied with, the authority may do the work in default and recover their reasonable costs from him.

WIRE ACROSS A PATH

It is an offence under the Highways Act 1980, s. 162 to place rope or wire across a highway, in such a way as to cause danger to a user of the highway. This is sometimes done on public paths temporarily to control movements of animals, but it can be dangerous to horseriders, pedestrians, and farm traffic which may have a private right of way along a bridlepath.

GATES AND STILES

If a highway has not been dedicated subject to gates or fences with stiles, the owner or occupier who puts up gates or fences with stiles on the way is committing a highway nuisance. A statutory notice may be served on him by the highway authority under the Highways Act 1980, s. 143 requiring him to remove the obstructions. If he fails to do so the authority may remove them and recover their reasonable expenses.

Farmers who wish to have gates, stiles or cattle grids in a public right of way in the interests of agricultural efficiency should apply to the highway authority for permission under the Highways Act 1980, s. 147.

DANGEROUS ANIMALS

It is unlawful to turn out animals known to be dangerous in fields crossed by public paths. It is possible that a bull may be in this class. In addition it is a statutory offence to turn out a bull in such fields, unless it is not more than ten months old, or is not of a recognised dairy breed, and is at large in a field or enclosure with cows or heifers (Wildlife and Countryside Act 1981, s. 59).

ANIMALS ON HIGHWAYS

A keeper of animals which are found straying on the highway commits an offence under the Highways Act 1980, s. 155 unless the highway passes over common land or waste or unenclosed ground. An offence under this section should not be confused with the owner's civil liability in negligence under the Animals Act 1971, s. 8 (see p. 174).

FIREARMS AND FIRES

It is an offence without lawful authority or excuse to discharge a firearm within fifty feet from the centre of a public carriageway if it results in damage to the highway (Highways Act 1980, s. 131). The Highways (Amendment) Act 1986 makes it an offence to light a fire on or over a public carriageway, or to discharge a firearm or firework within fifty feet of the centre of a public carriageway, if such activities result in injury, interruption or danger to a highway user. The Act also provides that it is an offence to light a fire near a public carriageway, which results in injury, interruption or danger to highway users (s. 161 of the 1980 Act) as amended by the 1986 Act.

PLOUGHING UP PATHS

Under the Highways Act 1980, s. 134 it is an offence to plough a public footpath or bridleway not dedicated subject to the right to plough, unless the surface is afterwards made good within two weeks.

DEPOSIT OF MATERIAL ON THE HIGHWAY

It is an offence under the Highways Act 1980, s. 148 to deposit dung, compost, fertiliser, or rubbish on a public carriageway without lawful authority or excuse. A notice to remove the material may be served on the offender by the highway authority and enforced by way of a complaint to a magistrates' court.

Cattle lawfully driven along a highway may occasionally drop dung on the road. That is not an offence or a highway nuisance.

INTERFERENCE WITH HIGHWAYS BY STATUTORY AUTHORITY

Statutory bodies such as highway authorities are given rights under statute to interfere with the highway. Apart from statute, such acts would amount to a nuisance, but as they are permitted or required under statute, there is no right to claim for damages. Instead a right to compensation is provided for by the statute. However, if a statutory power is exercised in a negligent way, the remedy is an action for damages.

The authority has a duty of care in the choice of place for carrying out a statutory work, and in the way in which the statutory power is exercised. It has been held that where a highway authority made a road in such a way that it acted as a catchwater for the hillside on which it was made, the authority was liable for the damage caused to nearby premises by stormwater (*Baldwin* v. *Halifax Corporation* [1916] 4 L.G.R. 787). Sometimes highway improvement works are carried out negligently causing damage to adjoining land by causing floodwater to pour onto the land.

ALTERATIONS TO THE LEVEL OF A HIGHWAY

A highway authority may interfere with the level of the highway so as to raise it or lower it. This may cause damage to property adjoining the highway. Owners or occupiers of such property are entitled to claim compensation for the damage sustained (Highways Act 1980, s. 77). Disputes about the compensation payable may be settled by arbitration or by the county court.

Dangerous places near a highway

If there is, near a street, a source of danger that is not properly fenced or not fenced at all, the owner or occupier of the land may be required to fence it by notice served by the highway authority. This provision was originally intended to deal with streets in towns, but a street is defined to include any highway (Highways Act 1980, s. 165).

If the highway authority raises the level of a highway so that there is a drop onto adjoining land, that would not count as a danger on adjoining land, which an owner or occupier could be required to fence.

Highway drainage

Disputes sometimes arise between owners or occupiers of farmland and the highway authority about drainage problems. Briefly, the position is that owners and occupiers of adjoining land are not required to drain the highway, but in draining their own land they are not entitled to discharge water over the highway so as to give rise to a highway nuisance. Thus farm ditches should not be allowed to overflow onto the highway, nor should farm drains discharge onto roads.

The highway authority has powers to drain the highway, but it does not have a duty to drain adjoining farmland. However, the highway authority does have extensive powers to drain a highway by carrying out works on adjoining land as well as on the highway. If the owner or occupier of the land suffers damage as a result of highway drainage works, he is entitled to compensation. It is an offence to interfere with any highway drainage works without the consent of the highway authority. Thus ditches, gutters, and drains made on farmland by the highway authority for the purpose of draining the highway should not be interfered with by the owner or occupier of the land (Highways Act 1980, s. 100).

DISCHARGE OF HIGHWAY DRAINAGE WATER ONTO ADJOINING LAND

Highway authorities are entitled to discharge highway drainage water into ditches on adjoining land, provided the ditches are capable of carrying the water. As a rule highway authorities are not entitled to discharge drainage water directly onto adjoining land, though where this has been done for a long period of years without objection, a prescriptive right to discharge drainage water in that manner may be claimed. Disputes about such discharges are not uncommon, especially where the amount of water discharged is suddenly and considerably increased owing to highway improvement works, for example widening of the highway with improvement of the surface leading to increased amounts of water collecting on the road and being rapidly discharged. A prescriptive right of discharge can be challenged where a sudden and substantial increase takes place.

DISCHARGE OF NOXIOUS MATERIALS

Highway authorities are not entitled to discharge noxious materials onto adjoining land. An authority was held liable for discharging road water carrying tarry acid onto adjoining land over watercress beds (*Dell* v. *Chesham U.D.C.* [1921] 3 K.B. 427).

An occupier of premises adjoining the highway is not entitled to drain any filth, dirt, or other offensive matter on to the highway (Highways Act 1980, s. 161). Thus a farmer should not discharge effluent from the farmyard onto the road.

FILLING IN ROADSIDE DITCHES

Highway authorities have powers to fill in roadside ditches if they consider they are a danger to road users, and are unnecessary, and if any occupier known to the authority agrees in writing that the ditch is not necessary for drainage purposes (Highways Act 1980, s. 101). A highway authority also has power to pipe a ditch on any land adjoining a highway, and thereafter to fill in the ditch. Compensation is payable to any owner or occupier of land who suffers damage. It is an offence to interfere with the highway authority's works, carried out under this provision.

Bicycles

CYCLISTS

The Countryside Act 1968 gave pedal cyclists the right to cycle on bridleways but not on public footpaths. The cyclists' right is subject to the superior rights of footpassengers and horseriders, and also to any orders and by-laws which may have been made by the local authority. The right does not affect any existing obligations of highway authorities or private individuals to maintain public bridleways, nor does it make them liable to make a bridleway fit for pedal cyclists to use.

The Cycle Tracks Act 1985 gave local authorities powers to make public paths into cycle tracks, but where such tracks cross agricultural land the consent of agricultural owners and occupiers must first be obtained.

CYCLE RACING

It is an offence to promote or take part in a trial of speed on a highway between pedal cyclists, unless the race or trial is authorised under regulations made under the Road Traffic Acts, and conducted according to the conditions laid down under the regulations. Highways include bridleways but not public footpaths. However, there is no right to ride a bicycle on a public footpath, and a race or trial of speed on a public footpath could amount to a public nuisance.

Motor vehicles

MOTOR VEHICLE TRIALS ON PUBLIC FOOTPATHS AND BRIDLEWAYS

It is an offence to promote or take part in a trial of any description between motor vehicles on a public footpath or bridleway unless the trial has been authorised by the local authority under the Road Traffic Acts. Such authorisation must not be given unless the written consent of the owners and occupiers of land over which the footpath or bridleway passes has been obtained. An authorisation may be made subject to conditions.

MOTOR RACING ON HIGHWAYS

It is an offence to promote or take part in a race or trial of speed between motor vehicles on a public highway. It is an offence to take part in any other competition or trial with a motor vehicle on a highway unless the trial or competition is authorised under and conducted in accordance with regulations made under the Road Traffic Acts.

DRIVING MOTOR VEHICLES NOT ON ROADS

Generally there is a prohibition against driving without a lawful authority a motor vehicle on any common land, moorland, or other land not forming part of a road, or on any public footpath or bridleway.

DAMAGE TO ROADSIDE FENCES ETC. BY VEHICLES

The driver of a motor vehicle who damages a roadside fence as a result of a motor accident, has a duty to stop and give his name and address if asked to do so by the owner of the fence or the occupier of the land, or any other person who has reasonable grounds for asking for it. If the driver for any reason does not give his name and address, he must report the accident at a police station or to a constable as soon as possible and in any case within twenty-four hours of the accident (Road Traffic Act 1972, s. 25; Road Traffic Act 1974, s. 24(2) Schedule 6).

Animals

ANIMALS STRAYING ONTO HIGHWAYS

As a result of the Animals Act 1971, owners of animals straying on to the highway are subject to the ordinary common law rules for liability for negligence. Where an animal strays onto the highway as a result of the owner's negligence, the owners will be liable for any damage done by the animal to a highway user. The burden of proving negligence will be on the person bringing the action. If the animal escapes owing to the act of a third party and not because of the owner's negligence, the owner will not be liable. An owner sued for negligence may be able to prove contributory negligence by the person bringing the action, for example he was driving too fast in an area where animals could be seen grazing. It is prudent to insure against risks arising from accidents caused on the highway by straying animals.

Fences alongside motorways are provided and maintained by the Department of the Environment on land acquired for making the motorway. The Department expects frontagers to report any fences found to be defective so that there is a risk of animals getting through them. If an animal does escape its owner can claim an idemnity. On new roads other than motorways, the adjoining owner or occupier is liable for maintaining the fence. In such cases there is no right of indemnity.

ANIMALS ON COMMONS AND OTHER UNFENCED LAND

There are special provisions for animals straying off common land onto highways. An owner of animals lawfully on common land, town or village green, or land where fencing is not customary, will not be held negligent because he has put them on that unfenced land to graze. If they stray onto the road and cause an accident he will not be held liable in negligence.

ANIMALS LAWFULLY ON A HIGHWAY

Where animals are lawfully on a highway and stray off it onto adjoining land, the owner will not be liable for any damage done, unless he can be shown to have acted without reasonable care. Animals being driven down a lane to the milking parlour would be lawfully on the highway, and provided they were being driven with reasonable care, the owner would not be liable if they strayed through an open gate into a garden, or into a field.

If cattle are *unlawfully* on the highway, having strayed there from the owner's land, and they then stray off the highway onto adjoining land, the owner of the cattle will be liable for damage done by them.

Stopping-up of highways

The general rule is 'once a highway always a highway' unless the highway is stopped-up by legal procedure. The modern method of closing a highway is by way of a stopping-up order or an extinguishment order made under statute. Such powers are contained in several Acts of Parliament. Under the

Highways Act 1980, a stopping-up order may be made by a magistrates' court on an application made by a highway authority. This procedure may be used for stopping-up or diverting public footpaths and bridleways or roads (other than trunk roads or special roads). The magistrates must be satisfied that the road is unnecessary or can be diverted to make it easier or more commodious to the public.

Public footpaths and bridleways may also be stopped-up or diverted by way of an order made by the highway authority under the Highways Act 1980, ss. 118–19. If an authority refuses to make such an order, the applicant may apply to the Secretary of State for the Environment to make such an order. Powers to stop-up highways are also contained in the Town and Country Planning Act 1971 to enable land to be developed in accordance with permission granted under the Act. There is also a power for the Secretary of State to extinguish highways under the Acquisition of Land (Authorisation Procedure) Act 1981.

EFFECT OF STOPPING-UP A HIGHWAY

In practice farmers are more likely to be interested in the stopping-up or diversion of a public footpath than in the extinguishment of other kinds of highways. However, it should be noted that where a highway is stopped-up for all purposes, the surface of the highway is no longer vested in the highway authority, and reverts to the owner of the soil of the highway. The highway authority will no longer be liable to maintain it. When a new road is made, the old road or part of it may be stopped-up. In such cases the owner of the land recovers control over the surface, and may use the old road for his own purposes.

Extinguishment of public paths

Farmers often feel that a public path which is not used much ought to be stopped-up. That is understandable, but it is often better to leave matters as they are. Extinguishment orders are rarely made in such cases, and when advertised will usually attract objections from organised footpath users. It is better in most cases to apply for a diversion order; these orders are not usually opposed provided a suitable alternative route can be agreed with the highway authority. It is advisable to discuss the alternative route proposed with the highway authority before making a formal application for diversion, and also to ensure that the parish council is agreeable to the alternative route so as to avoid local opposition to the order.

Applications for diversion orders can be made to the county council or district council. When the order is made it must be publicly advertised, and if representations or objections are made and not withdrawn, it must be submitted to the Secretary of State. If no objections or representations are made, the authority may itself confirm the order (Highways Act 1980, ss. 118–119).

COST OF THE ORDER

Before it decides to make a diversion order, the local authority may ask the owner to enter into an agreement for defraying or contributing to the cost of compensating any third part onto whose land the path may be diverted, and any expense incurred by the highway authority in making up the path. The authority is not entitled to require the applicant to contribute to the authority's administrative cost of making an order under the Highways Act 1980, ss. 118–119 but authorities will often ask an applicant to agree to contribute to or to pay the costs before they will agree to make an order.

Notice of the making of a diversion order (or extinguishment order) must be published in a local newspaper stating the effect of the order and the places in the district where the order and map may be inspected. Notices must be served on owners and occupiers affected, and posted on the path to be diverted. At least twenty-eight days must be allowed for objections to be made. If objections made by a local authority are not withdrawn, the Secretary of State must hold a local inquiry. If objections made by other parties are made and not withdrawn he may hold a local inquiry, but he is not obliged to do so. He must however consider all objections before deciding whether or not to confirm an order.

Chapter 8
Access to the Countryside

Abbreviations in this Chapter:
'1965 Act' – Commons Registration Act 1965.
'1968 Act' – Countryside Act 1968.
'1949 Act' – National Parks and Access to the Countryside Act 1949.
'1981 Act' – Wildlife and Countryside Act 1981.

Introduction

The public has a right to pass through the countryside along highways, that is along public carriageways and cartways, bridleways and footpaths (see Chapter 7). There is no common law right to wander at large in the country, not even over common land, but limited rights of access have been conferred by statute, or granted by the landowner by deed or under access agreements. The public increasingly seeks further rights of access, and the purpose of much countryside legislation is to reconcile this need with the basic use of the land for production of food.

Common land

Many people think that common land is land owned by the people at large, and that they are entitled to wander over it. In fact, common land is usually owned by private individuals, or by bodies such as the National Trust or the Church Commissioners. However, it is subject to rights exercised over it by third parties, that is, the commoners. Under the feudal system, the manorial lands were held by the lord of the manor. The agricultural tenants of the manor enjoyed rights of common grazing and certain other rights over some of the land of the manor set aside for that purpose. As the manorial system declined, common lands were enclosed, gradually at first, but eventually on a large scale during the eighteenth and early nineteenth centuries. In some counties very little common land was left unenclosed, while in others, particularly where the land was of poor quality, very large areas of common were left. The Royal Commission on Common Land which reported in 1958, recommended that common land, common rights, and ownership of common land should be registered. The Commons Registration Act 1965 introduced a system of registration. Registers were made by county councils and are held by them. The periods for making registrations and objecting to them have expired. Any common land which was not registered under the Act has ceased to be common land. Any common rights not registered under the Act have ceased to be exercisable, unless they had previously been registered under the Land Registration Act 1925. Where ownership of common land has not been registered, the Act requires the Commons Commissioners appointed under the Act to take steps to find the owner. The Commissioners also have to settle disputed claims arising from registrations which have been challenged by objections properly made under the Act.

RIGHTS OF COMMON

The rights of common which could be and have been registered under the Act are as follows: common of pasture; common of estovers; common of turbary; common of pannage; common of piscary; and common in the soil. Common of pasture is in practice the most important of the common rights to be registered, and claimants had to register a right to graze a specified number of animals of a specified kind. In many cases where claimants were not sure exactly what their rights were because there was no documentary evidence, a very large number of rights were registered, and many objections were made to such registrations. Common of pasture is the right to graze cattle, sheep, horses, or other animals on the common. The rights may be appendant, or appurtenant (attached to the farms originally in the manor) or they may exist in gross, that is independently from the land. Common of estovers is the right to cut and take tree loppings or gorse, bushes, underwood, heather or fern for the repair of the farmhouse, farm buildings, hedges, fences and farm implements or for fuel to burn in the commoner's house. Common of turbary is the right to dig turves and peat out of the common for use in the commoner's house. Common of pannage is the right to turn out pigs at certain times of the year to eat beech mast and acorns. Common of piscary is the right of fishing with others and sometimes with the owner of the soil in water owned by another. Common in the soil is the right to take gravel, sand, stone and other minerals from the soil.

Some common rights are exercisable only at certain periods of the year. For example, in the case of Lammas lands where the lord of the manor may take a hay crop off the land during the season, the commoners are not entitled to put their sheep on the land until Lammas, when the animals go on to graze the aftermath.

ACCESS TO COMMONS

Easements, such as private rights of way over the common, were not registrable under the 1965 Act, though they could be noted on the register. In addition to private rights of way over a common, there may also be public rights of way such as public footpaths or bridleways. The public may, of course, walk along such public rights of way, but there is no common law right to wander at will over common land. There is pressure from some amenity organisations for legislation to be introduced giving the public a legal right of access to all commons. A public right of access for air and recreation was granted by statute over metropolitan and urban commons by the Law of Property Act 1925, s. 193. The public may also enjoy a right of access over certain rural commons which have become regulated commons under the Commons Act 1899, or where rights have been granted by deed by the owners of the soil under the Law of Property Act 1925, or created by private Act or under an access agreement made under the National Parks and Access to the Countryside Act 1949. The inhabitants of towns and villages may enjoy a customary right of access to their town or village green.

FENCING OF COMMONS

The fencing of common land is restricted under the Law of Property Act 1925, s. 194. With certain exceptions, the section applies to any land which was subject to common rights on 1 January 1926. The consent of the Secretary of State for the Environment is required for any building or fence or the construction of any other work which interferes with access to the common. If unauthorised works are carried out, the county court may order them to be removed on the application of the local authority, the lord of the manor, or any other interested person.

RIGHTS OF THE OWNER OF THE COMMON

At common law the owner of the soil of the common may do what he likes with it provided he does not interfere with the rights of the commoners. Common land may be bought and sold like any other land, but subject to common rights. However, if common land is acquired by a statutory authority for statutory purposes, special rules apply. The owner of common land may plant trees on the common, graze cattle and grant licences to third parties to take the products of the soil. Although the owner may graze cattle on the common, that does not make him a commoner. The owner may shoot game on the common, and may grant the right of shooting to another. He may work minerals in the soil of the common, for example sand, gravel or chalk, though he would have to get planning permission for the commercial exploitation of such minerals.

Public access to open land

ACCESS AGREEMENTS

The National Parks Act 1949 and the Countryside Act 1968 provide for access agreements or orders to be made for land which is defined as open country in the Acts. Open country is land which is wholly or chiefly mountain, moor, heath, down, cliff or foreshore (including any bank, barrier, dune, beach, flat or other land adjacent to the foreshore). It also includes woodlands, any river or canal, and any expanse of water through which a river or part of a river flows. In the case of water, the local planning authority must consult with the water authority before making an access agreement with the owner of the land.

The effect of an access agreement or order is that a person entering land under it, for the purpose of open air and recreation, is not a trespasser, provided he enters without breaking or damaging any wall, fence, hedge or gate, but that does not apply to excepted land, for example agricultural land other than rough grazing, land covered with buildings, or used for a park, garden or pleasure ground and land used for getting minerals.

Access agreements may be made by the local planning authorities with any persons having an interest in the land defined as open country, and may include provision for making payments as a consideration for making the agreement, and towards the expenses of the person entering into the agreement. An access agreement may be recoverable or irrevocable. Local authorities may also make an access order.

Under the 1949 Act, farmers could convert moor or heathland which was subject to an access agreement or order, into agricultural land, by ploughing it. It then became excepted land not subject to access. The Countryside Act 1968 changed that. It provided that where land is subject to an access order, the Secretary of State has power to prevent the conversion of open land into excepted land by ploughing by making an order to the effect. The Secretary of State must consult the Countryside Commission before making such an order, and must hold a local inquiry or arrange for representation to be made to a person appointed by him.

ACCESS BY LONG-DISTANCE PATHS

In order to create long-distance paths giving a continuous route across a county, the county council, as highway authority, may enter into public path agreements or make a public path order, so as to create new lengths of paths to connect with existing paths. Public path agreements may be made under the Highways Act 1980, s. 25 between the authority and the owner of the land, on such terms as to payments and other matters as may be agreed. In entering into such an agreement, the local authority must have due regard to the needs of agriculture and forestry. If an owner is unwilling to enter into a public path agreement, the authority may decide to make a public path creation order. There is a right of objection under the 1980 Act to the making of such orders.

ACCESS BY PUBLIC PATHS AND BRIDLEWAYS

The National Parks Act 1949 introduced a system for registering public footpaths and bridleways on County Definitive Maps made and maintained by the county councils as highways authorities. The Act provided for surveys of paths by county councils after consultations with parish councils and district councils. The survey was followed by preparation of draft maps, to which objections could be made. After the objections and appeals had been settled, provisional maps had to be published, and it was open to owners, occupiers and lessees to challenge them by way of an application to Quarter Sessions. After all applications to Quarter Sessions were settled, a Definitive Map and statement had to be published.

The National Parks Act provided that the County Definitive Maps should be reviewed every five years by County Councils. That requirement proved to be unsatisfactory, and in many cases five year reviews were not regularly carried out. The Wildlife and Countryside Act 1981, introduced instead a continuous review procedure, whereby new paths could be put on the Definitive Maps by way of modification orders, or paths shown on the Map which were not public paths could be removed (see below).

A number of paths were marked on County Definitive Maps as 'roads used as public paths'. The designation was intended for ancient tracks, green lanes and unmetalled roads used chiefly as footpaths and bridleways. It proved to be an unsatisfactory designation, and the Countryside Act 1968, introduced a procedure for reclassifying such ways as either byways open to all traffic, bridleways or public footpaths. The duty to reclassify such paths is now contained in the Wildlife and Countryside Act 1981, Part III. A road used as a public path must be shown as a byway open to all traffic if a public right of way for vehicles has been shown to exist over it. Otherwise it will be shown as a bridleway unless public bridleway rights have been shown not to exist, in which case it will be shown as a public footpath.

Continuous reviews under the Wildlife & Countryside Act 1981

The Wildlife & Countryside Act 1981 made a fundamental change in the procedure for keeping the County Definitive Maps up to date. Instead of the five-yearly review procedure under the National Parks and Access to the Countryside Act 1949, there is now a continuous review procedure. County Councils may make orders amending the Map at any time that evidence is available showing that such an amendment ought to be made. For example, if a public path has been stopped up by way of a magistrates' court order, or diverted by way of a diversion order made by the local authority, the Definitive Map must be amended as soon as is practicable to show what has happened to the path. A new public path may have been created either under a public path agreement or a public path order. The new path must be shown on the Map as soon as is practicable. The public may have used a way as of right over twenty years so that it may be presumed to have been dedicated to the public. Evidence may be available that a way is public right of way though not on the Definitive Map, or that there is no public right of way where the Map shows such a way, or that a way shown as a bridleway should be shown as a footpath, or vice versa. Any of these matters can lead to an amendment of the Definitive Map.

Any person can apply to the County Council to have a modification order made so as to put on the Map a path not already marked on it. However, the applicant will have to produce evidence of the legal existence of such a path. Similarly any person (for example an owner or occupier of land) can apply to have a modification order made if he thinks that there is no public right of way over land shown in the Map, or that particulars shown in the Map and statement need to be modified. The procedure for making such applications is laid down in Schedule 14 to the 1981 Act. A map and copies of documentary evidence and statements of witnesses should accompany the application. *Notice must be served by the applicant on every owner and occupier of the land concerned.* In exceptional cases, where the names and addresses of owners and occupiers cannot be found, a suitable notice can be put up on the land. The applicant must certify to the highway authority that the proper notice has been served or posted on the land. Notices and certificates must be in the prescribed form. The provision ensures that owners and occupiers will be informed about proposals for paths over their land, and it should discourage frivolous applications by individuals for public path modification orders. Where an application is duly made, the highway authority must investigate the matters stated in the application, and decide whether or not to make an order.

If a highway authority decides not to make an order, the applicant has twenty-eight days in which to appeal against the decision to the Secretary of State. Notice of appeal must be served on the Secretary of State and on the authority. Where an authority fails to make a decision at all, there are provisions for making representations to the Secretary of State.

Where an authority decides to make a modification order, the procedure for making the order is laid down in Schedule 15 to the Act, but the form of the order is prescribed by regulation. The 1981 Act has abolished the requirement to publish notices of public path orders in the *London Gazette*, but notice of an order must be published in at least one local newspaper, and copies must be displayed on the path itself, and in local authority offices. Furthermore, *notice must be served on every owner and occupier of the land affected by the order*, though in exceptional cases the Secretary of State may direct that the notice shall be posted on the land instead. Notices must be given or displayed in sufficient time to allow forty-two days for objections to be made. The notice to owners and occupiers must be accompanied by a copy of the order or part of it. During the forty-two day period allowed for objections, an owner or occupier may ask the highway authority what documents (if any) were taken into account when preparing the order, and may ask permission to inspect them and take copies, or to be told where documents may be inspected (Schedule 15, para. 3(8), 1981 Act).

Unopposed orders may be confirmed by the highway authority, without modifications. Opposed orders must be submitted to the Secretary of State for confirmation. In such a case there will have to be either a local inquiry, or a hearing before a person appointed by the Secretary of State. The Local Government Act 1972, s. 250(2)–(5) applies to the giving of evidence and costs of local inquiries into public path amendment orders. Inspectors at public inquiries will be appointed by the Secretary of State, and as a rule the inspector will make the decision. Final decisions on public path modification orders must be publicised in the local Press and by notice to owners and occupiers of the land affected by the path, local authorities, etc. They will be entitled to receive with the notice a copy of the order or part of it.

Any aggrieved person who wishes to question the validity of a public path modification order, has six weeks from the date of publication of notice of confirmation of the order to appeal to the High Court.

Private rights of way

A private right of way for the benefit of one farm may be exercised over another farm or other land. A private right of way may be for all agricultural purposes, or for all purposes, or for certain limited purposes. Access to the way may be restricted to certain defined points, or may be exercised at any point along the way. A private right of way may be granted by deed, in which case it should be defined in the deeds of the properties concerned, and shown on a plan. However, a right of way may be claimed by prescription, or implied by law as in the case of a right of way of necessity.

Where there is a dispute about a private right of way, the deeds of the parties should be examined, and every effort should be made by the parties to get their solicitors to settle the matter. Sometimes occupiers take matters into their own hands by blocking the way or locking gates, or by removing obstructions and forcing locks. Disputes which could be settled quickly are allowed to drag on causing strain and bad feelings.

If there is no reference to a private right of way in the deeds, the person claiming to use the way may be able to establish a right based on prescription or lost modern grant. In order to establish such a claim, the claimant should generally be prepared to show that the way has been used as of right and without interruption continuously for a period of twenty years.

WAY OF NECESSITY

It may be possible to prove the existence of a right of way of necessity where land would be inaccessible apart from the right of way claimed. A right of way of necessity arises where a parcel of land sold off would be landlocked if a right of way was not available over the vendor's remaining land. Not every parcel of landlocked land is entitled to the benefit of a right of way of necessity over adjoining land, since it may never have been held together with the adjoining land over which a right of way is claimed.

REPAIR OF PRIVATE RIGHT OF WAY

A person who enjoys a private right of way over land owned by a third party is entitled to put the way into a condition fit for the purpose for which he is entitled to use it. Thus he can fill in pot holes on a farm track, or put down a hard surface if that is necessary in order to exercise his right of way over it for all agricultural purposes. He is not obliged, however, to maintain the right of way or to contribute to its maintenance unless he has contracted to do so.

INTERFERENCE WITH PRIVATE RIGHT OF WAY

The most usual type of interference is obstruction by means of a locked gate, or by continuous parking of large vehicles in the way. The person entitled to the right of way may abate the nuisance by removing the obstruction. In some cases this remedy leads to a breach of the peace. A person entitled to use the way may sue for an injunction to restrain the other party from interfering with his right of way, and he would be advised to do so where the other party persists in obstructing the way.

A person entitled to a right of way may sometimes use it excessively. An excessive user of a right of way may be restrained by an injunction. In *Jelbert v. Davies* [1968] 1 All E.R. 1182 a person who enjoyed a private right of way for all purposes over a drive was held to be entitled to use the way for access to land used as a caravan and camping site, but the court also held that use of the way for access to a site for 200 caravans was excessive, and made a declaration that the way should not be used in such a manner as to cause substantial interference with its use by a farmer entitled to use it for agricultural purposes.

A private right of way may exist over a highway, and an order made under the Highways Act to stop-up a highway would not affect a private right of way.

Chapter 9
Wayleaves

Abbreviations in this Chapter:
'CLA' – Country Landowners' Association.
'NFU' – National Farmers' Union.

The meaning of wayleave

The law does not define a wayleave, but it is a useful word to describe the package of rights acquired when an authority, company or other body or person exercises a power or right to construct, use, inspect and maintain something linear, like pipes or cables, routed through another's land. When the rights are acquired by a formal deed of grant from the landowner they are usually referred to as an easement.

A   General principles

Acts of Parliament give powers to numerous authorities and other bodies to construct pipelines, cables, etc. in, on or over land for public services, defence and commercial purposes. What can be done, and how, varies in each case, so that the Act or Acts under which the powers are exercised need to be examined in any particular instance. Guidelines on the more common types of wayleaves are given below, but first there are general principles for the protection of the owners and occupiers of the land which always apply (except in very rare occurrences such as national emergency).

Compensation

Two kinds of compensation will be payable:

(a) Compensation for loss and damage occasioned by the works, payable to the landowner or occupier suffering it.

(b) Consideration for the wayleave, payable to the landowner.

COMPENSATION FOR LOSS AND DAMAGE

This can be claimed for any damage not made good by the construction of the works and by any entry in connection with them, such as for preliminary survey or subsequent inspections, maintenance, repair, replacement or removal. It should cover, among other things, loss of crop (which might extend for some years) and any interference with farming programmes or other land use, such as sporting rights. Compensation for time necessarily spent by owners and occupiers in attending to the project can sometimes be obtained.

Professional fees. Owners and occupiers should engage a chartered surveyor experienced in this work to look after their interests and to negotiate for them. Professional fees reasonably incurred will be paid by (or recovered from) the acquiring authority or other promoters. The fee should be adequate remuneration for the work involved (see note in Chapter 5).

THE CONSIDERATION OR WAYLEAVE PAYMENT

Confusion can be caused by the several different ways used to describe this payment – 'recognition payment', 'payment for injurious affection', or 'for diminution in land value', or just 'compensation'. It is best looked on as payment for the bundle of rights acquired in and exercised over the owner's land. Where a formal easement is acquired by deed it will be described as the consideration for the grant.

The payment is commonly expressed as 'so much' per metre, with separate assessments for each above ground or surface structure, such as manholes, valve chambers, etc.

No confiscation. Frequently authorities exercising statutory powers enter into no deed or wayleave agreement with the owner. Contrary to what some have contended, they must still make a wayleave payment. The fundamental principle against confiscation, noted in Chapter 5, applies to wayleaves (*West Midlands Joint Electricity Authority* v. *Pitt* [1932] K.B. 1 – the Court of Appeal describing an electricity wayleave as 'an invasion of rights'). It is not enough to make good, or pay for, damage done. As the Lands Tribunal observed in *Griffiths* v. *Swansea Cpn.* (1960) 11 P. & C.R. 470, where the

Corporation had denied the landowner any consideration payment for a water main:

> I have no doubt at all that a pipeline laid through land does reduce the value of that land if only because the authority who have laid that pipe have powers under some form of legislation to enter the land in the future for the purpose of either inspection or repair and I do not consider that the form of procedure under which these powers can be exercised is of any moment. Compensation may be payable when the further entry takes place but the present value of the land is reduced because of the right of somebody else to have access to and powers over the land.

It can be pointed out to doubting authorities, also, that the High Court and the Lands Tribunal have said the exercise of statutory wayleave powers amounts to a compulsory purchase (see *Thurrock Grays and Tilbury Joint Sewerage Board* v. *Thames Land Co. Ltd.* (1925) E.G.D. 316; *Padfield* v. *Eastern Electricity Board* (1972) 24 P. & C.R. 423).

Interest on payments. It was common practice to pay interest on delayed payments until certain water authorities began to deny interest. The legal obligation is open to doubt. The decision of the Lands Tribunal in *Pattinson* v. *Finningley Internal Drainage Board* (1971) 22 P. & C. R.929, that it would not be full compensation without interest, has not been followed in later decisions of the Tribunal (see *Burlin* v. *Manchester City Council* (1976) 32 P.& C.R. 115 (L.T.). There is no room for doubt that denying interest on delayed compensation is inequitable, and the Government intend that the privatised Water Services P.L.C.s will be required to pay it (Green Paper 'Water and Sewerage Law', March 1986). Meanwhile, landowners and occupiers are advised to claim and insist on interest on the wayleave payment from the date of entry (as in compulsory purchase cases, which these are in effect). Interest on the loss or damage claim may not accrue until the claim is quantified, or, on another view, from the date the loss or damage occurred.

SETTLEMENT OF DISPUTES

If the parties cannot agree the payments the dispute can be referred to the Lands Tribunal for determination in virtually all cases, but where an easement is granted by deed it is quite common to provide for reference of disputes to arbitration.

CODES OF PRACTICE

The British Standard Code of Practice on 'Installation of Pipelines in Land' (CP2010 revised) lays down minimum standards of good practice which pipeliners can be expected to comply with. Unless expressly adopted in an agreement the code has no legal force.

More detailed codes of safeguards have frequently been agreed by pipelaying bodies with the Country Landowners' Association (C.L.A.) and the National Farmers Union (N.F.U.) jointy, in the form of undertakings. The C.L.A. and N.F.U. have also settled in many cases standard legal documentation (such as entry agreements and easement deeds) which have their approval. The codes deal with a catalogue of items to protect the interests of the landowners and occupiers before, during and after the installation of the works: preliminary consultations; notice of entry; supervision of the work; complaints procedure; re-instatement methods; maintenance of accesses and services during the work; safeguarding fixed equipment, livestock, land drainage, top soil, private roads, timber, sporting rights, watercourses, hedges, fences, minerals; and many other items. Anyone approached for impending pipeline works should enquire if such a code has been agreed and, if so, ask for a copy.

PRELIMINARY DISCUSSIONS

The importance of early discussions between the promoters of the project and the owners and occupiers cannot be over-emphasised, to give time for consultations about the route, safeguarding the land drainage, any special features of the land and the programme of events. Owners and occupiers should make sure they know in advance the name, address and telephone number of the project manager to contact in the event of anything untoward happening.

INDEMNIFICATION: LEAKAGES AND BURSTS

British Gas and the oil companies under agreements with the C.L.A. and N.F.U. include indemnity clauses in their standard easement deeds to secure that compensation will be paid for any damage caused in the event of leakage from their pipelines from any cause other than the fault of the landowner himself. Strict liability for damage caused by leakage from communication pipes or water mains (but not sewers) is placed on water undertakers by the Water Act 1981, s. 6, and there is also liability for escapes from Government oil pipelines. In the case of sewers, the sewerage authority will be liable (as will any undertaker) where the escape is due to negligence, and even where liability is denied, *ex gratia* payments can sometimes be obtained.

LOSS OF DEVELOPMENT VALUE

One of the hazards for the landowner having, say a pipeline or line of pylons across his land, is that one day it might hamper or frustrate permitted development of the land. If the development can be foreseen, the loss of development value can be taken into account in the wayleave payment. Some bodies will also agree in the wayleave agreement either to 'lift and divert' the line in the event of it later preventing unforeseen permitted development, or else pay compensation. The standard annual wayleave agreements settled by the C.L.A. and N.F.U. with the elctricity supply industry, tackles the problem by permitting the landowner at any time to convert the annual agreement into a permanent easement on payment of a lump sum which can then take into account any frustration of permitted development or any interference with amenity diminishing the land value.

RESTRICTION ON LAND USE

Where there is a written agreement for the wayleave, it will spell out the restrictions imposed on the use of the land for the protection of the buried works. Building, excavation, dumping, etc. is usually banned over a specified width above and adjacent to the pipeline or cable, and the landowner convenants not to do or permit anything on the land imperilling the pipe. Where the authority marches in in exercise of statutory powers with no written grant, it is less easy to know the extent of restrictions on land use because they are largely left to implications of law. Clearly the works may not be imperilled, nor may access to them be obstructed (*Abingdon B.C.* v. *James* [1940] 1 All E.R. 446 – see also Chapter 11, p. 161).

B Notes on specific wayleaves

1 Sewers and drains

THE RESPONSIBLE AUTHORITY

The Water Act 1973 transferred to the regional water authorities responsibility for sewerage and sewage disposal. When a public sewer or drain is constructed in private land the water authority will therefore be responsible, but they can, and usually do, get the local authority to carry out the works as their agents.

Note: If privatisation of the water authorities occurs (see Chapter 10) it will be necessary to study what duties and powers are given to the new W.S.P.L.C.s.

THE POWERS

The Water Act 1973, s. 14, imposes a duty on every water authority to sewer its area and gives them the powers contained in the Public Health Act 1936 to construct sewers and drains in private land. The powers are powerful. The authority requires no consent or agreement. The Act requires no more than reasonable notice to be served on the owner and occupier before entry to do the works. What is reasonable notice will depend on the circumstances and what, if any, forewarnings have already been given. It is suggested that less than three weeks' notice would usually be unreasonable.

SAFEGUARDS AND COMPENSATION

The C.L.A. and N.F.U. have negotiated codes of safeguards with nearly all the water authorities for the protection of owners and occupiers of agricultural land (see above).

By the Public Health Act 1936, s. 278, the authority is required to 'make full compensation to any person who has sustained damage' by the exercise of the statutory powers. The Lands Tribunal has given useful guidance on assessing the compensation in a number of cases (*Markland* v. *Cannock R.D.C.* (1973) 13 R.V.R. 379 is especially helpful as to the wayleave payment, specifying the main factors to take into account). As a permanent wayleave will be taken the wayleave payment will be 'once-for-all'.

2   Water mains

THE RESPONSIBLE AUTHORITY

A water supply duty is placed on the water authorities by the Water Act 1973, s. 11, but water companies still exist and function as agents for the water authorities (s. 12). See the note about privatisation and the proposed Water Services P.L.C.s in Chapter 10.

THE POWERS

Although there was some rationalisation at the time of the re-organisation in 1973, there are still a large number of Acts governing the powers of water undertakers to construct pipelines. The water companies each have their own Acts and Orders. The water authorities inherited powers from sundry

Acts but in the main will construct pipelines under the Water Act 1945. Under this Act the water authority again needs no consent or agreement. As with sewers (see above) no more than reasonable notice is required before entry (Local Authorities (Miscellaneous Provisions) Order 1977, S.I. 1977 No. 293).

SAFEGUARDS AND COMPENSATION

The codes negotiated by the C.L.A. and N.F.U. for sewer construction (above) apply equally to water mains.

Whatever Act the pipeline is constructed under there will be a compensation section. In the case of the Water Act 1945, Schedule 3, s. 19 requires compensation to be paid to any person interested in the land, for any damage or injurious affection suffered 'from time to time' by reason of the laying, inspection, repair, alteration, renewal or removal of the pipeline. As a permanent wayleave will be acquired the wayleave payment to the landowner will be 'once-for-all'.

3 Gas mains

THE RESPONSIBLE 'AUTHORITY'

At the time of writing the gas supply industry is in the process of being privatised. The Gas Act 1986 ('The 1986 Act') has abolished the monopoly of gas supply held by British Gas Corporation, and by Orders made under s. 49 of the Act, all the property, rights and liabilities of the Corporation were transferred on 24 August 1986 to a successor company, called British Gas PLC, except for rights and liabilities for British Gas Stock which on that date were transferred to the Treasury. A Director General of Gas Supply was appointed from 18 August 1986 (see S.I. s 1986, Nos. 1315, 1316, 1317, 1318).

The Secretary of State and the Director General are responsible for authorising public gas suppliers (1986 Act, s. 7) and unauthorised supply through pipes is an offence (s. 5). The Secretary of State and the Director General are responsible for securing all reasonable demands for gas, for protecting the interests of consumers, promoting efficiency, economy and safety (s. 4).

THE POWERS

Authorised public gas suppliers have the power to supply gas through pipes, with a duty to maintain an efficient, co-ordinated and economical system of gas supply (s. 9). They are given compulsory powers to acquire land and rights over land, such as pipeline wayleaves, under the Acquisition of Land Act 1981 (1986 Act, Schedule 3).

SAFEGUARDS AND COMPENSATION

For many years prior to privatisation the C.L.A. and N.F.U. had a comprehensive national agreement with the gas industry governing the terms, safeguards and standard documentation to be offered to owners and occupiers when gas mains were constructed in agricultural land. A code of undertakings was given to each owner and occupier along the route. Each occupier (whether tenant or owner-occupier) was offered a sum, expressed as a payment per metre, as a consideration for the early return of all the necessary consent forms to enable entry to the land (the rate varied with the diameter of pipe involved). This payment was additional to the easement payment and compensation for loss and damage.

Where the wayleave was granted by agreement a formal easement deed was entered into (including among the safeguards an indemnity clause and loss of development value clause (see above)). A once-for-all consideration equal to 75% of the capital value of the easement strip was offered to the landowner, subject to a minimum rate of payment, settled with the C.L.A. and N.F.U. for each pipeline. The width of easement varied with the diameter of pipe.

No doubt similar arrangements will be negotiated by the C.L.A. and N.F.U. with the privatised industry.

4   Electricity wayleaves

THE RESPONSIBLE AUTHORITY

The construction of electricity supply lines (which may be buried cables, or cables carried above ground by poles or pylons) is carried out by the Central Electricity Generating Board or by Area Electricity Boards. The Electricity Council has an overseeing role but no real powers.

THE POWERS

The procedure and powers are still largely governed by the Acts known as the Electricity (Supply) Acts 1882–1936 and Regulations made under them. The Boards have compulsory powers to acquire land or rights and the standard procedures and compensation rules apply (see Chapter 5).

An above-ground line may not be constructed without the Board first obtaining the consent of the Secretary of State. The Board first serves on each landowner and occupier a notice of intention to construct the line and seeks their agreement to it. If agreement is not given within twenty-one days, or is given with conditions unacceptable to the Board, the Board can apply to the Secretary of State both for consent to the line and for the compulsory grant of the necessary wayleaves. The owners and occupiers must be given the opportunity to make objection. If the local planning authority object to the line a public inquiry will be held, otherwise it is left to the discretion of the Secretary of State whether to hold one (Electric Lighting (Clauses) Act 1899, Schedule; Electricity (Supply) Act 1919, s. 22; Electricity Act 1947, s. 66; Electricity Act 1957, ss. 31, 32 and 34).

SAFEGUARDS AND COMPENSATION

The C.L.A. and N.F.U. have long had a national agreement with the electricity supply industry for wayleaves in agricultural land. It includes a code of practice for underground lines and a standard rate of payment to offer the landowner for wayleaves. Most lines are overhead. There are standard forms of wayleave agreements for these and scales of annual wayleave payments (described inaccurately as 'rentals') and annual compensation to the occupier for interference with agricultural operations. The scales are revised annually. Whilst the scales are convenient, it is open to any landowner to refer an assessment to the Lands Tribunal (cf. *Clouds Estate Trustees* v. *Southern Electricity Board* (1984) E.G.D. 682).

The standard wayleave agreement provides for termination by the landowner by six months' notice, though if the Board wanted it to continue they could and would apply to the Secretary of State for a compulsory wayleave. The agreement also allows the landowner to convert the wayleave to a permanent easement in return for a 'once-for-all' payment. This the landowner would want to do if he wanted, for example, to claim substantial compensation for injurious affection to the value of the land. On such a claim the compensation is assessed on a 'before-and-after' comparison of land value measuring the depreciation of land value caused by the electricity line, plus a capitalisation of the annual compensation for agricultural interference (see *Russell-Ross* v. *Central Electricity Generating Board* (1972) 223 E.G. 2051).

Actual or potential interference with aerial spraying of crops can also be taken into account (*Pryor* v. *Central Electricity Generating Board* (1968) 206 E.G. 1143).

In executing works the Boards must 'cause as little detriment and inconvenience and do as little damage as may be, and shall make full compensation to all bodies and persons interested for all damage sustained by them by reason or in consequence of the exercise of such powers' (Electric Lighting Act 1882, s. 17).

5   Government oil pipelines

THE RESPONSIBLE AUTHORITY

The Minister of Defence and other ministers are empowered to construct oil pipelines for defence purposes by making wayleave orders. Some government lines are leased or operated on an agency agreement by oil companies. The Property Services Agency of the Department of the Environment normally deals with the landowners and occupiers on behalf of the Ministry concerned.

THE POWERS

Government Departments can make compulsory wayleave orders under the Land Powers (Defence) Act 1958 giving them the right to construct, maintain, repair, replace or remove pipelines in private land. Oil pipelines constructed as war works in World War II may be maintained, removed or replaced under the Requistioned Land and War Works Act 1948, though in recent times relaying has been done by new wayleave orders under the 1958 Act.

SAFEGUARDS AND COMPENSATION

A code of safeguards has been agreed with the C.L.A. and N.F.U. for some government projects and the use of the code may become standard practice.

The Department concerned is required to pay compensation for any damage done by the installation of the works and for any dimunition caused to the value of the land (1958 Act, s. 18). Restrictions are imposed on the use of the land, prohibiting buildings, roads, deposits, excavations, etc. within ten feet of the pipeline (1958 Act, s. 16), or mining under the pipeline (1958 Act, s. 15). Compensation is payable for these restrictions.

The Department concerned is liable to pay for any injury or loss caused by failure to keep government oil pipelines in repair before abandonment (1948 Act, s. 15; 1958 Act, s. 15 and Regulations).

Claimants for compensation should beware the short time limits for making claims (Government Oil Pipelines (No. 2) Regulations 1959, S.I. 1959 No. 724 – claims for damage and disturbance must be made within twenty-one days; claims for depreciation in land value and in respect of restrictions, within six months of the wayleave order, or the coming into effect of the restrictions, as the case may be).

6 Telecommunications

THE RESPONSIBLE 'AUTHORITY'

The monopoly to run telecommunications systems, held first by the Post Office, then by British Telecom, was abolished by the Telecommunications Act 1984 ('the 1984 Act'). The 1984 Act repealed the Telecommunications Acts 1863 to 1916 and replaced them with a new Telecommunications Code (Schedule 2 of the Act). The 1984 Act provides for the appointment of a Director General of Telecommunications and for licensing all operators by the Director or Secretary of State.

THE POWERS

The Telecommunications Act 1984 provides for the Secretary of State to authorise, with the consent of the Director, the compulsory acquisition by *public* telecommunication operators, of land, easements or other rights (s. 34), and to authorise entry to survey (s. 37). The Secretary of State may also authorise *any* licensed operators to use the Telecommunications Code in Schedule 2, provided the operator is running a public system or one for the benefit of the public.

The Code is something of a muddle. Only a simplified sketch can be given here of the contorted way in which it enables operators to do works on land, whilst protecting to a degree the rights of owners and occupiers. The consent of the occupier (not necessarily the owner) is needed for an operator to install 'telecommunications apparatus' (widely defined in Schedule 2, para. 1(1)) on land (para. 2(1)). This consent will bind the owner and every other interest, not only if they agree, but also so long as the consenting occupier is the occupier, provided he had at least a lease for the term of one year when he consented (para. 2(3)). Further, where any person owning an interest in the land consents to the works, it will bind successors to that interest and also the owners of any other interest subsequently created (para. 2(4)).

Protection for owners not consenting to the works only appears later in the Code, where it deals with requirements to remove apparatus (see below). It is believed the ultimate effect is to make it worth the while of operators to negotiate both with owners and occupiers. If an operator cannot negotiate the required rights he can seek to obtain them by a court order (para. 5).

SAFEGUARDS AND COMPENSATION

Where there is a compulsory acquisition, compensation will be under the compulsory purchase code (see Chapter 5). Where rights are exercised under the 1984 Act Schedule 2 Code, compensation will no doubt be negotiated or ordered by the court, as the case may be. Before 1984 the C.L.A. and N.F.U. had negotiated a standard code and documentation for Post Office (subsequently British Telecom) lines and no doubt they will seek to make similar arrangements with licensed operators.

Where an owner has been bound, without his consent, by an occupier conferring rights on an operator, he will cease to be bound when that occupier's occupation ends. The landowner can then require the operator to restore the land to its former condition (Schedule 2, para. 4(2)) and require the removal of apparatus under a procedure set out in para. 21 of the code. Paragraph 21 is designed to see that an operator wishing to retain the works on the land will negotiate a grant from the owner. He will need to refer the issue to the court if agreement cannot be reached.

The original conferring of rights by the occupier might reduce the value of the owner's interest because of the procedures for applying for the ultimate removal of the apparatus. In that case the operator must pay compensation (para. 4), determined by the Lands Tribunal in default of agreement (para. 4(6)).

7   Commercial pipelines under Pipelines Act 1962

THE PIPELINES ACT 1962

This Act controls the construction of pipelines by private enterprise, enabling private companies to obtain powers to do so under the regulation of the Secretary of State. Pipelines constructed under this Act are mainly oil pipelines, though they may be constructed to transport different substances and at least one common-carrier pipeline has been laid under the Act. The Act also deals with safety in the construction and operation of pipelines.

The Act does not apply to water pipelines or sewers and the procedures do not apply to pipelines of the British Gas Corporation, the electricity boards, the U.K. Atomic Energy Authority, the railways, docks and the government, nor pipelines internal to any premises.

PROCEDURES

Different procedures are laid down for 'cross-country pipelines' (over ten miles) and 'local pipelines' (not exceeding ten miles), as follows:

(a) *Cross-country pipelines.* Before a cross-country pipeline can be constructed the promoters must obtain a pipeline construction authorisation from the Secretary of State, under a procedure which requires an approach to be made to all the landowners and occupiers along the proposed route before an application can be made for an authorisation. The application must state (among other things) what rights the company needs to obtain from landowners and whether they can be obtained. If the Minister allows the application to proceed, it must be advertised and notice must be given to each local authority affected, giving at least twenty-eight days for any objections to be lodged. If a planning authority objects the Minister cannot grant an authorisation without first holding a public inquiry. If no planning authority objects any other objector is entitled to be heard, but the Minister has a discretion whether it is to be at a public inquiry.

(b) *Local pipelines.* There is a simpler procedure for local pipelines. The promoter must give the Secretary of State sixteen weeks' notice before starting construction. No authorisation is needed and there is no provision for advertisement, objections or a public inquiry. The promoters again have to approach the landowners and occupiers before giving notice, however, as the notice must state whether the necessary rights can be obtained as in the case of an application for a cross-country pipeline application.

POWERS

The 1962 Act enables the promoters of the pipeline to apply to the Secretary of State for compulsory purchase orders to acquire land (s. 11), or compulsory rights orders to acquire wayleaves (s. 12). Companies cannot expect to get compulsory orders except as a last resort. The procedures are similar to the standard compulsory acquisition procedures (see Chapter 5), involving notices, advertisement, hearing of objections, etc.

SAFEGUARDS AND COMPENSATION

Anyone approached by a company should enquire whether terms, safeguards and documentation have been negotiated with the C.L.A. and N.F.U. In all likelihood the C.L.A. and N.F.U. will have been approached at an early stage and arrangements more favourable than in the case of statutory bodies will be made.

The Act requires compensation to be paid to the landowner for any depreciation in the value of his land by reason of the making of a compulsory rights order, and also requires compensation to be paid for any loss caused by damage to, or disturbance in the enjoyment of any land or chattels (s. 14). Compulsory rights orders are rare. The promoters almost invariably negotiate the grant of an easement by a deed containing covenants for the protection of the owner and occupier in return for restrictions placed on land use for the protection of the pipeline.

The Act also places a duty on the promoters to restore agricultural land, so far as practicable, 'as to be fit for use for the purpose for which it was used before the execution of the works was begun' (s. 45).

C Winning onshore resources

Petroleum in the land is vested in the Crown (Petroleum (Production) Act 1934) and coal is vested in the National Coal Board (Coal Act 1936 and Coal Industry Nationalisation Act 1946). 'Petroleum' is defined as including 'any mineral oil or relative hydrocarbon and natural gas'. Licences granted by the Secretary of State are required for surveying, exploring and winning 'petroleum' (Petroleum (Production) (Landward Areas) Regulations 1984, S.I. 1984 No. 1832) and planning permission is required for any exploration or development works.

The licences give no right of entry. The permission of the owner and occupier is required before any of these operations can be carried out, unless the operator obtains compulsory rights from the court under the lengthy and cumbersome procedure of the Mines (Working Facilities and Support) Acts 1966 and 1974.

Broadly the three stages of possible operations are:

(a) *Seismic surveys.* The operator requires an Exploration Licence under the above Regulations and permission of the owner and occupier for any entry onto private land. Normally this is a short and painless operation causing no appreciable damage to the land, and normally, too, nothing further happens. Some very minor temporary drilling may be involved. The C.L.A. and N.F.U. have negotiated standard payments and safeguards.

(b) *Appraisal.* If the operator wants to carry out further tests, an Appraisal Licence is required under the above Regulations, planning permission and a further Agreement with the landowner and occupier. The operations are likely to be more extensive, causing damage and disturbance, involving a drilling rig on the site for some time. A rent and more elaborate safeguards and restoration stipulations will need to be negotiated.

(c) *Development.* In the comparatively rare event of sufficient oil or gas being found to justify exploration, the operators will need a Development Licence, planning permission and a long-term agreement (usually a lease) with the landowner and occupier including comprehensive safeguards and substantial payments.

GEOLOGICAL SURVEYS

The Institute of Geological Sciences, a research body, carries out all kinds of geological explorations under the auspices of the National Environment Research Council. They have powers of entry, after notice to the owner and occupier, under the Geological Survey Act 1845 (as amended by the Science and Technology Act 1965).

Chapter 10
Water and Watercourses

Abbreviations in this Chapter:
'1963 Act' – Water Resources Act 1963
'1973 Act' –Water Act 1973.
'1976 Act' – Land Drainage Act 1976.
'Secretary of State' – Secretary of State for the Environment.
'The Minister' or 'Minister of Agriculture' – Minister of Agriculture, Fisheries and Food.
'I.D.B.' – Internal Drainage Board.

Responsibility for watery matters

WATER AUTHORITIES – IMPENDING PRIVATISATION?

Water resources and the whole 'water cycle' from water supply to sewage disposal are the responsibility of the water authorities. England is divided into nine water authority areas, each administered by a regional water authority and the Wales Water Authority has the responsibility in Wales. Control of water abstraction and pollution falls to the water authorities. They also have a land drainage function and a duty 'to maintain, improve and develop' the fisheries in their areas (Salmon and Freshwater Fisheries Act 1975, s. 28). The Water Act 1973 established the water authorities and governs their constitution and powers. Arrangements can be and are made for local authorities and water companies to carry out some of their functions.

Water authorities have power to acquire land and rights over land by agreement or compulsorily for the performance of any of their functions (Water Resources Act 1963, Part VI) and they have byelaw-making powers.

At the time of writing the Government has decided to privatise the water authorities (White Paper 'Privatisation of the Water Authorities in England and Wales', 1986, Cmnd. 9734) but keeping land drainage and flood protection in the public domain. However, the proposal to introduce a Bill to enable the water authorities to be floated as water services public limited companies (W.S.P.L.C.s) has been postponed. This chapter describes the present position before privatisation.

Riparian rights

Land alongside a river or other water is known as riparian land and the owners have certain rights at common law deriving from their ownership of riparian land. Riparian fishing rights are explained in Chapter 13.

RIGHTS TO USE WATER

The water flowing in a river is ownerless. The riparian owner, however, has a right at common law to have the water flowing through or past his land undiminished in quality or quantity, and has the right to take and use the water, so long as it is consistent with the rights of the riparian owners upstream and downstream of him. This means he can take the water for his own domestic purposes and for his livestock, even if by so doing he leaves insufficient for lower riparian owners, but if he takes it for other purposes and thereby leaves lower owners short to their detriment, the lower owners can claim damages and an injunction (*Chasemore* v. *Richards* (1859) 7 H.L. Cas 349).

Taking water for spray irrigation is not a riparian right (*Rugby Joint Water Board* v. *Walters* [1966] 3 All E.R. 497) but taking it for ordinary purposes in livestock buildings, such as washing down, would be within the riparian right.

UNDERGROUND WATER

The riparian right to receive water as described above applies to underground water only if it flows in a defined channel. In the more usual case of water percolating not in a defined channel there is no neighbourly obligation at law. There is no common law remedy against an abstractor drying up such groundwater whatever the purpose of the abstraction.

STATUTORY CURTAILMENT OF RIGHTS

The common law riparian rights are now subject to the laws regulating abstractions in the Water Resources Act 1963.

Water abstraction

The general rule is that water may not be abstracted from a 'source of supply' unless it is permitted by a licence granted under the Water Resources Act 1963, s. 23. There are exceptions, listed below, preserving to some extent common law riparian rights to take water.

WHAT IS A 'SOURCE OF SUPPLY'?

The meaning of 'source of supply' can be found from the combination of elaborate definitions in the 1963 Act (of this term and of 'inland water' ss. 2 and 135 (1)). In short it means any of the following in a water authority area: a river, stream or watercourse (whether natural, artificial, tidal or non-tidal); a lake, pond or reservoir unless it does not discharge into an outside water; a channel, creak, bay, estuary or arm of the sea; or water in any underground strata, or well, or borehole or similar work, including an adit.

EXCEPTIONS FROM LICENSING

No abstraction licence is needed in the following cases:

(a) Abstractions up to 1000 gallons, if they are not part of continuous, or a series of, operations (1963 Act, s. 24(1)).
(b) Abstractions not of underground water for use of the riparian occupier on the riparian holding for the domestic purposes of his household and agricultural purposes other than spray irrigation (s. 24(2)).
(c) Abstractions of underground water by an individual for the domestic purposes of his household – though not for agricultural purposes (s. 24(3)).
(d) Abstractions in the course of, or resulting from, land drainage operations (s. 24(4) (10)).
(e) Abstractions for fire-fighting purposes (s. 24(8)).
(f) Test boring for underground water with the prior consent of the water authority (s. 24(9)).
(g) Where the Secretary of State has by order exempted from licensing a source of supply (s. 25).

The exemption for the occupier's household does not extend to other dwellings on the farm or estate, such as workers' cottages.

ABSTRACTION LICENCES

Where a licence is required, it is an offence, punishable by a fine, to abstract the water, or to 'cause or permit any other person' to do so, or to construct or extend any well, borehole or other work for abstraction without a licence, or to contravene the conditions of a licence (1963 Act, s. 49).

There are two kinds of licences, namely licences issued at the discretion of the water authority and licences of right, which certain qualifiers were entitled to. It is now long past the final date for applying for licences of right (30 June 1965).

Every licence must state, among other things, the quantity of water that may be abstracted from the source of supply, over what period, by what means, where it may be used and for what purpose, and how it is to be measured (s. 30).

Charges are made for licences, based on the quantity of water authorised to be abstracted.

Application for licence. Application must be made to the water authority. It must be accompanied by a notice in a prescribed form and evidence must be produced showing:

(a) That the notice has been published in the *London Gazette* and in two successive weeks in at least one newspaper circulating in the locality.
(b) If the abstraction would be from an 'inland water' (that is, not an underground source), that the notice has been served on navigation, harbour and conservancy authorities concerned (if any) and on any internal drainage board.

The notice must also state where the application with its maps and plans may be inspected. The public must be allowed to inspect them free of charge at any reasonable hour during a period of twenty-eight days after publication of the notice and any person may make representations in writing to the water authority during the twenty-eight-day period (1963 Act, s. 28).

Determination by the water authority. The water authority must not make a decision on the application until the twenty-eight-day period for representations is up. They must have regard to any representations made and to the reasonable requirements of the applicant. They must also pay regard to other factors, including the character of any inland water affected and the minimum flow needed for safeguarding public health and for meeting the requirements of existing lawful uses of the water, whether for agriculture, industry, water supply or other uses and the requirements of land drainage, navigation and fisheries (1963 Act, ss. 19 and 29).

In particular, the water authority must not grant a licence for an abstraction which would derogate from the right of existing licence holders, or from rights to abstract which are exempt from licensing (s. 29(2)). Should the water authority derogate from such rights it will not invalidate the licence but the authority may be sued for damages for breach of statutory duty (s. 50).

Appeals and public inquiries. if the abstraction licence is refused or the applicant is dissatisfied with the conditions in a licence, he may appeal to the Secretary of State within twenty-eight days. All objectors must have a copy of the appeal served on them by the water authority and they may make further representations. The Secretary of State may hold a public inquiry, or give the applicant or the water authority an opportunity for a hearing before a person appointed by him, and must do so if the applicant or the water authority so request. The Secretary of State's decision on the appeal shall be final (1963 Act, s. 39).

Protective effect of licence. If any action is brought against a person in respect of an abstraction it shall be a defence to prove the abstraction was in accordance with an abstraction licence. The licence does not, however, protect the holder from an action for negligence or breach of contract (1963 Act, s. 31). Abstraction without a licence, when one is required, does not of itself give a neighbour a legal claim against the abstractor, or allow the neighbour to interfere with an easement to abstract water (*Cargill* v. *Gotts* [1981] 1 All E.R. 682).

Changes in occupation. The abstraction licence in respect of a holding will be in the name of the occupier. If he dies or there is a change in occupation for any other reason, the new occupier must notify the water authority within one month and he will then become the licence holder. Otherwise the licence will become invalid (1963 Act, s. 32).

Minimum acceptable flows. The 1963 Act imposed a statutory duty on the then river authorites (a duty inherited from them by the water authorities) to fix 'minimum acceptable flows' for each inland water which could be subject to licensing, so that there might be a yardstick for the proper determination of abstraction licence applications (s. 19). There has been a total dereliction of this duty. Not a single minimum acceptable flow has been set and the Government has announced an intention to abolish this duty.

Spray irrigation. Where a licence authorises spray irrigation, the water authority may impose temporary restrictions on the quantity of water that may be abstracted for this purpose in times of exceptional shortage of rain, or other emergencies. The water authority in so doing must be even-handed between abstractors from the same source of supply who are not far distant from each other (1963 Act, s. 45).

Impounding water

Most water authorities charge less if water is taken only in the winter when water is plentiful, and landowners are thereby encouraged to construct reservoirs. Before building a reservoir, or, say, a fishing lake, the water authority should be consulted because 'impounding works' may not be carried out without a licence (1963 Act, s. 36). Contravention is an offence punishable by a fine (s. 49).

'Impounding works' means any dam, weir or other works in an inland water whereby water may be impounded and any works for diverting the flow of an inland water in connection with the construction or alteration of such works (s. 36(6)).

IMPOUNDING LICENCE

The procedures for obtaining impounding licences and for appeals against the determination of the water authority are the same as for abstraction licences (described above).

FISHING LAKES

An owner who wishes to stock a lake or reservoir with fish should note that he will need the prior consent of the water authority before introducing any fish or spawn into the water. Contravention is an offence punishable by a fine (Salmon and Freshwater Fisheries Act 1975, s. 30 and Schedule 4). Further, the Wildlife and Countryside Act 1981 makes it an offence to release, or allow to escape, into the wild, certain non-indigenous creatures, including zander, wels and pumpkinseed fish (s. 14 and Schedule 9).

Land drainage works

OFFICIAL WORKS

There are two kinds of authorites with land drainage powers:

(a) Water authorities.

(b) Internal drainage boards.

The water authority's land drainage function is principally to ensure that watercourses designated as 'main rivers' carry away water efficiently. A 'main river' is one designated as such by the Minister of Agriculture (Land Drainage Act 1976, s. 9). The water authority has no power to do land drainage works to other watercourses. You can ascertain what are 'main rivers' in any area by inspecting maps at the offices of the Ministry of Agriculture or the water authority.

An owner or occupier cannot compel a water authority to undertake drainage works to a main river, but the Minister of Agriculture and the Secretary of State can direct the authority to carry out their land drainage (and other) functions (1963 Act, s. 107). Further, these Ministers can hold a public inquiry to see whether a water authority have failed to perform any of their functions and if they are found to be in default can take steps to see the default is remedied (1963 Act, s. 108).

INTERNAL DRAINAGE BOARDS

Internal Drainage Boards administer internal drainage districts within water authority areas, being districts which benefit, or avoid damage, from drainage operations (Land Drainage Act 1976), s. 6 (2)). An I.D.B. has power to carry out works of maintenance or improvement to any watercourse in its district.

Again, an I.D.B. cannot be compelled by an owner or occupier to do drainage works.

For powers of compulsory acquisition see 1976 Act, s. 37.

LIABILITY OF DRAINAGE AUTHORITIES

Water authorities and I.D.B.s are not legally liable for damages for failing to carry out drainage works. On the other hand if any 'injury' is caused to any person by works carried out by a drainage authority they 'shall be liable to make full compensation' (1976 Act, s. 17(5) and ss. 33(4) and 44(3)).

'Injury' has its usual legal meaning of loss or damage. The High Court has held that the injury caused must be 'an actionable wrong' for compensation to be payable (*Marriage* v. *East Norfolk Rivers Catchment Board* [1949] 2 All E.R. 1021). If there is any unncessary damage or interference with rights (such as fishing rights) it will be an actionable wrong (*Welsh National Water Development Authority* v. *Burgess* (1974) R.V.R. 395 (C.A.)).

Where a watercourse is widened or dredged the drainage authority may 'appropriate and dispose of any matter removed' without payment for it (1976 Act, s. 33(1)). The Act says matter may be deposited on the banks over such width as to enable it to be removed and disposed of in one mechanical operation, in which case the authority *may* pay compensation 'if they think fit' (s. 33(2)–(4) – not a satisfactory way of seeing fair play. The Lands Tribunal, awarding damages and interest in such a case, held that trees removed for widening a watercourse were not 'matter' and must be paid for, and although no payment was to be made for the land taken by the widening, as it was 'matter', compensation was payable to the farmer for the loss of use of it (*Pattinson* v. *Finningley I.D.B.* (1971) 22 P. & C.R. 929).

DRAINAGE REVENUE

Water authorities raise revenue for land drainage by a precept on local authorities and on I.D.B.s. They can also make a general charge on occupiers of agricultural land and buildings within I.D.B. districts (1976 Act, s. 48) and may make a special drainage charge on such occupiers where special schemes are approved by the Minister of Agriculture (s. 50).

Within its district an I.D.B. raises revenue by an owners' and an occupiers' drainage rate. Both are levied on the occupier, who, if he is a tenant, is entitled to deduct the owners' rate from the rent (1976 Act, s. 63).

GETTING NEIGHBOURS TO DO DRAINAGE WORKS

A landowner or occupier can apply to the Agricultural Land Tribunal for an order requiring another owner or occupier to cleanse, or remove obstructions from, a ditch. The Tribunal will consider whether work is necessary to the ditch to enable the applicant to drain or improve his land and may, after hearing the parties, make such order as it sees fit. If it orders a person through whose land the ditch passes or abuts to do work to the ditch and he defaults, after three months the Ministry of Agriculture or a drainage authority may carry out the work and recover the cost from the defaulter (1976 Act, ss. 40–44).

The Tribunal also has power, on the application of an owner or occupier, to authorise him to go on to another's land to carry out drainage works or to alter a ditch. The authorised person can then, after giving at least seven days' notice, enter with men and equipment to do the necessary work. If the land is unoccupied, it must be left secure against trespass, and in any case, if unnecessary damage is done he will be liable to pay compensation (1976 Act, s. 44).

There is also power for the Minister of Agriculture to authorise an owner or occupier to enter on the land of others who object to desirable drainage works, to do the works. If there is an objection to the application, the Minister must first hold a public inquiry (1976 Act, s. 93).

A drainage authority has power of its own volition, by notice, to require landowners and occupiers to remedy the condition of watercourses (1976 Act, s. 18).

Chapter 11
Public Health

Abbreviations in this Chapter:
'1936 Act' – Public Health Act 1936.
'1961 Act' – Public Health Act 1961.
'1974' Act' – Control of Pollution Act 1974.

Introduction

District Councils as public health authorities have statutory powers and duties designed to safeguard the health of persons living in the neighbourhood. Some of these powers and duties have been taken over by water authorities under recent legislation (see Chapter 10). The principal public health statutes are the Public Health Act 1936, the Public Health Act 1961, and the Control of Pollution Act 1974, which replaces some of the provisions of the 1936 Act.

Among their many duties, public health authorities have to deal with statutory nuisances. It has been said that a nuisance is incapable of definition, but the word itself is descriptive. A statutory nuisance is one which a local authority may deal with summarily under powers in the Public Health Act 1936, s. 92. These powers are in addition to any common law remedies for nuisance (for example an action in the courts). In order to count as a statutory nuisance, the nuisance in question must affect the public health. It is a question of fact for the magistrates whether in any case there is a nuisance or not.

Abatement of a statutory nuisance

Where a local authority is satisfied that a statutory nuisance exists, they must serve an abatement notice on the person causing it. If he cannot be found, they must serve the notice on the owner or occupier of the premises on which the nuisance arises. Where it is clear that the owner or occupier is not causing the nuisance, the local authority may enter and abate it, and take steps to prevent it recurring. If a nuisance arises from a structural defect, for example from an unsafe wall of a house, the notice must be served on the owner of the premises.

If an abatement notice is disregarded, the local authority can make a complaint to a magistrates' court, which has powers to make a nuisance order, and to impose a fine. The local authority has power to abate the nuisance if the order is not complied with, and to recover their reasonable costs.

Some examples of statutory nuisances

Where premises are allowed to become prejudicial to health or a nuisance, they will amount to a statutory nuisance. Premises include buildings and land, and also tents, vans and sheds. Prejudicial to health means injurious or likely to cause injury to health. The provision is intended to deal with cases where the premises are decayed, dilapidated, dirty or out of order (*R.* v. *Parlby* (1889) 22 Q.B.D. 520).

Any animal kept in such a place or manner as to be prejudicial to health or a nuisance, can be dealt with under the 1936 Act, s. 92. It has been held that noisy animals are not covered by the section (*Galer* v. *Morrisey* [1955] 1 All E.R. 380), but that pigs kept so near to houses as to cause a nuisance from effluent would be. An accumulation or deposit may amount to a nuisance. An accumulation of manure from stables which was so offensive that the neighbours had to keep their windows shut was held to be a nuisance (*Smith* v. *Waghorn* (1863) 27 J.P. 744).

Even in the country a pond, ditch, gutter or watercourse may become foul or otherwise in a state prejudicial to health. It has been held that mere failure by a landowner to keep a natural stream flowing freely from obstruction brought about by natural causes was not an act of default for which he could be held liable under the 1936 Act, s. 92.

WELLS, TANKS, CISTERNS AND WATER BUTTS
Any of the above used for the supply of water for domestic purposes which is so situated, made or kept, that it is liable to contamination. may amount to a statutory nuisance, and may be dealt with summarily under the 1936 Act.

A local authority also has power to close or restrict the use of water from a polluted well, tank or other source of supply not vested in them. The water in question must be or be likely to be used for domestic purposes, or the preparation of food or drink for human consumption. The local authority may obtain a magistrates' court order directing that the well, or other source of water supply, must be permanently closed, or cut off, or the water used for certain purposes only. Any user of the water can be heard by the court, and the court may order the water to be analysed at the cost of the local authority. If an order to restrict or close a supply is not complied with, the local authority may do the work and recover their reasonable cost.

SEPTIC TANKS AND CESSPOOLS

While septic tanks require little attention, cesspools need to be emptied regularly and sometimes frequently. Local authorities have powers to arrange for the emptying of cesspools for which they are entitled to make a reasonable charge. Occupiers of premises not connected to the public sewer are not liable to pay the sewerage charge collected with the general rates (*Daymond* v. *Plymouth City Council* [1975] 3 All E.R. 134). If the contents of a cesspool soak or overflow, the local authority or water authority may serve a notice on the person responsible, requiring him to take steps to put the matter right. There is a right of appeal to a magistrates' court against such a notice.

A local authority has powers to examine a cesspool which is prejudicial to health or a nuisance, and may open the ground for that purpose.

RUBBISH

Rubbish in the countryside may consist of litter, rubbish dumps left by trespassers, abandoned vehicles left in bridleways or woodlands, or waste deposited in old pits and quarries with the owners' consent.

Litter. It is an offence under the Litter Act 1983 to drop or deposit and leave litter in, into or from any place in the open air to which the public are entitled or permitted to come without payment. The Act is difficult to enforce because litter is often scattered or deposited after dark from minor roads or bridleways.

Rubbish dumps. Where rubbish such as rubble, waste paper, crockery and metal has accumulated on land and spoils the country or rather the amenities of the neighbourhood, the local authority may remove it. However, an authority must first serve notice on the owners and occupiers of the land stating their intention to remove the rubbish, so as to give owners and occupiers an opportunity to serve notice on the authority that they intend to remove the rubbish themselves, or to appeal to a magistrates' court against the order (Public Health Act 1961, s. 34).

Local planning authorities have powers to deal with waste land which is in such a condition that it seriously injures the amenity of the area. The authority may deal with any garden, vacant site or other open land, by serving on the owner and occupier a notice requiring him to abate the injury. If the works of abatement are not done within the period specified by the notice, the authority may enter and do the work in default, and recover their reasonable expenses from the owner.

Abandoned vehicles and other refuse. Abandoned vehicles left by trespassers in the countryside became such a nuisance that powers to deal with them were introduced by the Civic Amenities Act 1967, now consolidated in the Refuse Disposal (Amenity) Act 1978. It is an offence to abandon a motor vehicle on any land in the open air or on any other land forming part of a highway. The rule applies to part of a motor vehicle, and also to any other refuse abandoned on such land. The penalty is a substantial fine, and in the case of a second or further offence, a term of imprisonment can be imposed.

In order to discourage dumping of vehicles, local authorities have a duty to provide dumps for the deposit of refuse other than business refuse. These dumps must be reasonably accessible to local residents. However, in spite of the provision of dumps, there still may be cases where old vehicles are left on land in the open air or on part of the highway. In such cases, the local authority has a duty to remove them. First they must serve a notice of intention to remove on the occupier of the land if there is one. The authority will not be entitled to remove the vehicle if the occupier objects. Second, unless the vehicle is on a public carriageway, the authority will not be obliged to remove it if it would be too costly to do so. Local authorities have similar duties to remove other rubbish abandoned on land in the open air, or on part of a highway, and they may sell refuse removed by them. In the case of abandoned vehicles and other rubbish, the authority may recover the costs of removal from any person who put them on the land, that is if they can find him.

Disposal of waste

Owing to the demand for land on which to dispose of waste products, and to some cases where poisonous chemicals have been deposited on land, a system for licensing disposal of controlled waste and forbidding unlicensed disposal of such waste was introduced by the Control of Pollution Act 1974. 'Controlled waste' means household, industrial and commercial waste. Farmers are sometimes approached by contractors looking for land on which to deposit waste. Controlled waste should not be deposited on land unless the land is occupied by a person holding a licence under the Act. Licensing regulations have been made under the Act, and there are certain exemptions under those regulations. As a rule, planning permission is required for depositing waste, and where it is required, a disposal licence will not be issued unless planning permission has been obtained.

Sewers and drains

Under the Water Act 1973, water authorities now have a duty to provide and maintain public sewers and sewage disposal works (see Chapter 10). They have taken over duties and powers which used to be exercised by local authorities under the Public Health Act 1936. Water authorities may construct a sewer under a street, or under or over any land not forming part of a street, but they must give reasonable notice of their intention to do so, to every owner and occupier of the land in question. There is no prescribed period of notice but it is suggested that at least twenty-eight days' notice in writing should be given. The notice should state the dimension of the sewer and the situation proposed. It may be, but need not be, accompanied by a map. There is no provision in the 1936 Act for objections by owners and occupiers. Provided the water authority complies with the Act, an owner or occupier cannot object to the laying of a sewer in his land.

Compensation for statutory works

A water authority is not obliged to purchase land or an easement in order to lay a sewer. However, it has been held that the laying of a sewer in land amounts in substance to a compulsory acquisition of land. The 1936 Act, s. 278 provides that the authority must make full compensation to any person who has sustained damage resulting from the statutory works. The section does not restrict compensation to injury or physical damage done to the land. For example in *Lingke* v. *Christchurch Corporation* [1912] 3 K.B. 595), a sewer authority was made to compensate the plaintiff for obstruction of his access by the carrying out of sewerage works. The section provides for compensation for almost every kind of loss caused by the carrying out of the works by the authority. Thus, in addition to a claim for the permanent depreciation of the land, the claim for compensation can include surface damage to the land, loss of crops, damage to trees, cost of reseeding and returfing, interference with land drainage, and any other loss due to the inability of the authority to re-instate the land to its former condition (see also Chapter 5).

APPEALS TO LANDS TRIBUNAL

An authority is not obliged to pay compensation before entering and carrying out the work. If there is a dispute about the amount of compensation, it may be referred to the Lands Tribunal. In settling the matter, the Tribunal must take into account the amount, if any, by which the value of the claimant's land has been enhanced by the construction of the pipe. The amount of the enhancement can be set-off against the compensation payable under the 1936 Act, s. 278. Where a sewer is put through agricultural land, and there is no planning permission for development, there is unlikely to be any enhancement. Claims for enhancement should not be admitted unless it is certain that the sewer will lead immediately to an enhancement in the value of the land. Speculation about possible future development of the land is not sufficient to sustain a claim for enhancement. If there is no right connect to the sewer, there will not be any ehancement.

COMPENSATION FOR MINERALS

Where a sewer has been laid under the Public Health Act 1936, the sewer authority has a right of support for the pipe by statute. The owner of the subsoil must not jeopardise the support by the removal of the minerals without first giving notice of his intention to the authority. Within thirty days of receiving such notice, the authority may require that the minerals should be left unworked, but if they do, they must pay compensation. If the sewer authority does no take any action within thirty days of receiving the notice, the minerals may be worked, but only in a responsible manner.

Water supply

Water authorities have a duty under the Water Act 1973, s. 11 to supply water in their area. Local authorities have a duty to see to it that the water supply in their area is wholesome and sufficient and to notify the water authority when the supply is inadequate or unwholesome. Any dispute on the matter between the authorities must be settled by the Secretary of State for the Environment, who also has power to decide whether a supply of water can be provided at reasonable cost. He may be asked to decide such a question at the request of a local authority, or ten or more local government electors.

In areas where there is a statutory water company, the water authority can supply water through the company.

The water authorities' powers to lay water mains are regulated by Schedule 3 to the Water Act 1945, modified by Order made in 1977. A water authority has powers to lay a water main in private land on giving notice to every owner and occupier of the land. As in the case of sewers, the authority does not have to get the consent of the owner or occupier of the land, nor does the authority need to acquire land or an easement. Compensation is payable to every person interested in the land for any damage or injury done to the land as a result of the laying, repair, alteration, renewal or removal of the main. Compensation is payable not only for surface damage to the land, but also for depreciation in its value resulting from the laying of the main and its presence in the land. Disputes as to the amount of compensation payable for a water main may be referred to the Lands Tribunal.

Although it is not necessary for a water authority to acquire easements for mains, there have been cases where easements have been acquired. Also, even where an easement is not acquired, it is the practice to pay compensation for depreciation in the value of the land at so much per yard or metre.

Building over a water main or sewer

There is no express prohibition on buildings over sewers or water mains in either the Public Health Act or the Water Act. However, the Building Act 1984, s. 18 provides that where plans of buildings are deposited with the local authority for approval under the building regulations, and it is proposed to erect a building over a sewer or drain, the authority must reject the plans unless it is satisfied that in the circumstances it could properly consent to the erection of the building either with or without conditions.

In practice it would usually be difficult or even impossible to build over sewers and water pipes without interfering with them or damaging them, because pipes are often laid at depths of two to three feet. Anyone who damages a sewer or main in the course of a building operation would risk being held liable in negligence or in trespass and damage.

In the case of *Abingdon B.C.* v. *James* [1940] All E.R. 446, it was held that the authority's right of access to water mains for inspection, maintenance and repair had been prevented by the building of two houses over the mains. The authority was entitled to an injunction to prevent the houses remaining on the land.

Chapter 12
Liability of the Occupier of Land

Abbreviations in this Chapter:
'1957 Act' – Occupiers' Liability Act 1957.
'1971 Act' – Animals Act 1971.
'1984 Act' – Occupiers' Liability Act 1984.

Impact of land use

The use of land can have a far-reaching impact – on the occupier, invited visitors, neighbours, the endless band of officials authorised to enter land, trespassers and the general public. A glance through the law reports is enough to demonstrate the almost limitless ways in which unpleasant happenings can lead to claims against the occupier of land. The courts and the legislature try, with varying success, to balance the scales of justice between people who suffer injury, loss or discomfort on or near the land of others and the occupiers who can reasonably expect them to take some care of themselves.

This chapter summarises the legal duties owned to others by occupiers of land. It is mostly concerned with the laws of negligence, nuisance and animal trespass.

INSURANCE
The importance of taking out adequate insurance against civil liability cannot be over-stressed. Accidents will happen, and they can be very expensive.

Negligence

Everyone has a duty to take reasonable care not to harm others. Negligence is a breach of the duty to take that care. Where damage is caused to someone by another's failure, by act or omission, to take the care the law expects of him, the injured party will have a claim. Damage here generally means physical harm to persons or property, but it may include loss caused to someone. The standard of care expected is that of an ordinary reasonable man (whom judges used to believe could be found 'on the Clapham omnibus'). The degree of care owned may range from the highest (where dangerous animals are kept) to almost none (for example to a burglar). Being a commonsense test, it depends on the circumstances, all of which need to be taken into account in each case.

OCCUPIERS' LIABILITY ACTS 1957 and 1984

The 1957 Act sets out the legal duty owed by the occupier of premises to 'visitors' (as defined in the Act) and the 1984 Act the duty owed 'to person other than his visitors'. 'Premises' in the Act does not have its colloquial meaning. It includes land and waters and in effect means the property of the occupier.

Visitors and non-visitors. The visitors the 1957 Act applies to are invitees or licensees 'using the premises' – that is, anyone entering with permission or at the direct invitation of the occupier, or who enter under a right conferred by law (1957 Act, s. 2(6)). This covers most people lawfully on property, from relatives of the occupier, to tradesmen and the gas man. It includes persons lawfully using a private right of way, but not users of a public footpath (*Greenhalgh* v. *British Railways Board* [1969] 2 Q.B. 286). The 1984 Act applies to anyone else on the property, such as trespassers and lawful entrants under an access order or agreement made under the National Parks and Access to the Countryside Act 1949, except for persons using the highway (1984 Act, s. 1(7)), and it does not apply 'to any person in respect of risks willingly accepted as his by that person' (s. 1(6)). Neither Act, therefore, applies to users of a footpath across the occupier's land.

Duty owed to 'visitors'. The 1957 Act lays down that the occupier owes what it calls 'a common duty of care' to all visitors, except in so far as he can and does alter this obligation towards particular entrants by agreement. The duty is described as follows:

'The common duty of care is a duty to take such care as in all the circumstances of the case is reasonable to see that the visitor shall be reasonably safe in using the premises for the purposes for which he is invited or permitted by the occupier to be there (1957 Act, s. 2(2)).

Elaborate protection of visitors is not expected. It is very much a duty of sweet reasonableness. If there are dangers on the land the visitor might get to, the occupier should either guard them or give sufficient warning of them. Although a warning will be taken into account in judging whether there is liability for a mishap (1957 Act, s. 2(4)(a)), a warning will not always be sufficient protection. The Act admonishes occupiers to expect children to be less careful than adults (s. 2(3)(a)).

The occupier is allowed to rely on visitors to take reasonable care of themselves, especially if the visitors are adults. Where someone is engaged to enter the property to exercise his calling (for example an agricultural worker, or a steeple-jack) the occupier is not expected to protect him against the risks that go with the job (s. 2(3)(b)). Further, if a visitor suffers damage due to faulty work by an independent contractor engaged by the occupier, it will normally be the contractor who is liable and not the occupier, provided it was reasonable for the occupier to assume a competent job had been done by him (s. 2(4)(b)).

Agreements changing the duty. The 1957 Act allows the occupier to 'restrict, modify or exclude' the common duty of care, if he is free to do so. It is therefore open to him to say 'enter at your own risk' unless the Unfair Contract Terms Act 1977 applies. This 1977 Act applies 'only to business liability'. This will usually be where there is a contract entered into for a consideration. Where the 1977 Act applies the occupier cannot effectively exclude by agreement liability for death or personal injury resulting from his negligence. Any agreement or notice to that effect would be a nullity. As regards a notice excluding liability for loss or damage (other than death or personal injury), this would be effective only if 'it should be fair and reasonable to allow reliance on it having regard to all the circumstances obtaining when the liability arose or (but for the notice) would have arisen' (s. 11(3)). This leaves it all rather uncertain, as fair and reasonable tests always will.

The 1977 Act, however, proved too much of a deterrent to allowing recreational access to land where a business was carried on, such as agriculture or forestry. The 1984 Act therefore amended the 1977 Act. The effect is that occupiers may restrict, modify or exclude their duty of care towards anyone entering the land for recreational or educational purposes, unless granting the access 'falls within the business purpose of the occupier' (1984 Act, s. 2). For example, someone running a safari park could not say 'enter at your own risk', but a farmer allowing orienteers on to his land, could.

Duty owed to non-visitors. Where the 1984 Act applies, namely when 'persons other than visitors', such as trespassers (see above) enter land, a duty is owed to the entrant if (a) the occupier knows of a danger on his land, or has reasonable grounds to believe it exists; (b) he knows, or has reasonable grounds to believe, the entrant is in, or may come into, the vicinity of the danger, and (c) 'the risk is one against, which, in all the circumstances of the case, he may reasonably be expected to offer the other some protection' (s. 1(3)). Where those three conditions apply the duty owed 'is to take such care as is reasonable in all the circumstances of the case to see that he (the entrant) does not suffer injury on the premises by reason of the danger concerned' (s. 1(4)). 'In an appropriate case' the duty may be discharged by giving a warning or discouragement from incurring the risk (s. 1(5)). 'Injury' here means death or physical or mental injury (s. 1(9)) not loss or damage to property (s. 1(8)).

Again, therefore, the law is somewhat vague, depending on ordinary concepts of what is reasonable. It may well be that in most cases the occupier would not have to safeguard the *adult* trespasser beyond putting up notices warning of the more torrid and accessible dangers. If, however, *child* trespassers can be expected, greater safeguards must be taken to see that they do not fall foul of hazards. Warnings will not be enough if, for example, there are gaps in protective fences children can get through (see *Pannett* v. *P. G. Guiness & Co. Ltd* [1972] 2 Q.B. 599 – child burned on demolition site). Before the 1984 Act, where a child got through a gap in a railway fence and was injured on the line, British Rail were held liable (*British Railways Board* v. *Herrington* [1972] A.C. 877) but not when an adult did so (*Titchener* v. *British Railways Board* [1983] 3 All E.R. 770). Occupiers should remember small boys are attracted to certain hazardous places such as waters and derelict buildings.

EMPLOYEES

The occupier has specific obligations for the well-being of his employees laid down in statutes and regulations, in particular the Health and Safety at Work, etc. Act 1974 and 'health and safety regulations' made under it (see s. 15 for health and safety regulations generally; s. 30 for agricultural health and safety regulations; s. 47 for extent of employer's civil liability).

LANDLORDS

A landlord not in possession may be liable for dangers he himself creates (*Anns* v. *Merton London Borough* [1978] A.C. 728) and under the Defective

Premises Act 1972 a duty is placed on the landlord to take reasonable care to protect the tenant and 'all persons who might reasonably be expected to be affected' from defects if the landlord is responsible for maintenance and repairs under the tenancy, provided he knew or ought to have known of the defects (s. 4(1) and (2)).

Nuisance

The law of nuisance gives a right to an injured party to claim a remedy at law regardless of negligence. If the owner or occupier of land creates a nuisance it is no defence to prove reasonable care was taken. Nuisance at law is what one might expect, namely causing a substantial nuisance to others. A nuisance may be public or private, as explained below. Typical of nuisances a countryman may suffer from or create are pungent smells, excessive noise from, for example, bird-scarers or saw mills, tree roots undermining neighbouring property and pollution of air, earth or water.

SOME TYPES OF NUISANCE

Livestock. In farming districts some noise and smell from animals is to be expected and to some extent must be tolerated. However, it has been held that a large number of pigs kept in premises adjoining a village street amounted to a nuisance (*A. G.* v. *Squire* (1906) 5 L.G.R. 99). Farmers who are tempted to make use of farm buildings near residential areas for intensive keeping of livestock should note that decision. In a later case where extensive poultry farming was carried on in a rural area which was also residential, it was held by the court that a large number of cockerels crowing in the early morning amounted to a nuisance (*Leeman* v. *Montagu* [1936] 2 All E.R. 1677).

Smells. A typical agricultural nuisance is smell from manure or effluent. In *Peaty* v. *Field* [1970] 2 All E.R. 895 manure spread on the land near a housing estate was held to amount to a statutory nuisance under the Public Health Act 1936, but the farmer could have been held liable at common law if a neighbour's ordinary health and comfort was affected by the smell. In *Bone* v. *Seale* [1975] 1 All E.R. 787 neighbours did bring an action for damages against a farmer because of the smell of pig manure, and the boiling of pig swill. In spite of undertakings made by the farmer, he did not take steps to make the smell less offensive. Substantial damages were awarded.

Game. An owner or occupier of land over-run with rabbits is not liable at common law for the damage they may do on adjoining land, unless he brought the rabbits on to the land or deliberately encouraged them. Under statute he may be required to clear the land of rabbits, if a rabbit clearance order is made under the Pests Act 1954, or a notice is served on him by the Minister of Agriculture under s. 98 of the Agriculture Act 1947.

Pheasants bred for sport are sometimes regarded by farmers as pests. As between landlord and tenant, the farmer's remedy is compensation under the Agricultural Holdings Act 1986, s. 20 (see p. 179 below). There must be mutual reasonableness between the owner or tenant of sporting rights and the owner and occupier of the land (*Peech* v. *Best* [1931] K.B.1). As between the farmer and his neighbour, overstocking with game can give rise to liability for damages (*Farrer* v. *Nelson* (1885) 15 Q.B.D. 528). An occupier who kept pheasants on his land was held not liable to the adjoining owner when the pheasants increased naturally because it was a good season for them (*Seligman* v. *Docker* [1948] 2 All E.R. 887).

Straw and stubble burning. Especial care must be taken by farmers who burn straw or stubble, particularly near boundaries or highways. They are strongly advised to comply meticulously with the N.F.U. Code. In some years there has been such an outcry against nuisance from burning that byelaws to control it have been made in many areas and Parliament has passed the Highways (Amendment) Act 1986. There is therefore a risk of committing criminal offences. The local byelaws should be checked before burning.

Under the Highways (Amendment) Act 1986 it is an offence to injure, interrupt or endanger a user of a highway (being a carriageway) by lighting a fire on or over it, or on land off the highway, or directing or permitting the fire to be lit.

Civil liability for damages can arise where neighbouring property (such as a hedge) is burnt, or if a substantial nuisance from smoke or smuts is caused. Smoke causing an accident on a road can be a public nuisance and negligence (*Tysoe* v. *Davis, The Times,* 21 June 1983).

PUBLIC NUISANCES

A public nuisance is in essence criminal, not giving the individual a right of action except in special circumstances. It is an interference with the rights, comfort or convenience of the public or a section of the public. Normally it is for the Attorney General or the local authority to take proceedings to stop it on behalf of the public. It is open to an individual to take an action only if he suffers some particular damage over and above that suffered by the public generally. For example, obstructing the highway is a public nuisance, but an individual may sue if it obstructs access to his house, or prevents customers getting to his shop.

Control by local authorities. Local authorities have powers to deal with 'statutory nuisances' by serving abatement notices, which, if disregarded may be followed by nuisance orders made by a magistrates' court under the Public Health Act 1936 Part III (see Chapter 11). Local authorities have powers to deal with noise nuisance under the Control of Pollution Act 1974 Part III. Contravention of a noise abatement notice is an offence, but if the noise is caused in the course of a trade or business it is a defence 'to prove that the best practical means have been used for preventing, or for counteracting the effect of, the noise' (s. 58(5)).

PRIVATE NUISANCES

A private nuisance is 'an unlawful interference with a person's use or enjoyment of land or some right over, or in connection with it' (*Read* v. *Lyons & Co. Ltd* [1945] K.B. 216). As with negligence, the tests the courts apply in deciding whether something is an actionable nuisance are tests of reasonableness and commonsense. A balance must be struck between the right of the occupier to do what he likes on his own property and the right of his neighbour not to have the enjoyment of his property interfered with (*Sedleigh-Denfield* v. *O'Callaghan* [1940] A.C. 880). People must expect farm land to be farmed and expect it to smell and sound like the countryside – but within reason.

THE MAIN RULES

From the mass of decided cases the following main principles emerge.

(a) *The nuisance must be unreasonable* if it is to justify a legal remedy. The interference must be substantial. There must be too much of it. A farmer is allowed a manure heap, for example, but in *Bland* v. *Yates* (1914) 58 Sol. Jo. 612 it was held to be too much of a good thing and 'a serious inconvenience and interference with the comfort of the occupiers of the dwelling-house according to notions prevalent among reasonable English men and women'.

(b) *The claimant must have a legal interest in the land.* The essence of private nuisance is an interference with another in respect of his property – so that the wife of the tenant of land was once held to have no claim when vibrations from a neighbour's engine caused a water tank in their house to fall on her (*Malone* v. *Laskey* [1907] 2 K.B. 141). Today she would probably be held to have a sufficient possessory title.

(c) *The character of the locality must be considered where no physical damage is done.* Where there is actual injury to property, it is no defence that the offending act was in keeping with the usual activities of the neighbourhood (*St. Helens Smelting Co. Ltd* v. *Tipping* (1865) 11 H.L. Cas. 642). However, where the complaint is interference with enjoyment of property with no physical injury done to it, the character of the neighbourhood must be considered 'and in particular with regard to the trades usually carried on there' (*Polsue and Alfieri* v. *Rushmer* [1907] A.C. 121) to decide whether it is reasonable to allow the thing complained of to continue.

(d) *It is no defence that the claimant moved to the nuisance.* Provided the offending act would be a nuisance in any event, the claimant is not barred from a remedy even if he knew it existed before he went there. This is well illustrated by *Miller* v. *Jackson* [1977] Q.B. 966. The plaintiff bought a house on the edge of a cricket field and was awarded £400 damages for the nuisance of sixes being hit into his garden.

(e) *Excessive sensitivity does not give rise to a claim.* If the complaint arises only because of the particularly sensitive nature of the complainant or his activities, no remedy may be claimed. On the other hand, if the nuisance would be actionable in any event, the claimant will not be barred from an action because of any over-sensitiveness on his part (*McKinnon Industries Co. Ltd* v. *Walker* [1951] 3 D.L.R. 577, 581), and a right to the high degree of light required for a greenhouse may be acquired by long enjoyment (*Allen* v. *Greenwood* [1979] 2 W.L.R. 187).

(f) *It is no defence that injury was due to a natural cause.* When a landslip from Barrow Mump, a National Trust property, damaged a neighbouring house down the hill, the National Trust were held liable even though the slip was not their fault but a quirk of nature, as they were aware of the danger (*Leakey* v. *National Trust* [1980] 1 All E.R. 17). This case overruled *Giles* v. *Walker* (1890) 24 Q.B.D. 656, which had held there was no liability for thistles spreading from a field onto neighbouring land. Liability can arise from encroachment by tree roots, and if the tree is in the highway verge the highway authority will be liable (*R.* v. *Brophy, The Times,* 26 June 1981). There will be no liability for an 'Act of God' (see p. 172 below).

REMEDIES

The usual remedy for a private nuisance is an action for damages and, if appropriate, an injunction, but self-help is allowed within limits.

Damages. Where loss or injury is proved the claimant is entitled to damages, whether the claim is for negligence or nuisance. It is often made up of two elements:

(a) Loss or damage which can be quantified (such as loss of crop, or the cost of replacing broken window panes after a game of cricket).
(b) Compensation for matters involving no pecuniary loss (such as for pain and suffering and loss of libido).

An important and often difficult rule to apply is that the damage claimed must not be too remote from the wrong complained of. The wrong must be the direct, though not necessarily the immediate, cause of the damage. The general test adopted is that any damage that the defendant could be reasonably expected to have foreseen as a result of the wrongdoing can be recovered (*The Wagon Mound (No. 2)* [1967] A.C. 667). In cases of strict liability (see below) the remoteness rule is less stringent.

Injunctions. An injunction is a court order to stop it. To disregard an injunction is a contempt of court likely to be visited with condign punishment. Unlike damages, there is no entitlement to an injunction as of right.

It is a discretionary remedy the court will grant where justice so requires. In the cricket ball nuisance case (*Miller* v. *Jackson*, above) the court refused an injunction so that cricket could continue. Injunctions may be granted not only to restrain existing wrongs but also threatened unlawfulness. An interim injunction will sometimes be made, especially in an emergency, to preserve the status quo until the legal implications can be properly examined by the court.

Self-help. The injured party is allowed to abate a nuisance, but it is a remedy to be resorted to with caution. It is only too easy for the wronged person to put himself in the wrong. If he resorts to self-help the method adopted to remove the nuisance must be a sound one doing no unnecessary harm or damage and the abater must not cause a riot. Like Shylock, he must go thus far and no further. He must not enter the offender's land if it can be avoided and only after notice if entry is unavoidable. If these rules are followed, you may, for example, cut off tree branches overhanging your land (*Lemmon* v. *Webb* [1896] A.C. 1) though the branches may not be kept.

Where something potentially dangerous is kept on land the law allows the occupier hardly any excuse to avoid liability should it escape from the land. This rule of strict liability was expounded in the case of *Fletcher* v. *Rylands* (1866) L.R. 1 Ex. 265 (confirmed in the House of Lords under its more familiar name of *Rylands* v. *Fletcher* (1868) L.R. 3 H.L. 330) in the famous words of Mr Justice Blackburn:

> The person who for his own purposes brings on his land and collects and keeps there anything likely to do mischief if it escapes, must keep it in at his peril, and, if he does not do so, is *prima facie* answerable for all the damage which is the natural consequence of its escape.

In that case water escaped from a reservoir and flooded a mine – the court held there was strict liability. The rule only applies to non-natural uses of land – some special act of bringing something onto the land or accumulating something there.

Defences. The law recognises only three possible defences if damage is caused by the escape:

(a) That the escape was due to the claimant's own fault; or
(b) It was an 'Act of God' – that is, a happening so unusual nobody could be expected to anticipate it, such as an earthquake; or
(c) It was caused by a stranger over whom the occupier had no control.

Statutory authority. In reality there can be a fourth defence, because the courts have held that where a body carries out duties required by statute, the statutory body is not liable for any damage caused in the absence of negligence, unless the statute expressly removes this exoneration. This can work unfairly. For example, a sewerage authority is not liable, in the absence of negligence, for damage caused by leakage from its sewers (*Smeaton* v. *Ilford Corporation* [1954] Ch. 450).

Straying animals

A typical case of strict liability (see above) arises when a dangerous animal escapes from captivity and causes damage or injury. Much of the law about escaping animals is now to be found in the Animals Act 1971. Section 2(1) imposes strict liability on the keeper of an animal of a 'dangerous species' for any damage caused by it. This is defined as animals of a species which is not commonly domesticated in the British Islands and when the animals are fully grown are likely to cause severe damage, or else any damage they may cause is likely to be severe (s. 6(2)). The Dangerous Wild Animals Act 1976, provides for licensing the keeping of the animals listed in it (S.I. 1981 No. 1173 substituted a new list). See also the Zoo Licensing Act 1981.

BULLS

A bull is a *domestic* animal and therefore not one of a dangerous species. The courts always had the odd notion that bulls have at heart a kindly disposition and they must not be classed as likely to attack man (see *Lathall* v. *Joyce & Sons* [1939] 3 All E.R. 854). Liability therefore turns, as with all other animals not of a dangerous species, on whether a particular animal was known to have a vicious tendency before it attacked.

ANIMALS NOT OF A DANGEROUS SPECIES

The keeper is liable for damage done by these animals if three conditions are fulfilled:

(a) The damage done is of a kind the animal was likely to cause if not restrained, or which if caused by such an animal was likely to be severe.
(b) The likelihood of that kind of damage is due to a characteristic in the particular animal which is not normally found in animals of the species, or is not normally found except at particular times or in particular circumstances.
(c) Such characteristic was known to the keeper of the animal (or a servant in charge of the animal).
Thus, where a horse with a known nervous and unpredictable temperament injured a groom leading the horse into a horsebox, the groom recovered damages (*Wallace* v. *Newton* [1982] 2 All E.R. 106).

Where the keeper is the head of a household, knowledge of the characteristic by another keeper of the animal in the household under sixteen years of age, counts as his knowledge (1971 Act, s. 2(2)).

STRAYING LIVESTOCK

The 1971 Act also imposes strict liability for damage done to land or property on land (though not for personal injuries) by trespassing livestock

(s. 4). 'Livestock' here means cattle, horses, asses, mules, hinnies, sheep, pigs, goats, poultry, and deer not in the wild state (s. 11).

If the damage is the fault of the person suffering it there is no liability, but it must be remembered that in the absence of an express obligation to the contrary, it is the occupier's responsibility to keep in his own animals and not his neighbour's duty to fence them out.

The Act gives the occupier of land the right to detain and sell livestock straying on his land if nobody is in control of them. As with other remedies of self-help (see above) and because special rules have to be complied with (set out in s. 7), it is a remedy to be resorted to with caution and usually best avoided.

ANIMALS STRAYING ON TO OR OFF THE HIGHWAY

The 1971 Act changed the law by creating a legal duty of care to prevent animals straying on to the highway (s. 8(1)). This is not strict liability, so that if, for example, an accident was caused by a horse bounding out of a field on to a road, the person in charge of the horse would be liable if it was due to carelessness, but not if reasonable care had been taken to prevent it.

Further, if there is a right to place animals on common land, or on a town or village green or on land where fencing is not customary, the 1971 Act states it is not a breach of the duty of care to place the animals on such unfenced land.

Nor is there strict liability when animals lawfully on the highway stray from it and cause damage (s. 5(5)). In the absence of negligence there will be no liability for the damage. A famous incident is recorded in *Tillett* v. *Ward* (1882) 10 Q.B.D. 17, where a bull being driven to market along the street plunged into an ironmonger's shop and by the time it was extricated, forty-five minutes later, not a little havoc had been wreaked. It was held the shopkeeper's claim failed as no negligence was proved. The law is the same today.

DOGS WORRYING LIVESTOCK

The keeper of a trespassing dog is liable if it kills or injures livestock (1971 Act, s. 3). The farmer is allowed to protect his livestock from a worrying dog by shooting it, provided it is on his land (or his employer's) and the dog is in the act of worrying livestock, or is about to, and there are no other reasonable means of preventing or ending the attack. He may also shoot the dog if it has been worrying livestock, has not left the vicinity, is not under anyone's control and there is no practical means of ascertaining who the owner is (or he reasonably believes he cannot find out). He should notify the

Police within forty-eight hours of shooting the dog, because if he does so he will have a defence against a civil action if one is brought against him.

'Livestock' has the meaning given above with the addition of pheasants, partridges and grouse while in captivity (s. 11).

Boundary disputes

Boundary disputes between occupiers of farmland are not uncommon. There may be doubt about the ownership of a boundary hedge or ditch, or the position of a boundary where two farms are divided by a river. An occupier who has relied on his neighbour's hedge to keep his own animals off his neighbour's land may find the hedge has been removed and not replaced.

There is no common law duty to mark a boundary on the ground by a fence, hedge or ditch, but in practice boundaries are usually marked by some more or less permanent barrier. An owner would often mark his boundary by a hedge, planting the hedge on his land on a mound of earth dug out from a ditch made by him on his side of the boundary. From this practice has come the common law presumption that where a property is bounded by a hedge and ditch, the hedge and ditch are owned by the same owner. However, the common law presumption may be rebutted by evidence to the contrary.

In the case of a dispute, the deeds of both parties should be examined, and it should be possible for the solicitors on both sides to settle the dispute without resort to the courts. The common law presumption as to ownership of a hedge and ditch may be rebutted by the deeds, though the deeds may not define the boundary precisely. In some cases the Ordnance Survey practice of marking the boundary down the centre of a hedge or ditch is adopted, and in those cases, the boundary would follows the Ordnance Survey practice (*Davey* v. *Harrow Corporation* [1957] 2 All E.R. 305).

Where land adjoins a highway, the general rule is that the boundary runs down the centre of the highway. However, that would not be the case where a highway authority had actually purchased the land on which to lay out a highway.

Where land adjoins the sea shore, the general rule is that the boundary runs along the line of the medium high tide between the ordinary spring and neap (lowest) tides. In the case of tidal rivers the boundary between the bed of the river and the adjoining land is generally the line of medium high water mark.

Where land abuts onto a non-tidal river the boundary is generally a line down the middle of the stream. In the cases where land is gradually added by the river to the land at the side of it, that land belongs to the owner of the land on that side, and the boundary remains down the centre of the river. The rule does not apply where a river suddenly changes course, for example, as a result of an extraordinary storm or landslip (see *Hindson* v. *Ashby* [1896] 2 Ch. 1).

Although there is no common law duty to put a fence or hedge on a boundary, there may be a contract to do so. Under an agricultural tenancy agreement, a tenant will generally be liable to keep his landlord's fences in repair under an express covenant or under the statutory repairs clauses made under the Agricultural Holdings Act. Where land has been sold a purchaser may have a covenanted to erect and maintain fences against the vendor's remaining land.

A duty to fence may arise by prescription (*Jones* v. *Price* [1965] 2 All E.R. 625), but the fact that one party has repaired a boundary fence for many years does not necessarily mean that he is under a duty to do it. He may have done it for his own convenience.

Owners of young plantations often fence the land to protect the young trees and when the trees mature the fences are allowed to fall into disrepair. Owners of animals kept in adjoining land then complain that their animals wander into the woods. However, it is the duty of an owner of animals to keep them on his own land. He is not entitled to rely on his neighbour's fences unless he can show that the neighbour has a duty to fence, for example, under contract or statute.

Trespass

Entry onto the land of another without consent or lawful authority is trespass. If a trespasser declines to leave the land on request, the occupier does not break the law if he physically ejects him, provided no more force is used than is reasonably necessary. It is generally advisable, however, not to resort to this remedy. A trespasser may be sued even if no damage has been done. Normally there is no point in taking proceedings unless significant damage has been done, or the offender is a persistent trespasser or further trespass is threatened. The Court may be asked to award damages and/or issue an injunction to restrain trespass in the future.

Trespass is not a crime of itself. Unless an offence is committed Police help will not be forthcoming. Wilful trespass in numbers, for example by 'hippy convoys', has presented severe problems for occupiers. The Public Order Bill aims to strengthen the hands of the Police by creating new offences and, at the time of writing, it is expected the Government will introduce new clauses giving the Police new powers to deal with the problem. It is also intended to review the Rules of the Supreme Court to enable occupiers suffering wilful mass trespass to get an eviction order quickly.

PUBLIC ORDER ACT 1986

Section 39 of the Public Order Act 1986 gives powers to the police to order trespassers to leave land. A person who fails to leave land when directed to do so, commits an offence. The new provision applies where two or more persons have entered land as trespassers, and have the common purpose of residing there. Reasonable steps must have been taken by or on behalf of the occupier to ask them to leave, and the trespassers must have done damage to property on the land or used threatening behaviour, or have brought twelve or more vehicles on to the land. A trespasser who fails to leave the land as soon as reasonably practicable or who re-enters as a trespasser within three months of a direction to leave being given, commits an offence. Land is defined in the section to include farm buildings and scheduled monuments.

Chapter 13
Sporting

This chapter deals with the right to hunt for, take and kill animals, birds or fish in the wild.

Sporting rights

SPORTING RIGHTS ARE PROPERTY

Sporting rights are legal property. From this simple point of jurisprudence much flows. The rights may be owned together with or separately from the land. They may be sold or leased or given away. They may be defended against trespass or interference (*Mason* v. *Clarke* [1975] A.C. 778) and on a compulsory acquisition must be paid for. They can be rated. In exercising the rights the owner, whether or not on his own land, must comply with the laws concerning close seasons, protected species, cruelty to animals, licensing and firearms.

WHO MAY EXERCISE SPORTING RIGHTS?

To carry out sporting lawfully a person must own the sporting rights or have obtained the necessary right or permission from the owner by lease or licence. In certain places the public can exercise public fishing rights.

Who owns the sporting rights over any land is a question of history. If they have never been disposed of separately from the land, the landowner will own them.

FARM TENANTS

When land is leased to a tenant, the tenant obtains a tenancy of the sporting rights as well unless the landlord reserves them (*Pochin* v. *Smith* [1887] 52 J.P. 4) or they are owned by someone else. The usual practice in a farming tenancy is for the landlord expressly to reserve them.

Game damage. The tenant of an agricultural holding can claim compensation from his landlord if his crops are damaged by any wild animals or birds the landlord (or anyone claiming under him) has the right to kill, provided the tenant has not permission in writing to kill them (Agricultural Holdings Act 1986, s. 20). The compensation can only be claimed if notice in writing is given to the landlord within one month after the tenant first became, or ought reasonably to have become, aware of the damage and a reasonable opportunity is given the landlord to inspect the damage before the crop reaping begins (or if the damage is to a gathered crop, before it is removed). Written particulars of the claim must also be given 'within one month after the expiry of the year in respect of which the claim is made', the 'year' ending on 29 September, unless otherwise agreed. In cases where the landlord does not have the sporting rights, he is entitled to be indemnified by whoever has them against claims for game damage. See also Chapter 12 for game damage nuisance.

Occupier's right to ground game. No matter who may have the sporting rights the occupier of the land has the right conferred by the Ground Game Act 1880 to take and kill ground game (namely, hares and rabbits) so that he may protect his crops. Any agreement to relinquish this right will be null and void. If someone else has the right to ground game (for example the landlord or the shooting tenant) it will be exercised along with the occupier of the land.

Where the occupier does not have the shooting rights, his right to take ground game under the 1880 Act is subject to restrictions. Only the occupier and one other person, who must be authorised by the occupier in writing, may use firearms to kill ground game under the Act. More than one other may be authorised (in writing) by him to take ground game by other methods (for example, with snares or ferrets), but a person can only be authorised by the occupier if he is:

(a) A member of his household resident on the land; or

(b) An employee in ordinary service on the land (for example a farm worker); or

(c) Any one other person *bona fide* employed by the occupier for reward to destroy ground game.

Any such authorised person must, if required by anyone having a concurrent right to ground game, produced his written authority.

A person with a right of common over common land does not have the benefit of an occupier under the Act, nor does a person who occupies 'for the purpose of grazing or pasturage of sheep, cattle or horses for not more than nine months' (s. 1). The occupier and one other person authorised by him may now shoot ground game at night with the written authority of any one other person so entitled (Wildlife and Countryside Act 1981, Schedule 7).

Rating. The when and how of rating sporting rights is explained in Chapter 4.

Shooting and game laws

Abbreviations in this part of this Chapter:
'1831 Act' – Game Act 1831.
'1981 Act' – Wildlife and Countryside Act 1981.
'1968 Act' – Firearms Act 1968.

NO PUBLIC RIGHT OF SHOOTING
In English law there is no such thing as a public right of shooting.

The foreshore. The foreshore belongs to the Crown unless it was disposed of by the sovereign before Magna Carta 1215 stopped such things. There are only two public rights over Crown foreshore, namely fishing and navigation and no public rights over private foreshore. However, shooting is tolerated by the Crown over much foreshore, provided others are not endangered, but the wildfowler cannot claim to shoot as a public *right*. (*Fitzhardinge (Lord) v. Purcell* [1908] 2 Ch. 139).

Shooting on highways. Again there is no public right to shoot on roads and rights of way (*R. v. Pratt* (1855) 4 E. and B. 860) the public right being limited, in the phrase beloved of lawyers, to 'passing and repassing'. The soil of a highway, however, belongs to the adjoining landowner, so it is permissible for the property owner to shoot from the highway provided an offence is not committed against the Highways Act 1980, s. 161, which forbids the discharge of a firearm within fifty feet of the centre of a highway comprising a carriageway if in consequence 'a user of the highway is injured, interrupted or endangered'.

PROTECTION OF WILDLIFE
The protection of birds and animals in the wild is now dealt with largely by the Wildlife and Countryside Act 1981 and various Acts dealing with game and deer.

Birds. All birds in the wild are protected in Great Britain at all times, except in so far as the 1981 Act (and the game laws, see below) allow specified species to be killed or taken (1981 Act, ss. 1–8 and Schedules 1 and 2). It is generally a defence to a charge if a bird is killed of necessity to prevent serious damage to livestock, foodstuffs for livestock, crops, vegetables, fruit, growing timber or fisheries, or to prevent spread of disease (1981 Act, s. 4(3)). Other exceptions include certain official action (s. 4(1)) and acts of mercy to disabled birds (s. 4(2)).

The general scheme for the protection of birds is to create offences of killing, injuring or taking birds, and of taking, damaging or destroying nests or eggs, and of having possession of birds, nests or eggs. There are also offences concerned with selling them. Birds listed in Part I of Schedule 1 of the 1981 Act are protected by special penalties at all times, those listed in Part II of Schedule 1 are protected by special penalties in the close season for the bird in question. The close seasons are in s. 2(4), but may be varied (s. 2(5)). There are also special penalties for disturbing Schedule 1 birds while they are nesting, building nests or are dependent young (s. 1(5)). Birds listed in Part I of the Schedule 2 may be killed or taken only outside the close season. Those in Part II of Schedule 2 may be killed or taken by authorised persons at all times. 'Authorised persons' include the landowner or occupier (s. 27(1)). The Schedules may be varied by order.

Provision is made for temporary orders protecting birds that could otherwise be shot, for up to 14 days (s. 2(6) and (7)) and for specifying areas of special protection (s. 3). Schedule 2 birds may not be killed on Sundays or Christmas Day in Scotland nor on Sundays in England and Wales where orders are made prohibiting it (s. 2(3)).

Animals. The 1981 Act affords protection to certain species of wild animals (see ss. 9–12 and Schedules 5–7) none of which would normally be the prey of legitimate sportsmen. Rabbits and hares are dealt with by the game laws (see below). The Deer Act 1963 provides a close season for four species of deer, and prohibits the use of certain weapons (see firearms section below). The Deer Act 1980 creates offences against poaching and in relation to sales of venison.

GAME LAWS

'Game'. Unfortunately 'game' means something different in nearly every Act referring to it. The definition must be checked in each case.

There is no close season for killing rabbits and hares, but game, including hares, may not be killed on Sundays or Christmas Day (Game Act 1831, s. 3).

Game licences. It is an offence to pursue, take or kill any game, or to assist in doing so, or to use any dog, gun, net or other engine or instrument for the purpose (including a snare – *Allen* v. *Thompson* (1870) L.R. 5 Q.B. 336) without a game licence. 'Game' here means pheasants, partridges, grouse, blackgame, moorgame, hares, woodcock, snipe, rabbits and deer (1831 Act, s. 23 and Game Licences Act 1860, s. 4).

None of the following need a game licence: beaters or persons assisting a licence holder, provided they are not carrying guns; persons killing ground game under the Ground Game Act 1880 (see above pp. 179–180); the owner or occupier killing hares or deer on enclosed lands; or taking rabbits at a warren on enclosed lands; persons coursing or hunting hares with dogs or hunting deer with hounds; anyone required by the Minister of Agriculture to kill game by order under the Agriculture Act 1947.

Anyone paying the licence duty is entitled to a game licence as of right. It is obtainable from Post Offices. The licence comes into force from the moment it is issued and it cannot be retrospective. It is not transferable.

Dealing in game. Anyone dealing in game must have two licences, one from the local authority and the other an excise licence. This does not mean the owner of shooting rights holding a game licence cannot sell the bag, lawfully shot, to the butcher. He may do so provided the butcher is a licensed dealer in game.

POACHING

The laws against poaching are in a muddle. No attempt has been made to rationalise or consolidate the laws, which are still mainly found in the venerable Night Poaching Acts 1828 and 1844, the Game Act 1831 and the Poaching Prevention Act 1862 with a little grafting on to them in modern times (Game Laws (Amendment) Act 1960, Deer Acts 1963–1980 aided and abetted by the Firearms Act 1968). We have attempted to unravel the laws by the tables in Appendix B setting out the powers of the police and others against poachers under the various statutes.

Theft. Although sporting rights are property, the owner of land or sporting rights does not own creatures in the wild until they are killed or otherwise brought under his control, even if he reared them. Ownerless things cannot be stolen. Hence the laws against poaching are not about theft but about criminal trespass and possessing the booty or the wherewithal for poaching. However, pheasants in a rearing pen are owned and can be stolen. The Theft Act 1968 summaries the position thus: 'wild creatures, tamed or untamed, shall be regarded as property, but a person cannot steal a wild creature, unless ... it has been reduced into possession by or on behalf of another person' (s. 4(4)).

Night poaching. Poaching at night is a more serious offence, carrying heavier penalties, than day-time poaching. Under the Night Poaching Acts 1828 and 1844 it is an offence unlawfully by night to take or destroy game or rabbits on open or enclosed lands, highways or gateways. It is a separate offence to enter or to be present on open or enclosed lands (though not a highway) with a gun, net or instrument for taking or destroying game.

'Night' means from one hour after sunset to one hour before sunrise. 'Game' in these Acts means hares, pheasants, partridges, grouse, heath or moorgame, blackgame and bustards.

Although the second mentioned offence cannot be committed by being on a highway after game, a person with a gun on a highway helping others poaching on private land is equally guilty of the offence (*R.* v. *Whittaker* (1848) 17 L.J.M.C. 127).

Three or more armed persons entering land at night for taking game or rabbits commit a more serious offence under the 1828 Act, s.9 with heavier penalties.

Day-time poaching. It is an offence under the 1831 Act, s. 30 to trespass in pursuit of game (as defined for night poaching above), woodcock, snipe and rabbits in the day-time. An extra fine may be imposed if violence is used. The offence is committed by the trespassers whether or not they find or take any quarry. Any defence to an action for trespass will be a defence to a charge under s. 30.

A farm tenant not holding the sporting rights cannot, of course, trespass on the land he occupies, but he commits an offence under the 1831 Act, s. 12 if he unlawfully takes or kills game (*Spicer* v. *Bernard* (1859) 23 J.P. 311), though not if the booty is woodcock, snipe or ground game.

Armed trespass. Although in some cases it may be doubtful whether the court will be convinced that a plausible defendant was in pursuit of game when trespassing, it is often overlooked that it is an offence under the Firearms Act 1968, s. 20(2) to trespass on land with a firearm. No poaching motive need be proved for a conviction of armed trespass. The Act also makes it an offence to carry a loaded gun in a public place (s. 19). A highway, including a public footpath or bridleway, is a public place.

Powers of arrest, seizure, etc. The steps the police and private persons may take against poachers are summarised in Appendix B. It will be observed that in some instances owners or occupiers of land and their gamekeepers have powers of arrest, and in some circumstances they may seize from poachers their equipment (but not guns), dogs and any game taken. They (and anyone else having the sporting rights) may require a day poacher to give his name and address and they may require him to leave the private land. An offender who refuses may be arrested.

The power of arrest should be exercised with discretion by the private citizen, possibly with less circumspection by the police. The powers of arrest by constables have been drawn together and clarified in the Police and Criminal Evidence Act 1984, Part III.

FIREARMS

Offences under the Firearms Act 1968 which may be committed by poachers, and the steps that can be taken against offenders under the Act are included in the tables in Appendix B.

Firearm and shotgun certificates. A firearms certificate is not needed to possess lawfully a shotgun, but a shotgun certificate is needed (1968 Act, s. 2(1)). A shotgun is defined as a smooth bore gun, other than an air weapon, with a barrel not less than twenty-four inches in length. It is an offence to give a shotgun to anyone under fifteen years of age and a person under fifteen years of age may have an assembled shotgun with him only under the supervision of an adult over twenty-one (unless the gun is covered so that it cannot be fired). A person under seventeen is not allowed to buy or hire a shotgun or its ammunition. Shotgun certificates are issued by the police.

It is an offence for anyone to have in his possession, or to purchase or acquire a firearm (other than a shotgun or air weapon), or ammunition for one, without holding a firearm certificate in force at the time (1968 Act, s. 1). The police must issue a firearm certificate to an applicant for one, provided they are satisfied he has a good reason for possessing the firearm, he will not be a danger to public safety or to the peace and he is not disqualified from having a firearm (s. 27). An officer serving in Germany was properly refused a firearms certificate, where he owned a house in Warwickshire but let it and did not reside in it (*Burditt* v. *Joslin* [1981] 3 All E.R. 203).

Firearms and deer. The Deer Act 1963 makes it an offence to use for the purpose of killing, injuring or taking deer any smooth bore gun; or any rifle less than 0.240 inches calibre or muzzle energy less than 1700 ft lbs; or any air gun, air rifle or air pistol; or any cartridge for a smooth bore gun; or any arrow, spear or similar missile; or any rifle bullet other than soft-nosed or hollow-nosed; or any missile containing poison, stupefying drug or muscle-relaxing agent. It is also an offence to possess any firearm or ammunition for the purpose of committing an offence against the Deer Act or to possess any trap, snare, poisoned or stupefying bait, net, arrow, spear or prohibited missile for this purpose.

OTHER WEAPONS, SNARES, ETC.
The 1981 Act has elaborate provisions prohibiting the use of certain weapons and devices for killing, taking, stunning, frightening or decoying birds (s. 5) and animals (s. 11).

Fishing

Abbreviation in this part of the Chapter:
'1975 Act' – Salmon and Freshwater Fisheries Act 1975.

PROTECTING FISHING RIGHTS
Fishing rights and fisheries being property, the owner can take legal action against any person, body or authority unlawfully interfering with them. An unauthorised interference with them is a trespass. Over the centuries the courts have been strong in affording protection. They will give a remedy (usually damages and an injunction) against such people as polluters (for example *Pride of Derby Angling Association* v. *British Celanese* [1953] 1 All E.R. 179 where the well-named pub angling club got injunctions against British Celanese, Derby Corporation and the British Electricity Authority), unauthorised canoeists (*Rawson* v. *Peters* (1973) E.G.D. 259) or careless land drainage authorities (*Welsh National Water Development Authority* v. *Burgess* (1974) R.V.R. 395).

Who owns the fishing? Tracing the ownership of fishing rights can involve difficult and expensive investigations through the labyrinths of history. Fortunately this is rarely necessary because the law provides aids by way of certain presumptions which prevail unless the contrary is proved. These presumptions are:

(a) *The owner of the river bed owns the fishing.* The law presumes the owner of the soil of a non-tidal river or a lake owns the fishing rights. Likewise the owner of the fishing is presumed to own the soil (*Hanbury* v. *Jenkins* [1901] 2 Ch. 401). Ownership of the soil and fishing can be severed but the burden of proof is on the party seeking to rebut the presumption.

(b) *The ownership to the middle line of the river.* Where a non-tidal river bounds land, the law presumes the riparian owner on each side owns the soil (and therefore the fishing) up to the middle line of the river. The middle line is taken at the mean average flow of the river (*Hindson* v. *Ashby* [1896] 2 Ch. 1). Again the presumption can be rebutted by evidence to the contrary, but the burden of proof is on the party seeking to displace the presumption. Where both banks are in the same ownership the owner is presumed to have the fishing rights across the river. Where the middle line is the boundary however, it is permissible to cast across it in Scotland (*Fotheringham* v. *Kerr* (1984) 48 P. and C.R. 173) and a similar flexibility is likely in English law (see *Long* v. *Gowlett* [1923] 2 Ch. 177, 196.

(c) *The ownership by the Crown of tidal rivers.* The law presumes the Crown owns the soil (and therefore the fishing) of tidal rivers and of the foreshore. This can only be rebutted if the soil or the fishery was disposed of by the King before Magna Carta 1215 stopped the sovereign doing such things. Riparian ownership of land adjoining a *tidal* river or estuary does not therefore raise a presumption of ownership to the middle line. A river affected by tides is tidal up to the point where ordinary sea tides cease to cause the flow of water to fluctuate both horizontally along the banks and vertically up and down them (*West Riding of Yorkshire River Board* v. *Tadcaster U.D.C.* (1907) 97 L.T. 436).

(d) *Long use and the Prescription Act 1832.* The legal presumption that if a right is exercised for many years without challenge it is lawful provided it could have had a legal origin, applies to fishing rights. It is known as a prescriptive right. Without going into all the complexities of the law of prescription, in outline it is this. The common law presumes the right is lawful and absolute if it has been exercised 'since time immemorial'. It also presumes the right has been enjoyed since time immemorial if there has been twenty years' uninterrupted and unchallenged use, but this presumption could be rebutted by proof that at any time after the year 1189 (Richard I's accession) the right did not exist. Also, a claim to a prescriptive right can always be defeated by proving the right was enjoyed under a grant which had been, or could be, ended (for example, a grant for a fixed period). The Prescription Act 1832 modified the law by providing that:

(i) When fishing rights have been enjoyed continuously for thirty years, the claim to them can no longer be defeated by proving there was a time since 1189 when they did not exist, but it could be defeated by disproving the rights in other ways.

(ii) When fishing rights have been enjoyed continuously for sixty years, the claim can be defeated only by production of a written grant showing the right has ended or could be revoked.

Neither the public nor any other 'fluctuating and uncertain body' can obtain fishing rights by prescription (*Goodman* v. *Saltash Cpn.* (1882) 7 App. Cas. 633).

FISHING LEASES

Fishing may be leased with or without land. If it is leased separately from the land it should be by formal deed and the same applies if there is a sale or grant of fishing rights (*Neil* v. *Duke of Devonshire* (1882) 8 App. Cas. 135). As mentioned above, when there is a lease of land with no reservation of the fishing rights, they are deemed to be included in the lease unless there is clear evidence that the parties intended the contrary (*Browne* v. *Marquis of Sligo* (1859) 10 I Ch.R. 1).

It is open to the landlord to include stipulations in the letting regulating the way the fishery is to be enjoyed, such as restricting the number of rods, imposing bag and size limits and prohibiting assignment or subletting. If the fishing is let separately from the land (for example to an angling club) it is prudent for the parties to agree and include in the lease the means of access, fishing paths and where the anglers may park vehicles.

It should be noted that rating liability can sometimes be avoided by granting a licence instead of a lease (see Chapter 4).

PUBLIC FISHING

The public has a right to fish in tidal waters and on the foreshore, except where the right was lost before Magna Carta 1215 by the King granting the rights away (probably with the land). For the extent of tidal water in rivers see p. 186 above. The foreshore is the land between the high and low water marks of ordinary tides, discounting spring and neap tides (*Att.-Gen.* v. *Chambers* (1854) 23 L.J. Ch. 662).

On the other hand the public has no right to fish non-tidal waters and cannot get it (*Smith* v. *Andrews* [1891] 2 Ch. 678). On some major rivers public fishing is tolerated in non-tidal reaches and in some places the public have fished for centuries, but even so the acquiescence of the riparian owners does not turn the concession into a right.

Access. The right of public fishing in tidal waters does not automatically carry a right of access across adjoining land. Permission is required to get to the water if there is no public right of way, or else access must be by boat.

CLOSE SEASONS

The 1975 Act (s. 19 and First Schedule) lays down detailed laws specifying standard close seasons (and weekly close times for salmon and trout) for taking freshwater fish, trout and salmon, with differing close seasons for rod and line fishing, putts and putchers (baskets) and other means (mostly nets). All this is not set out here because in reality the fishery owner and the angler will need to consult the fishery byelaws to ascertain the close season in any place.

Byelaws. Each water authority has a duty to make close season byelaws for its area. The byelaws can depart from the standard close seasons, provided they comply with the minimum periods required by the Act (Schedule 1, para. 3). The close seasons often vary in different parts of a water authority area.

Compliance with close seasons. It is an offence to fish for, take, kill or attempt to take or kill a fish during the close season for using the method employed for taking the species of fish concerned. However, there are periods when, say, putts and putchers are forbidden for taking salmon, but rod and line fishing is allowed.

It is no defence for the landowner or occupier to plead he was fishing on enclosed waters on his own land (unless it is an excepted case, see below).

Salmon. The minimum close season for rod and line fishing is ninety-two days and the weekly close time must be at least forty-two hours.

Trout. The minimum close season for rod and line fishing for trout other than rainbows is 153 days and the minimum close time (only for rod and line) is forty-two hours.

Rainbow trout. The rule for rainbows is odd. There need be no close season, but if one is made by byelaws it must be at least ninety-three days.

Freshwater fish. 'Freshwater fish' in the 1975 Act means 'any fish living in fresh water exclusive of salmon and trout and of any kinds of fish which migrate to and from tidal waters and of eels' (that is, coarse fish; s. 41). As with rainbows, the close season may be dispensed with, but if there is one it must be at least ninety-three days. Nearly always it is the standard close season between 14 March and 16 June (you can fish on both dates mentioned, but not in-between).

Exceptions. With the permission of the water authority or the Ministry of Agriculture, salmon and trout may be taken during the close seasons for artificial propagation or for some scientific purpose, or, in the case of trout, for stocking waters.

Freshwater fish and rainbow trout have special exceptions:

(a) They may be removed by the owner or occupier during their close seasons from any exclusive fishery where salmon or trout are specially preserved.

(b) They may be fished for (by rod and line only) with the previous written permission of the owner or occupier, in any such fishery.

(c) They make be taken for scientific purposes (no need for official permission).

(d) They may be taken for bait in any exclusive fishery with the written permission of the owner or occupier, or in any other fishery so long as no byelaw is contravened (1975 Act, s. 19 (3)–(5) and (8)).

Miscellaneous. There are special rules for eels (1975 Act, s. 19(6), (7) and (8); s. 2, and Schedule 1) and for the removal of fixed devices for taking salmon and migratory trout during the 'nets' close season (s. 20). There are also times when selling salmon and trout is prohibited, and when having possession of them for sale between certain dates is unlawful, unless the fish have been canned, frozen, pickled or otherwise preserved (s. 22). Restrictions on exporting salmon and trout are in s. 23.

UNCLEAN AND IMMATURE FISH

It is an offence 'knowingly' to take, kill or injure (or to attempt to) any salmon, trout or freshwater fish which is unclean or immature, though no offence is committed if the fish is taken accidentally and returned to the water with the least possible injury (1975 Act, s. 2).

'Unclean' means a fish about to spawn, or which has recently spawned but not yet recovered. 'Immature' means fish below the sizes specified locally by byelaws, or a salmon less than twelve inches from the tip of the snout to the fork of the tail.

FISHING LICENCES

It is an offence to fish for or take fish without a fishing licence in any water where a licence is needed for the fish concerned and the method used (1975 Act, s. 27). A fishing licence is always needed for salmon and trout fishing. There are still some places where a licence is not needed to fish for coarse fish.

Fishing licences are issued by the water authority. They fix the licence duties for waters in their areas. The Minister's approval is required if there is a written objection to a proposed duty. The duty differs from area to area and it usually varies for trout, salmon and freshwater fish licences. The licence will state what kind of fishing it authorises and for what kind of fish (separate licences are needed for rod and line, basket and net fishing) and the period of validity, which may be, for example, a day, week, month or year.

A rod and line licence also authorises the use with it of a gaff, tailer or landing net (s. 25(4)). A salmon fishing licence also authorises fishing for trout, and a salmon or trout licence also authorises fishing for freshwater fish and eels (s. 25(5) and (6)). The procedure the water authority must follow for fixing or altering licence duties is laid down in the 1975 Act, Schedule 2.

The points to note with relevance to fishing licences are:

(a) A fishing licence does not confer a right to fish. The angler must also have the fishing rights or the owner's permission to fish (1975 Act, Schedule 2, para. 16).
(b) A rod and line licence is not transferable (s. 25(2)), and it cannot take effect before the moment it is issued (*Wharton* v. *Taylor* (1965) 109 S.J. 475 (D.C.)).
(c) Anyone tendering the duty is entitled to a licence unless disqualified by a court for fishing offences, or unless an order has been made limiting the number to be issued (s. 26 and Schedule 2, para. 15).
(d) Production of licence. Any person holding (and producing) a fishing licence, or any constable or official bailiff, may require anybody found fishing to produce his licence and to give his name and address. Failure to comply is an offence (s. 35).

General licences. A person or association entitled to an exclusive right of fishing may be granted a general licence for the fishery under which the licence holder or any person authorised in writing by him (or by the secretary of the association) may fish there, subject to any conditions agreed with the water authority (s. 25(7)). The duty payable is negotiated with the water authority. A general licence is useful where the landowner wishes to allow guests to fish who may not hold fishing licences. The water authority may not withhold a general licence without a good reason (*Mills* v. *Avon and Dorset River Board* [1953] 1 All E.R. 382).

ILLEGAL FISHING METHODS

Prohibited instruments. It is an offence to use any of the 'instruments' or modes of fishing prohibited by the 1975 Act. The prohibited instruments are any firearm; an otter, lath or jack, wire or snare; a crossline or setline; a spear, gaff, stroke-haul, snatch or other like instrument; and a light. With the exception of gaffs and tailers, none of these instruments may be used for taking or killing salmon, trout or freshwater fish, nor may they be in the possession of anyone with the intention of so using them (s. 1). A gaff or tailer may be used as auxiliary to angling with rod and line, or be in possession for that purpose (s. 1(4)).

Definitions of the prohibited instruments are given in the 1975 Act. The instruments will be familiar to poachers. They are mainly devices for foul-hooking fish, or for running out baits or lures, or for leaving them across or in waters without rods.

Nets. The Act prohibits the shooting or working of any seine or draft net for salmon or migratory trout across more than three-quarters of the width of any water and there are restrictions on the size of mesh (s. 3).

Prohibited modes. It is an offence to throw or discharge any stone or other missile for the purpose of taking or killing, or facilitating the taking or killing of any salmon or trout or freshwater fish (s. 1(1)(c)). It is also illegal to use any fish roe for bait (s. 2); or to use any explosive or poisonous substance or any electrical device with the intent to take or destroy fish, unless it is done with the written permission of the water authority for scientific purposes, or for protecting, improving or replacing fish stocks (s. 5).

POACHING

Just as there are special statutory offences for poaching game because of difficulties about proving theft by poachers, as explained above (pp. 182–183) the same applies to illegal fishing. Offences are laid down by the Theft Act 1968, which deals separately with night and day-time poaching.

Night poaching. It is an offence unlawfully to take or destroy at night fish in a private fishery, or a water in which there is a private right of fishing. It is also an offence to attempt to. 'Night' is from one hour after sunset to one hour before sunrise. To some extent this is not only a night offence, because the Act states that the offence is committed if it is done (or attempted) in the day-time by a means other than angling (Theft Act 1968, s. 32(1) and Schedule 1, para. 2).

Day-time poaching. If the unlawful taking or destruction of fish, or an attempt, is done by angling in the day-time, a different offence is committed for which the penalties are ligher (Theft Act 1968, s. 32(1) and Schedule 1, para. 2).

Remedies against poachers. The old remedy of confiscating the poacher's tackle is no longer allowed, but 'any person' may seize for production in court anything the poacher has with him for taking or destroying fish, and the court may order forfeiture of it. Any person may also arrest without a warrant anyone caught committing the offence described above under 'night poaching' (including the non-angling offence by day), but not offenders poaching by angling in the day-time. The powers of fishery bailiffs are unaltered by the Police and Criminal Evidence Act 1984 (see above).

The poacher will also be a trespasser liable in the civil courts for an action for damages and an injunction.

The Salmon Act 1986 has created a new offence of 'handling' illegally taken salmon in suspicious circumstances, and provides for a scheme of dealer licensing to be brought in by order.

Water Authorities. Water authorities have fisheries responsibilities including a duty 'to maintain, improve and develop' the fisheries in their areas in consultation with statutory fishery advisory committees (1975 Act, s. 28). As noted in Chapter 10 it is proposed to privatise these authorities, the new W.S.P.L.C.s retaining their fisheries functions – how, and with what safeguards, remains to be seen.

Hunting

Trespass. It was once widely believed a hunt could cross land without permission. It cannot lawfully do so. Members of a hunt entering land without permission commit a trespass (*Paul* v. *Summerhayes* [1878] 4

Q.B.D. 9 (D.C.)) and a Master of Hounds, or other hunt official, may be held liable for trespass even if he does not enter the land himself (*Robinson* v. *Vaughan* (1838) 8 C. and P. 252) though not if entry was made against his will (*Baker* v. *Berkeley* (1827) 3 C. and P. 32). Although a Master of Hounds is only liable for trespass if he intends hounds to enter land unauthorised, or if he negligently fails to prevent it, persistent hunting close to land where it is effectively impossible to prevent hounds entering can be evidence of an intention to trespass (*League Against Cruel Sports* v. *Scott* [1985] 2 All E.R. 489). A member of a hunt holding no official position cannot be held responsible for the trespass of other hunters (*Paget* v. *Birkbeck* (1863) 3 F. and F. 683).

Trespass is also committed by allowing or sending hounds on to another's land without permission, even if no person enters the land (see *Read* v. *Edwards* (1864) 17 C.B.N.S. 245).

It is necessary, therefore, for a hunt to get prior consent from the occupiers before they can hunt over any land. This, of course, is the usual practice and arrangements are made about compensation for damage done.

Fresh pursuit. The Game Act 1831, s. 35, provides that the offences of trespassing in pursuit of game do not apply to anyone hunting with hounds (or coursing with greyhounds) in fresh pursuit of any deer, hare or fox already started upon some other land. Although the section gives a defence to a charge of poaching, it is no defence to an action for trespass (*Paul* v. *Summerhayes*, above).

APPENDIX A
Compensation for Agricultural Tenants' Improvements

As explained in Chapter 3, the tenant requires the landlord's consent to improvements listed in Part I of the Seventh Schedule of the 1986 Act, and the consent of the landlord, or the approval of the Agricultural Land Tribunal in lieu, to improvements in Part II of the Seventh Schedule. Without the required consent or approval no compensation is payable by the landlord. The items listed in the Seventh Schedule are as follows:

1986 Act Schedule 7

PART I: IMPROVEMENTS TO WHICH CONSENT OF LANDLORD REQUIRED
1. Making or planting of osier beds.
2. Making of water meadows.
3. Making of watercress beds.
4. Planting of hops.
5. Planting of orchards or fruit bushes.
6. Warping or weiring of land.
7. Making of gardens.
8. Provision of underground tanks.

PART II: IMPROVEMENTS TO WHICH CONSENT OF LANDLORD OR APPROVAL OF THE TRIBUNAL REQUIRED
9. Erection, alteration or enlargement of buildings, and making or improvement of permanent yards.

10. Carrying out works in compliance with an improvement notice served or an undertaking accepted, under Part VII of the Housing Act 1985 or part VIII of the Housing Act 1974.

11. Erection or construction of loading platforms, ramps, hard standings for vehicles or other similar facilities.

12. Construction of silos.

13. Claying of land.

14. Marling of land.

15. Making or improvement of roads or bridges.

16. Making or improvement of water courses, culverts, ponds, wells or reservoirs, or of works for the application of water power for agricultural or domestic purposes or of works for the supply, distribution or use of water for such purposes (including the erection or installation of any structures or equipment which form part of or are to be used for or in connection with operating any such works).

17. Making or removal of permanent fences.

18. Reclaiming of waste land.

19. Making or improvement of embankments or sluices.

20. Erection of wirework for hop gardens.

21. Provision of permanent sheep-dipping accommodation.

22. Removal of bracken, gorse, tree roots, boulders or other like obstructions to cultivation.

23. Land drainage (other than improvements falling within paragraph 1 of Schedule 8 to this Act).

24. Provision or laying-on of electric light or power.

25. Provision of facilities for the storage or disposal of sewage or farm waste.

26. Repairs to fixed equipment, being equipment reasonably required for the proper farming of the holding, other than repairs which the tenant is under an obligation to carry out.

27. The grubbing up of orchards or fruit bushes.

28. Planting trees otherwise than as an orchard and bushes other than fruit bushes.

APPENDIX B
Powers to Apprehend Poachers: Search, Seizure, Confiscation etc.

Table B. 1   Arrest

Firearms Act 1968 Police and Criminal Evidence Act 1984	Night Poaching Acts 1828 & 1844 Game Laws (Amt.) Act 1960 Police and Criminal Evidence Act 1984	Game Act 1831 Wild Creatures and Forest Laws Act 1971 Police and Criminal Evidence Act 1984
Offence Trespass on land with a firearm (s. 20). Carrying a firearm in public place (including highway) (s. 19). Failure to produce certificate (s. 48). A constable has powers of arrest under s. 25, Part III of the Police and Criminal Evidence Act 1984. A constable has powers of entry and search under s. 46, Firearms Act 1968. He has power to demand production of firearm certificate or shotgun certificate (s. 48, 1968 Act). If it is not produced, a constable may ask for the person's name and address. Failure to provide the information or providing false information is a ground for arrest.	Police constables have powers of arrest under the Police and Criminal Evidence Act 1984. Owners, occupiers, Lords of the manor, their gamekeepers and servants may apprehend offenders found on any land committing an offence under s. 1 of the 1828 Act. If pursuit is made, the offender can be apprehended in the place to which he has escaped (s. 2, 1828 Act). (S. 1 makes it an offence to take or destroy game or rabbits by night or enter land for taking game.) If an offender assaults a person trying to arrest him, he is liable to 6 months imprisonment, or a fine, or both (s. 2. 1928 Act). The Act also applies to taking rabbits or game on the highway – and adjoining owners, occupiers, etc. can arrest as above (1844 Act). The Game Laws (Amt.) Act 1960 gives police constables powers of entry for purposes of arrest under the Police and Criminal Evidence Act 1984.	Any person found trespassing on land in search of game in the daytime may be required to leave and give his name and address by any of the following: (a) the person who enjoys the sporting rights (b) the occupier (c) any gamekeeper or servant of either of the above (d) any police constable Any offender who refuses to give his name and address may be arrested by any of the above (ss. 31, 31A). A police constable has powers of entry under the Game Laws (Amt.) Act 1960, s. 2, for the purpose of ss. 31, 31A above and to arrest offenders under s. 25, Police and Criminal Evidence Act 1984.

Table B. 1   Arrest (cont.)

Deer Act 1963
Deer Act 1980

A constable may arrest without
warrant a person suspected of
committing an offence under the
1963 Act (s. 5) and for the
purpose may enter any land other
than a dwelling house.

A constable has similar powers of
arrest without warrant under s. 4
of the Deer Act 1980, and similar
powers of entry.

A constable has powers of arrest
where he suspects an offence is
being committed, under s. 25,
Police and Criminal Evidence Act
1984.

Table B. 2   Seizure of guns etc.

Firearms Act 1968	Night Poaching Act 1828 Game Laws (Amt.) Act 1960 Police and Criminal Evidence Act 1984	Game Act 1831
s. 47 Power of constables to stop and search. A constable who suspects that a person is committing armed trespass on private land under s. 20 may require him to hand over the firearm or any ammunition for examination. A constable may also search and detain a person he suspects is committing or about to commit armed trespass on private land under s. 20. The same powers may be exercised with respect to a person suspected of having a firearm in a public place under s. 19. A person convicted of an offence under ss. 19, 20, 48 may have his firearm forfeited by the court and his firearm certificate or shotgun certificate may also be cancelled (s. 52). s. 47(4). A constable has powers to stop and search vehicles which he suspects are being used for armed trespass under s. 20. s. 48(2). A constable may seize and detain firearm, ammunition and shotgun if a person refuses to produce his certificate. Powers of Search with Warrant A constable with a warrant granted under s. 46 may enter premises, if necessary by force, and search the premises or place and every person found there. He may also seize and detain any firearm or ammunition.	Where a person is apprehended in accordance with s. 25 of the Police and Criminal Evidence Act 1984 for an offence under ss. 1, 9 of the Night Poaching Act 1828, a police constable by or in whose presence he was apprehended may search, seize and detain any: (a) game or rabbits (b) gun, part of gun, or cartridges or other ammunition (c) nets, traps, snares, etc. (s. 4, 1960 Act, as amended by Schedule 6 of 1984 Act) If a person is convicted, the court may order the forfeiture of any or all of the above items.	s. 13. Lords of the Manor may appoint gamekeepers to act within limits of the manor. Such gamekeepers may be authorised to seize and take dogs, nets, and other engines and instruments for the killing or taking of game within the manor by persons not having a game licence. This does not give power to seize guns but includes snares. What is seized may be kept. s. 36. Game may be demanded from trespassers and seized if not delivered up when demanded. This right is for the person enjoying the sporting rights, the occupier of the land, and their gamekeepers and servants. Where a person is apprehended under s.31 (see note above), a police constable by or in whose presence he was apprehended may search him and seize any: (a) game or rabbits; (b) gun or part of a gun, or cartridges, or other ammunition; (c) nets, traps, snares etc. If the person is convicted, the court *may* order the forfeiture of any or all of the above items (s. 4 of 1960 Act).

Table B. 2   Seizure of guns etc. (cont.)

Deer Act 1963 Deer Act 1980	Poaching Prevention Act 1862 [as amended by Game Laws (Amt.) Act 1960]
Where a person is convicted of an offence under the Act, the court may order the forfeiture of any vehicle, animal or other thing used or capable of being used to take, kill or injure the deer (s. 6, 1963 Act), and any deer which was the subject of the offence. A constable may seize any vehicle, animal, weapon, etc. under s. 5, 1963 Act.	s. 2 Constable has power in any highway, street or public place to search any person he suspects has been poaching and has in his possession any poached game, gun, or part of a gun. A constable also has power to stop and search any vehicle which he suspects is carrying game, and if he finds game, gun or part of a gun, he can seize and detain them., By the Game Laws (Amt.) Act 1960, the section is made to apply to cartridges and other ammunition and to nets, traps, snares etc. Where a person is convicted under this section, a court may order forfeiture of game guns, etc. seized under the section (s. 3, 1960 Act).

Table B. 3   Fines and other penalties

Firearms Act 1968	Night Poaching Acts 1828 & 1844 [amended by Game Laws (Amt.) Act 1960 and Criminal Law 1977]	Game Act 1831 [as amended by Wild Creatures and Forest Laws Act 1971 and Game Act 1970]
Schedule 6. Part I Possessing etc. firearm or ammunition without firearms certificate. (s. 1) Summary – six months or a fine or both. On indictment – aggravated offence five years or fine or both in other cases three years or a fine or both.	s. 1 of 1828 Act. Taking or destroying game or rabbits by night or entering land for that purpose. Penalty: a fine (1977 Act Schedule I). s. 2 Assaults by persons committing offences under the Act –Summary – six months or a fine or both. (offence triable only summarily) (1977 Act, Schedule 12).	s. 3 Killing or taking game on Sunday or Christmas Day. Fine plus costs. Taking or killing game in the close season. Fine plus costs. For laying poison to kill game. Fine plus costs.
Possessing shotgun without certificate, (s. 2(1)) six months or a fine or both.		For killing or taking game without a licence. Fine plus costs (see also Game Licence Act 1860, s. 4).
Use of firearm to resist or prevent lawful arrest. On indictment life imprisonment (s. 17) or fine or both.	s. 9 Entering land with others armed and for the purpose of taking or destroying game or rabbits – summary – 6 months or a fine or both (1977 Act, Schedule 12).	Trespassing in the day time in search of game, woodcock, snipe, rabbits. Fine plus costs. Trespass as above by five or more persons. Fine plus costs s. 30.
Carrying loaded firearm in public place – s. 19 Summary – six months or a fine or both. Indictment (except for air weapon) five years or fine or both.	The above penalties applying to persons destroying rabbits or game at night, apply to persons destroying rabbits or game by night on any public road, highway, path and openings and gates leading onto them (s. 1 Night Poaching Act 1844).	Trespass as above by five or more persons using violence. Fine in addition to any other penalty s. 32.
Trespassing with a firearm on land (s. 20(2)). Summary – three months or a fine or both.		
Failure to hand over firearm or ammunition on demand by a constable (s. 47(2)) Summary – three months or a fine or both.		

Table B. 3   Fines and other penalties (cont.)

Poaching Prevention Act 1862 [as amended]	Deer Act 1963 Deer Act 1980 Criminal Law Act 1977
Where a person searched by constable on highway, street or public place under s. 2 of Act, found to have game unlawfully obtained on land, or gun or part of gun for unlawfully obtaining game. Penalty: a fine.	Any offence under the Act. The penalty is a fine or 3 months imprisonment or both (s. 6, 1963 Act as amended).

Table of Cases

Table of Statutes and Statutory Instruments

Statutory Instruments

Index